FOR ORGANS, PIANOS & ELECTRONIC KEYBOARDS

E-Z PLAY® TODAY

211

THE BIG BOOK OF
Nursery Rhymes
& Children's Songs

D1326636

 Music Sales America

EXCLUSIVELY DISTRIBUTED BY

HAL•LEONARD®
CORPORATION

7777 W. BLUEMOUND RD. P.O. BOX 13819 MILWAUKEE, WI 53213

E-Z Play® Today Music Notation © 1975 by HAL LEONARD CORPORATION
E-Z PLAY and EASY ELECTRONIC KEYBOARD MUSIC are registered trademarks of HAL LEONARD CORPORATION.

Visit Hal Leonard Online at
www.halleonard.com

Contents

A-Hunting We Will Go

Registration 4
Rhythm: March

Traditional

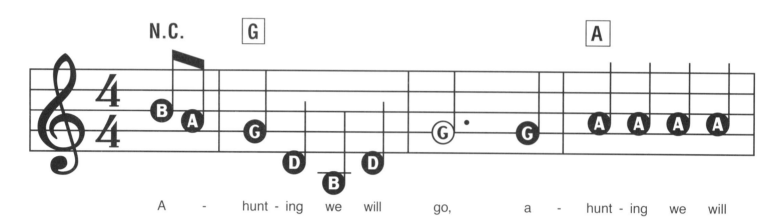

A - hunt - ing we will go, a - hunt - ing we will

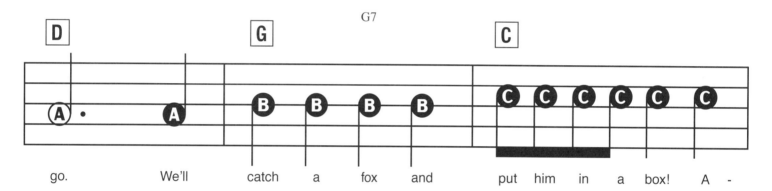

go. We'll catch a fox and put him in a box! A -

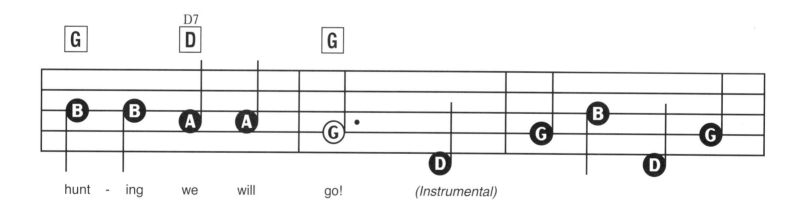

hunt - ing we will go! *(Instrumental)*

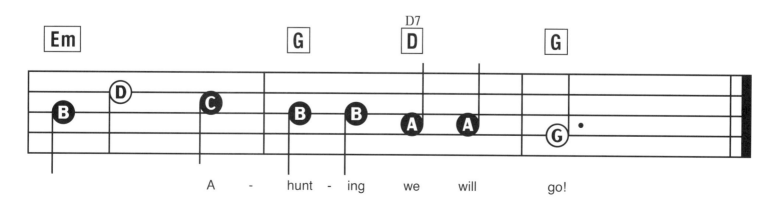

A - hunt - ing we will go!

A-Tisket A-Tasket

Registration 9
Rhythm: Fox Trot or Swing

Traditional

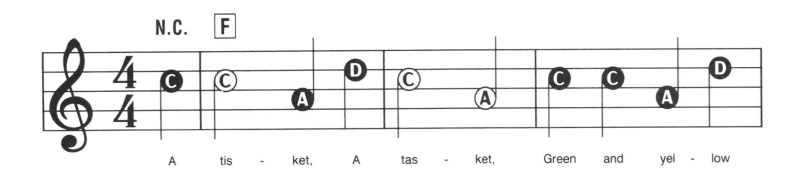

A tis - ket, A tas - ket, Green and yel - low

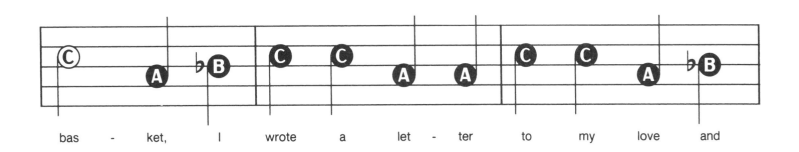

bas - ket, I wrote a let - ter to my love and

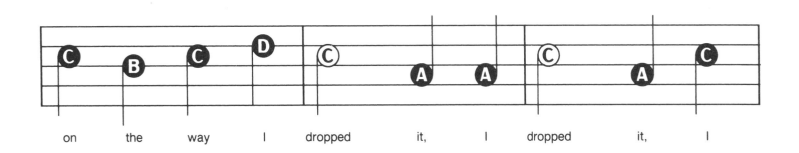

on the way I dropped it, I dropped it, I

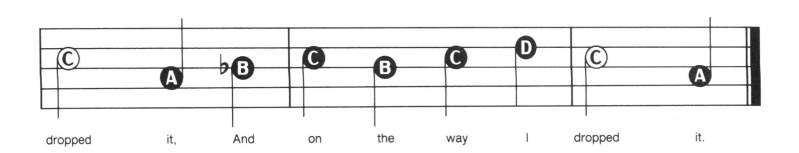

dropped it, And on the way I dropped it.

Alice the Camel

Registration 9
Rhythm: March or Fox Trot

Traditional

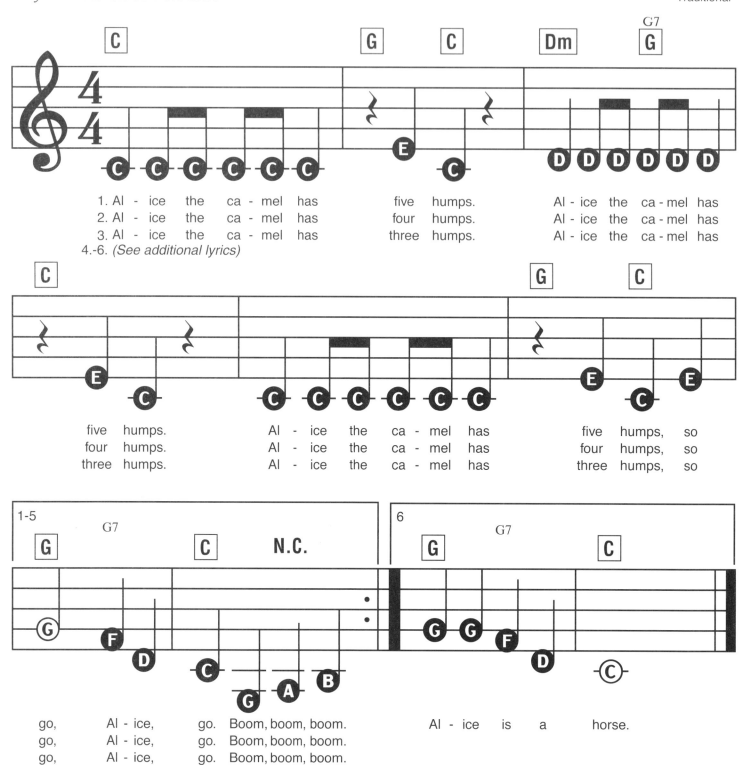

1. Al - ice the ca - mel has five humps.
2. Al - ice the ca - mel has four humps.
3. Al - ice the ca - mel has three humps.
4.-6. *(See additional lyrics)*

five humps.
four humps.
three humps.

Al - ice the ca - mel has
Al - ice the ca - mel has
Al - ice the ca - mel has

five humps, so
four humps, so
three humps, so

go, Al - ice, go. Boom, boom, boom.
go, Al - ice, go. Boom, boom, boom.
go, Al - ice, go. Boom, boom, boom.

Al - ice is a horse.

Additional Lyrics

4. Alice the camel has two humps, *etc.*

5. Alice the camel has one hump, *etc.*

6. Alice the camel has no humps, *etc.*
   So Alice is a horse!

All the Pretty Little Horses

Registration 1
Rhythm: Fox Trot

Southeastern American Folksong

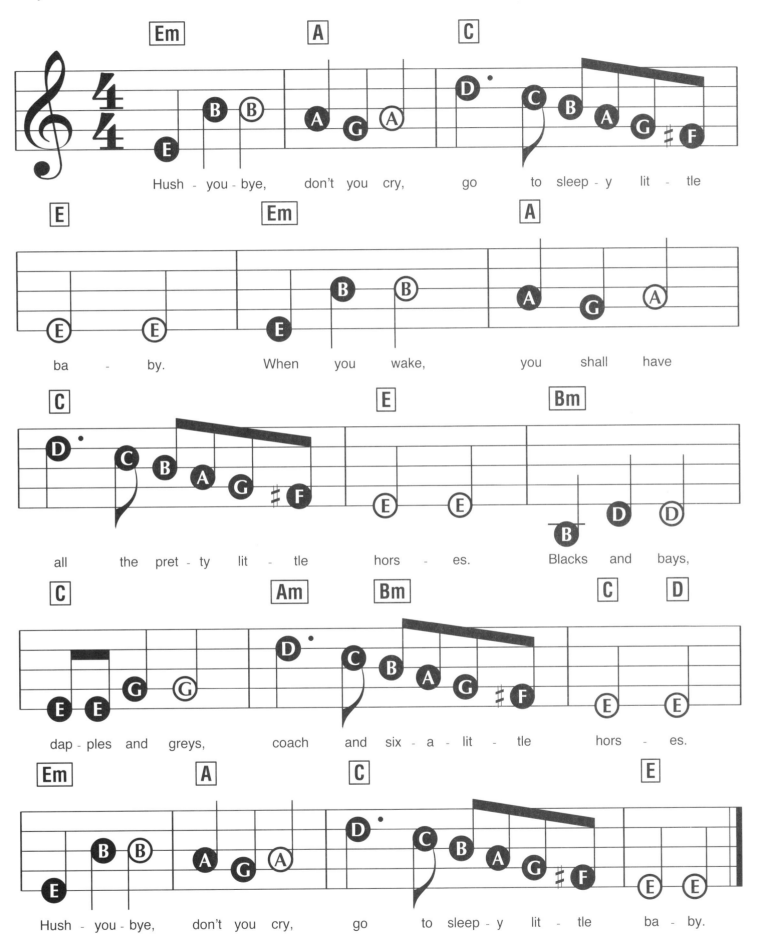

Alouette

Registration 3
Rhythm: Fox Trot

Traditional

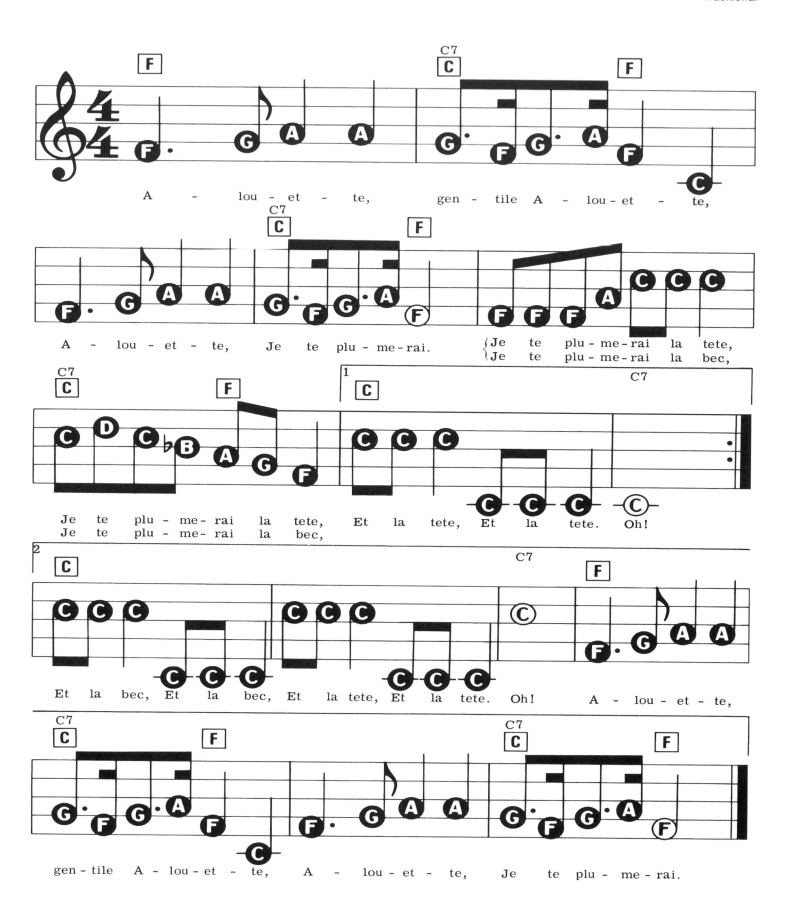

Animal Fair

Registration 4
Rhythm: 6/8 March

Traditional

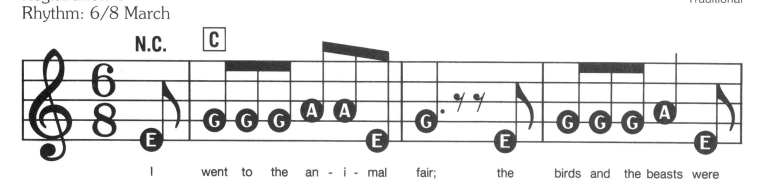

I went to the an-i-mal fair; the birds and the beasts were

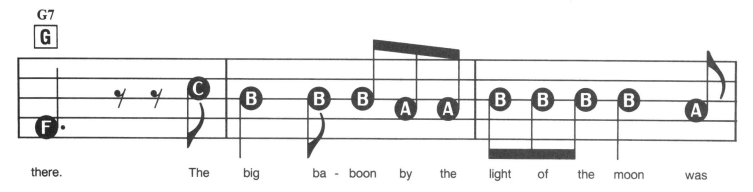

there. The big ba-boon by the light of the moon was

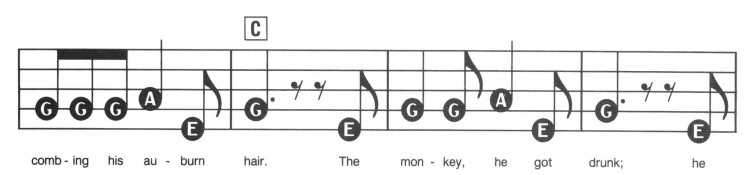

comb-ing his au-burn hair. The mon-key, he got drunk; he

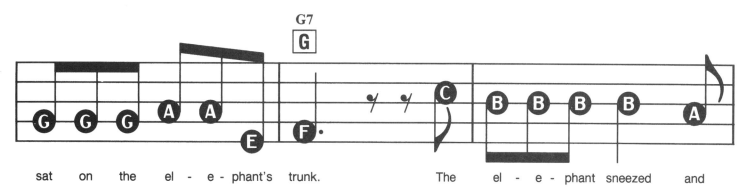

sat on the el-e-phant's trunk. The el-e-phant sneezed and

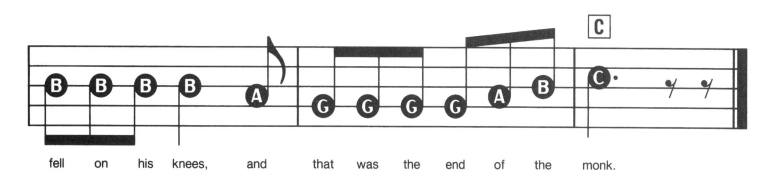

fell on his knees, and that was the end of the monk.

The Ants Came Marching

Registration 2
Rhythm: 6/8 March

Traditional

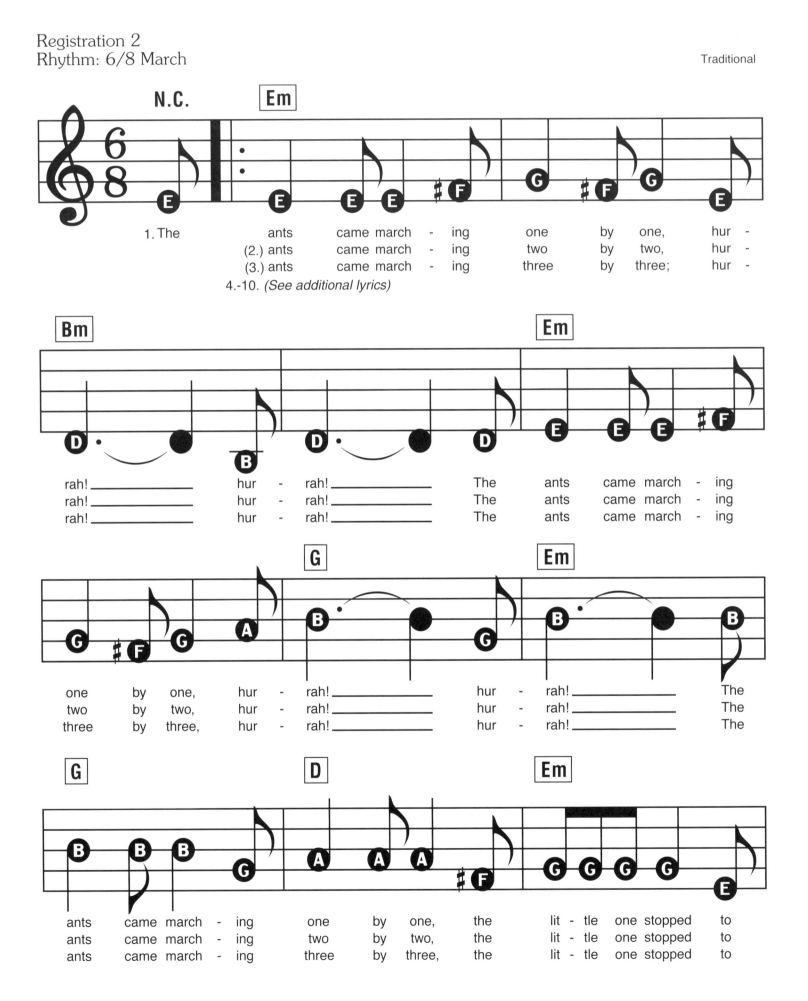

11

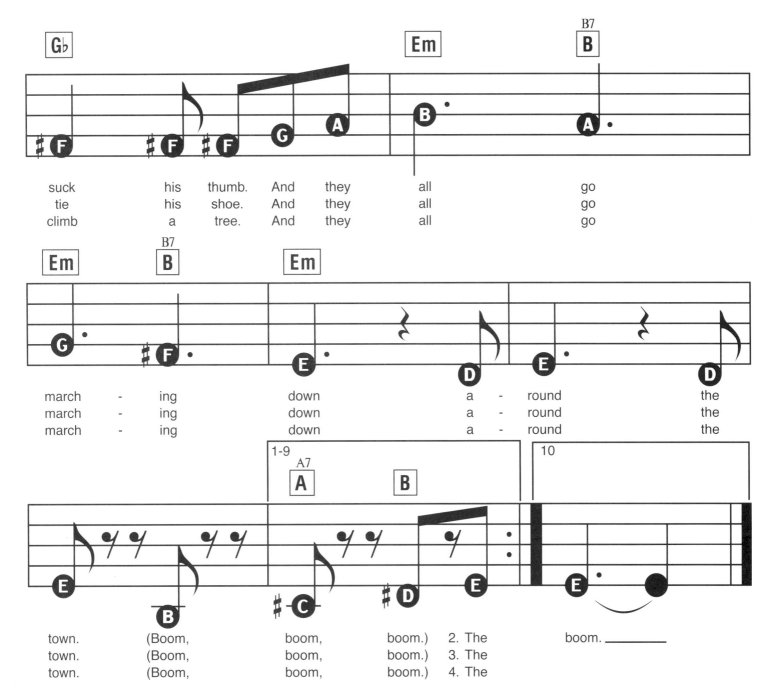

suck his thumb. And they all go
tie his shoe. And they all go
climb a tree. And they all go

march - ing down a - round the
march - ing down a - round the
march - ing down a - round the

1-9   10

town. (Boom, boom, boom.) 2. The   boom. _____
town. (Boom, boom, boom.) 3. The
town. (Boom, boom, boom.) 4. The

Additional Lyrics

4. The ants came marching four by four…
   The little one stopped to shut the door…

5. The ants came marching five by five…
   The little one stopped to take a dive…

6. The ants came marching six by six…
   The little one stopped to pick up sticks…

7. The ants came marching seven by seven…
   The little one stopped to go to heaven…

8. The ants came marching eight by eight…
   The little one stopped to shut the gate…

9. The ants came marching nine by nine…
   The little one stopped to scratch his spine…

10. The ants came marching ten by ten…
    The little one stopped to say "the end"…

Baa Baa Black Sheep

Registration 2
Rhythm: Fox Trot

Traditional

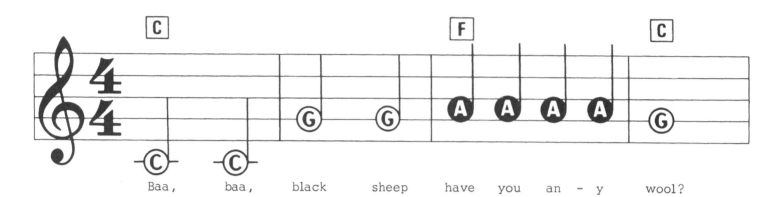

Baa, baa, black sheep have you an - y wool?

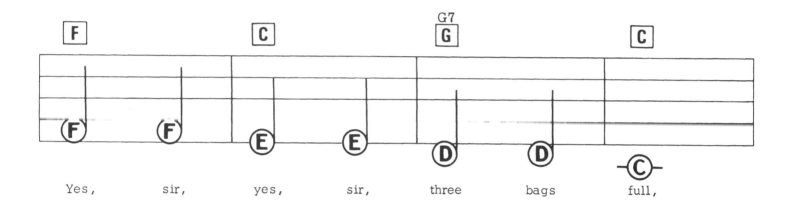

Yes, sir, yes, sir, three bags full,

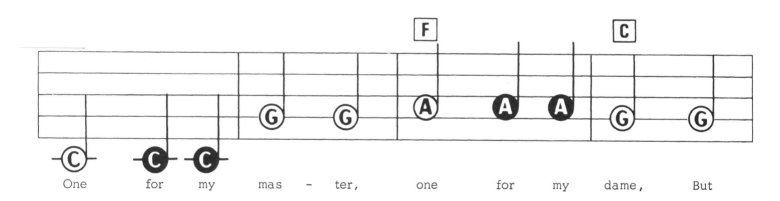

One for my mas - ter, one for my dame, But

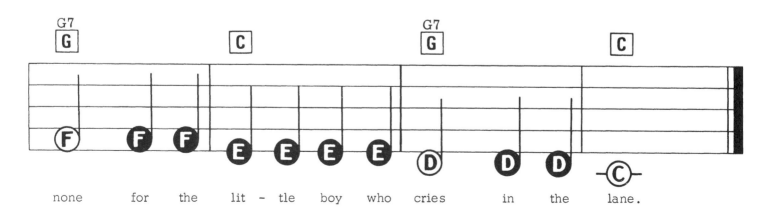

none for the lit - tle boy who cries in the lane.

Baby Bumble Bee

Registration 9
Rhythm: March or Fox Trot

Traditional

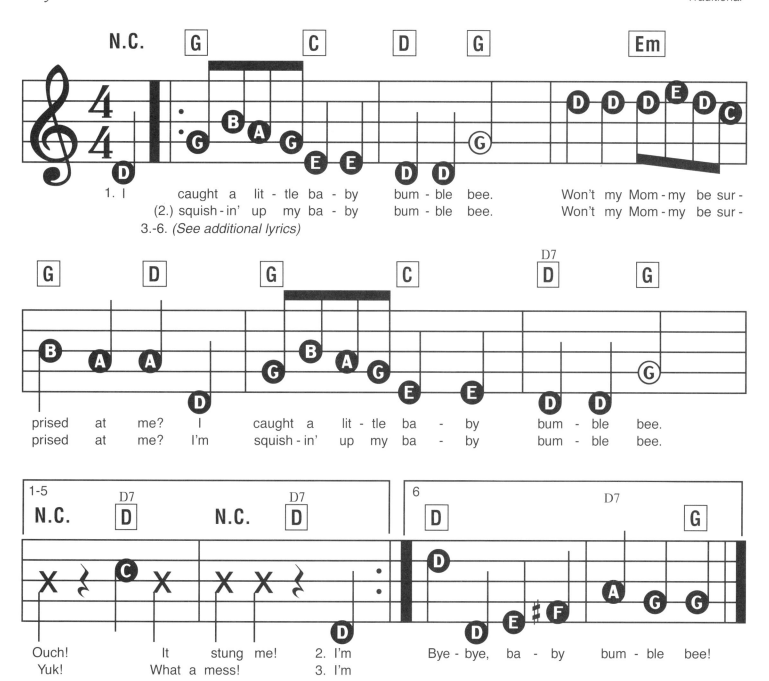

1. I caught a lit - tle ba - by bum - ble bee. Won't my Mom - my be sur -
(2.) squish - in' up my ba - by bum - ble bee. Won't my Mom - my be sur -
3.-6. *(See additional lyrics)*

prised at me? I caught a lit - tle ba - by bum - ble bee.
prised at me? I'm squish - in' up my ba - by bum - ble bee.

Ouch! It stung me! 2. I'm Bye - bye, ba - by bum - ble bee!
Yuk! What a mess! 3. I'm

Additional Lyrics

3. I'm lickin' up my baby bumble bee.
   Won't my Mommy be surprised at me?
   I'm lickin' up my baby bumble bee.
   Ick! I feel sick!

4. I'm barfin' up my baby bumble bee.
   Won't my Mommy be surprised at me?
   I'm barfin' up my baby bumble bee.
   Oh! What a mess!

5. I'm wipin' up my baby bumble bee.
   Won't my Mommy be surprised at me?
   I'm wipin' up my baby bumble bee.
   Oops! Mommy's new towel!

6. I'm wringin' out my baby bumble bee.
   Won't my Mommy be surprised at me?
   I'm wringing out my baby bumble bee.
   Bye-bye, baby bumble bee!

Barnyard Song

Registration 8
Rhythm: Waltz

Traditional

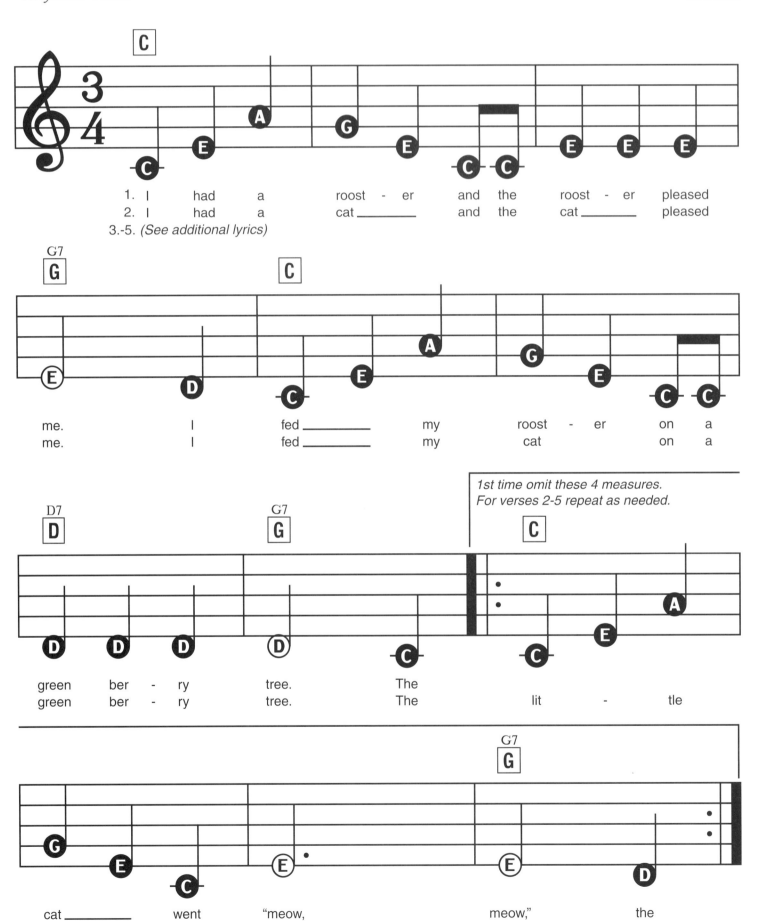

1. I had a roost - er and the roost - er pleased
2. I had a cat _____ and the cat _____ pleased
3.-5. *(See additional lyrics)*

me. I fed _____ my roost - er on a
me. I fed _____ my cat _____ on a

1st time omit these 4 measures.
For verses 2-5 repeat as needed.

green ber - ry tree. The
green ber - ry tree. The lit - tle

cat _____ went "meow, meow," the

15

Chorus

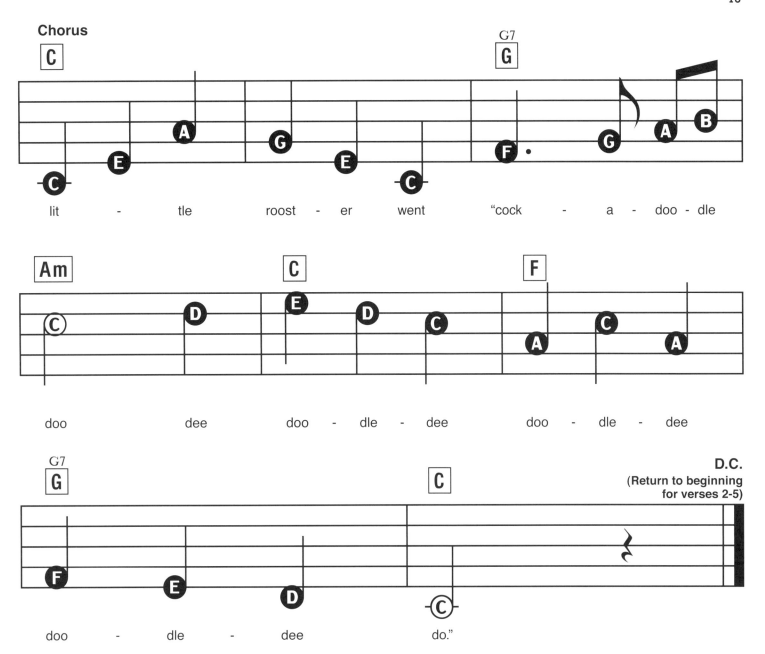

lit - tle roost - er went "cock - a - doo - dle

doo dee doo - dle - dee doo - dle - dee

doo - dle - dee do."

D.C.
(Return to beginning
for verses 2-5)

Additional Lyrics

3. I had a pig and the pig pleased me.
I fed my pig on a green berry tree.
The little pig went "oink oink."
The little cat went "meow meow."
Chorus

4. I had a cow and the cow pleased me.
I fed my cow on a green berry tree.
The little cow went "moo moo."
The little pig went "oink oink."
The little cat went "meow meow."
Chorus

5. I had a baby and the baby pleased me.
I fed my baby on a green berry tree.
The little baby went "waah waah."
The little cow went "moo moo."
The little pig went "oink oink."
The little cat went "meow meow."
Chorus

The Bear Went Over the Mountain

Registration 9
Rhythm: Waltz

Traditional

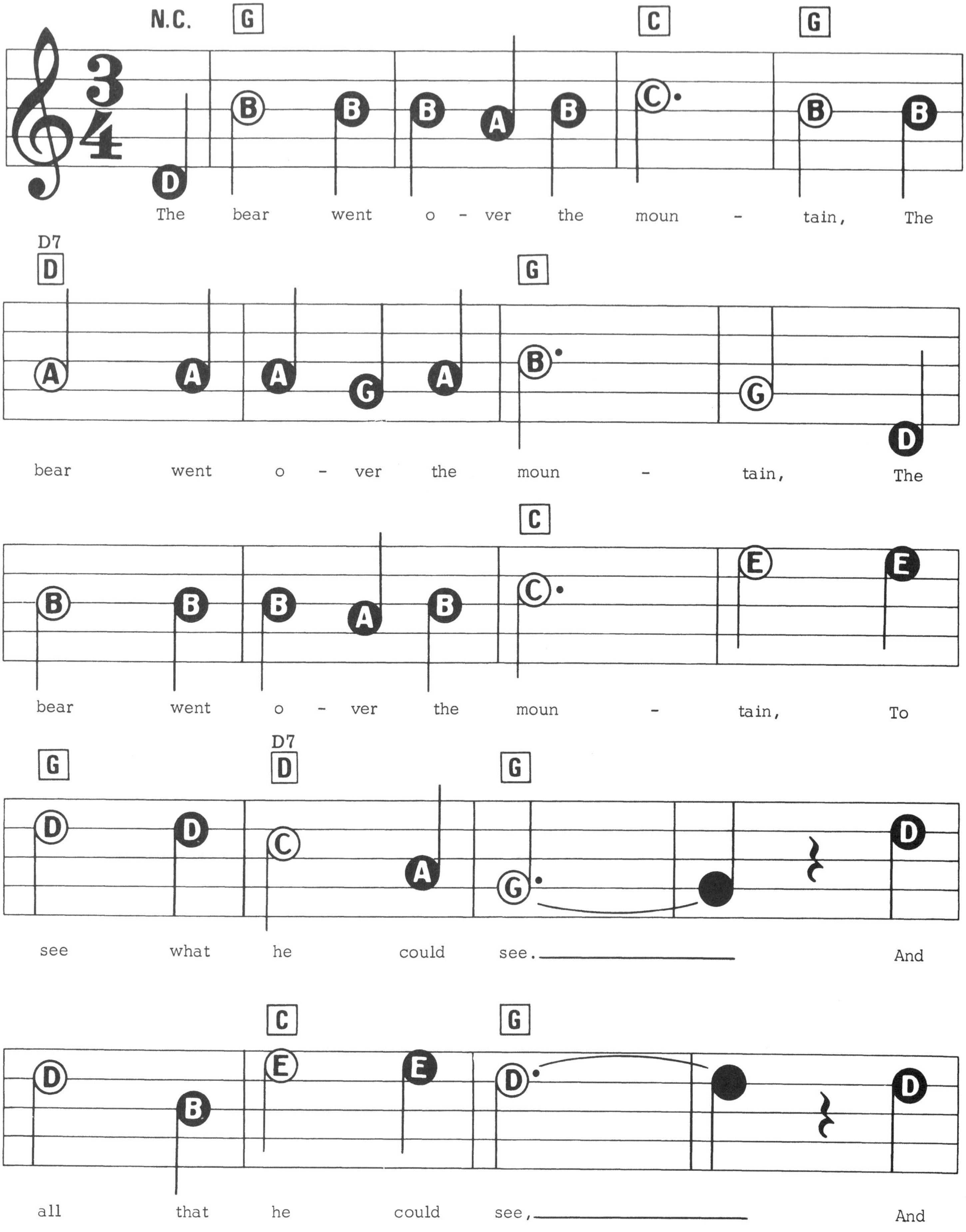

N.C. | G | C | G

The bear went o - ver the moun - tain, The

D7
D | G

bear went o - ver the moun - tain, The

C

bear went o - ver the moun - tain, To

G | D7
D | G

see what he could see._____ And

C | G

all that he could see,_____ And

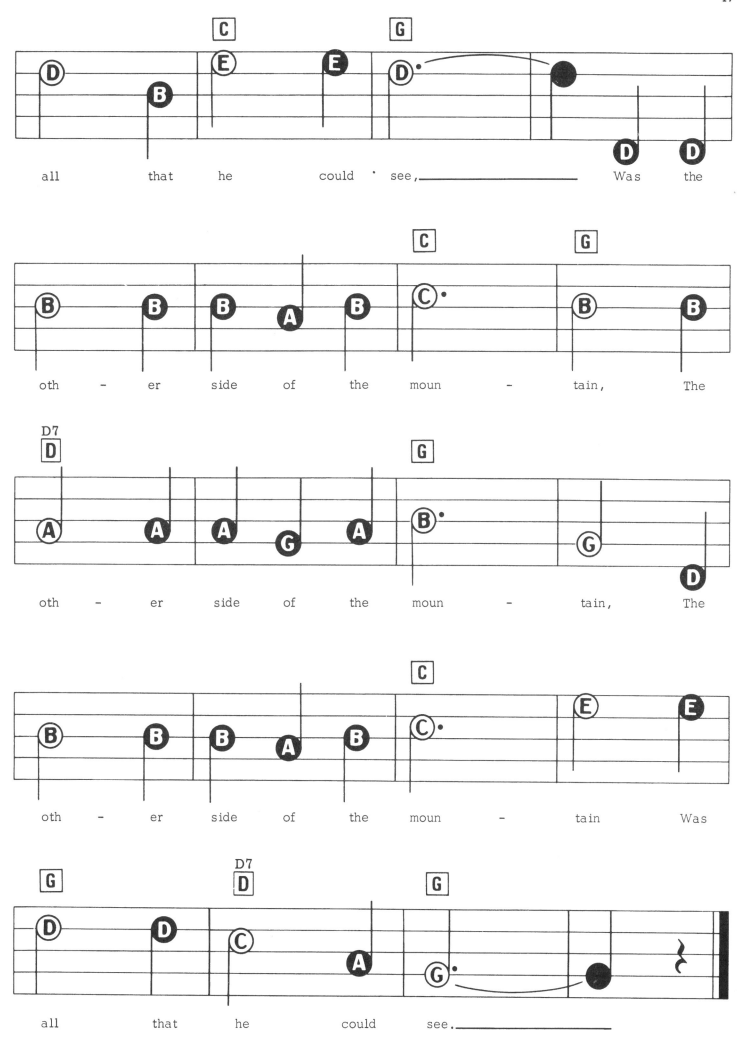

Blowing Bubbles

Registration 7
Rhythm: March or Fox Trot

Traditional

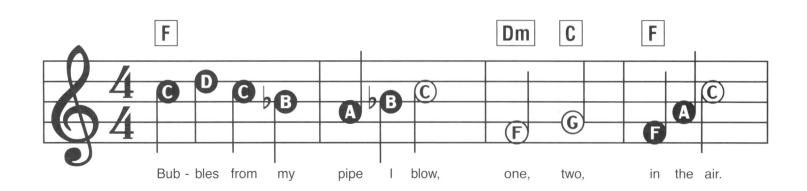

Bub - bles from my pipe I blow, one, two, in the air.

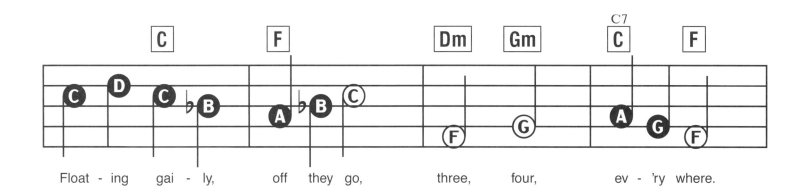

Float - ing gai - ly, off they go, three, four, ev - 'ry where.

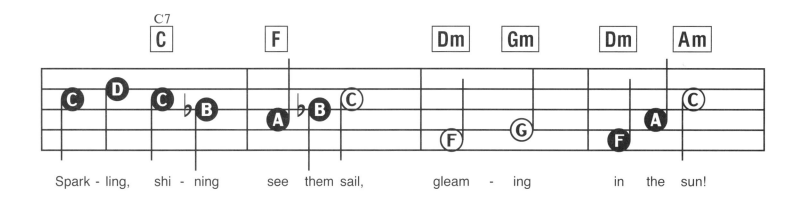

Spark - ling, shi - ning see them sail, gleam - ing in the sun!

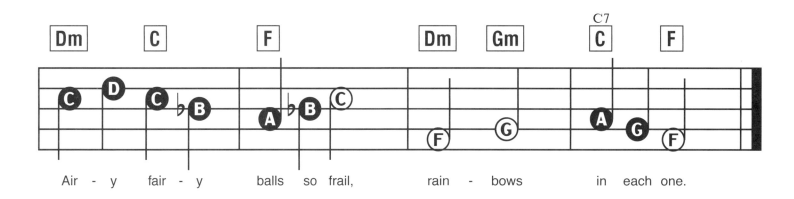

Air - y fair - y balls so frail, rain - bows in each one.

Bobby Shaftoe

Registration 2
Rhythm: March

Traditional

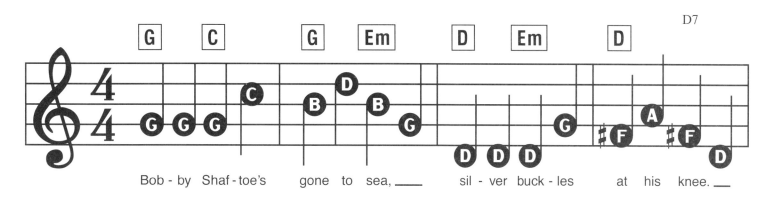

Bob - by Shaf - toe's gone to sea, ___ sil - ver buck - les at his knee. ___

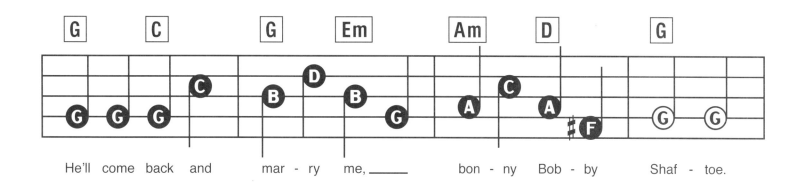

He'll come back and mar - ry me, ___ bon - ny Bob - by Shaf - toe.

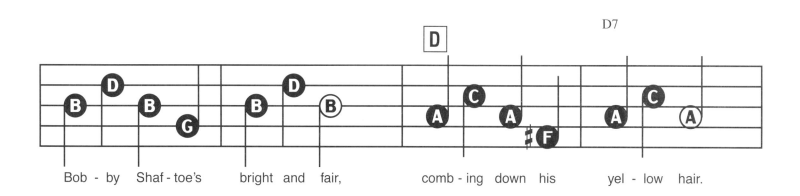

Bob - by Shaf - toe's bright and fair, comb - ing down his yel - low hair.

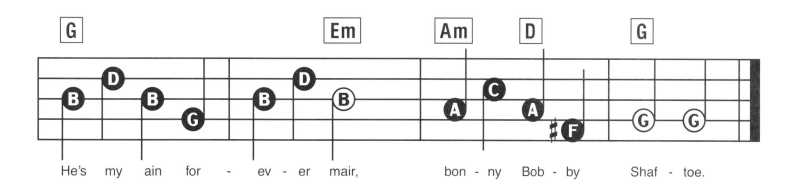

He's my ain for - ev - er mair, bon - ny Bob - by Shaf - toe.

Bye, Baby Bunting

Registration 3
Rhythm: Waltz

Traditional

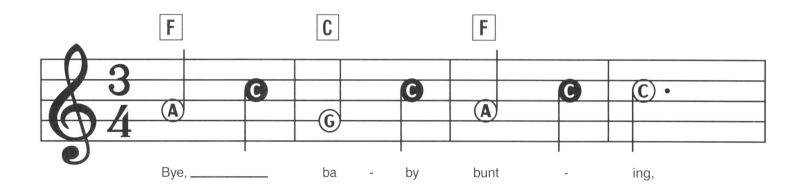

Bye, _____ ba - by bunt - ing,

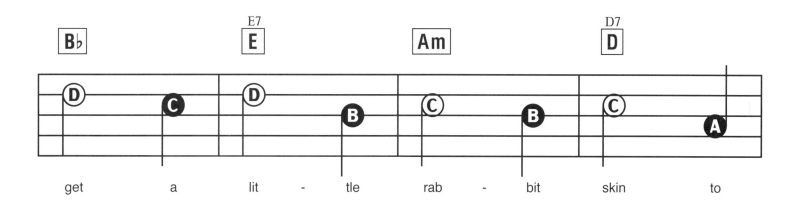

dad - dy's gone a - hunt - ing, to

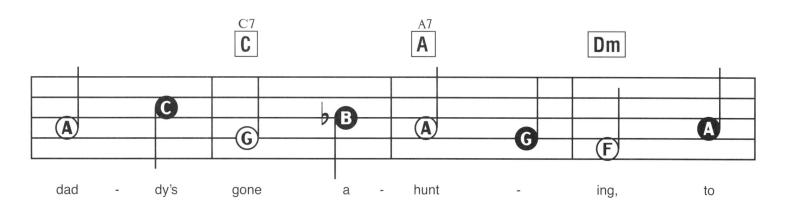

get a lit - tle rab - bit skin to

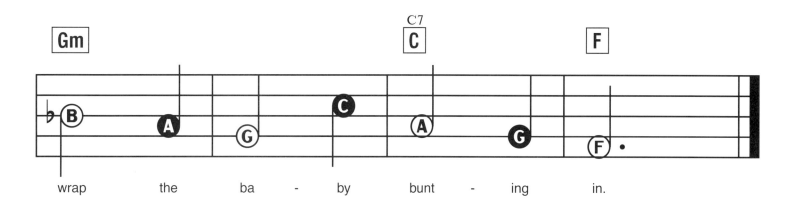

wrap the ba - by bunt - ing in.

Chook Chook

Registration 9
Rhythm: March or Fox Trot

Traditional

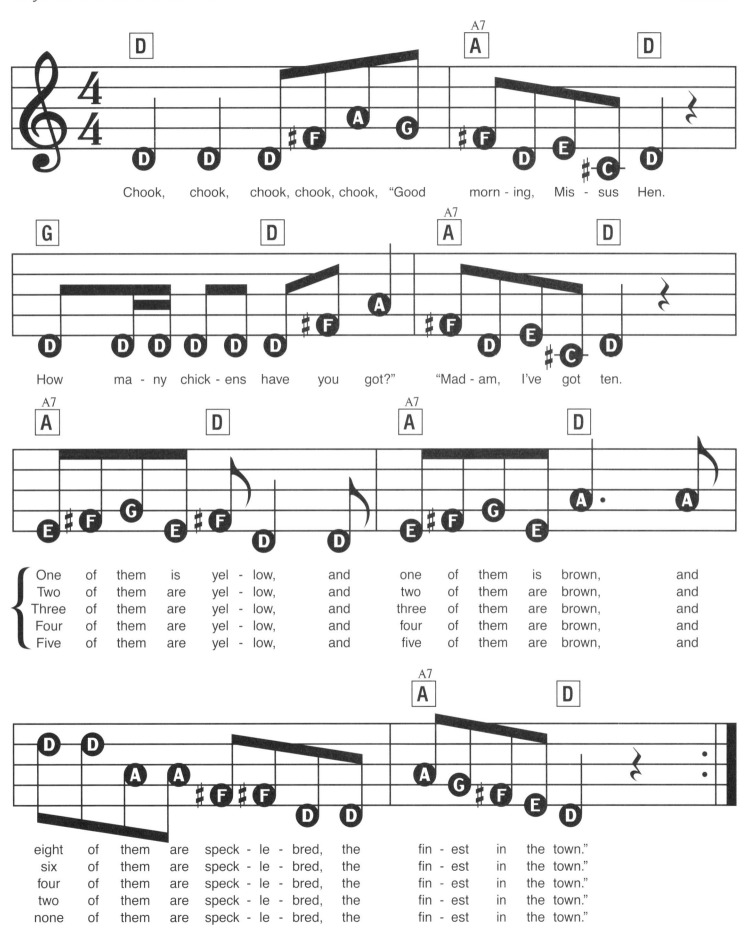

Chook, chook, chook, chook, chook, "Good morn - ing, Mis - sus Hen.

How ma - ny chick - ens have you got?" "Mad - am, I've got ten.

One of them is yel - low, and one of them is brown, and
Two of them are yel - low, and two of them are brown, and
Three of them are yel - low, and three of them are brown, and
Four of them are yel - low, and four of them are brown, and
Five of them are yel - low, and five of them are brown, and

eight of them are speck - le - bred, the fin - est in the town."
six of them are speck - le - bred, the fin - est in the town."
four of them are speck - le - bred, the fin - est in the town."
two of them are speck - le - bred, the fin - est in the town."
none of them are speck - le - bred, the fin - est in the town."

Camptown Races

Registration 4
Rhythm: Polka

Words and Music by
Stephen C. Foster

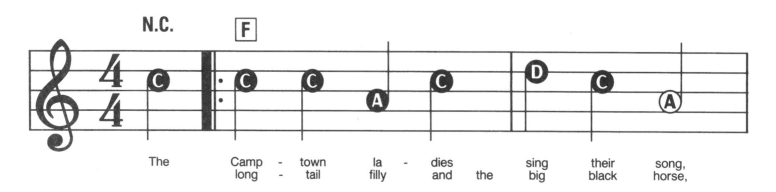

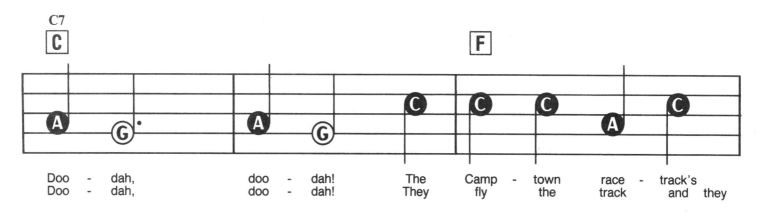

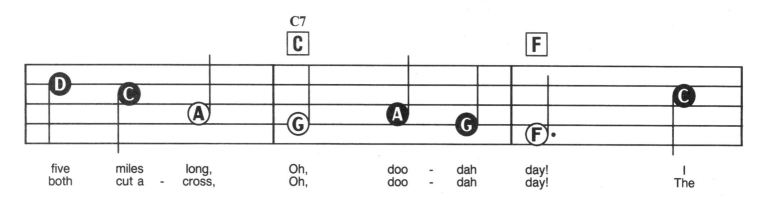

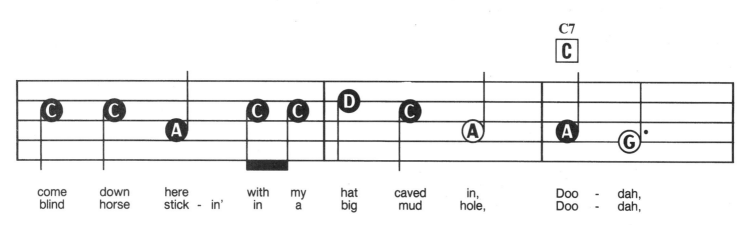

23

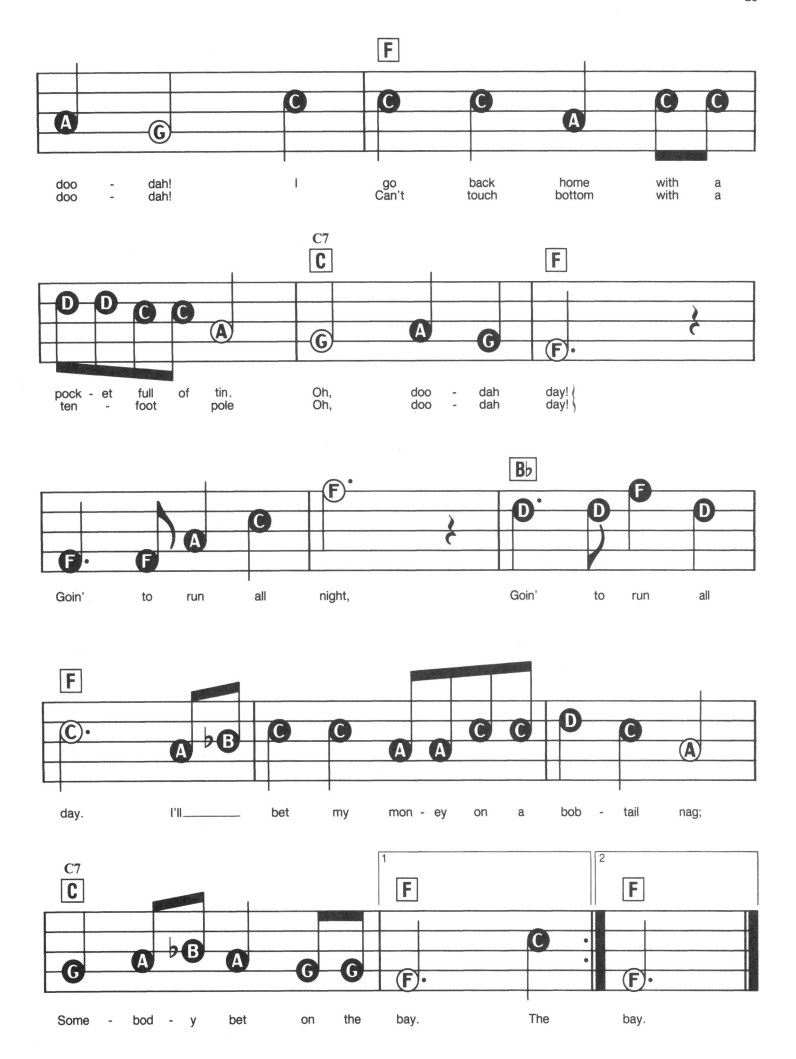

Cock-a-Doodle-Doo

Registration 3
Rhythm: 6/8 March

Traditional

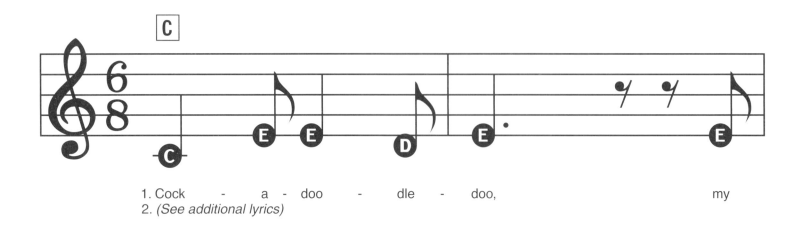

1. Cock - a - doo - dle - doo,   my
2. *(See additional lyrics)*

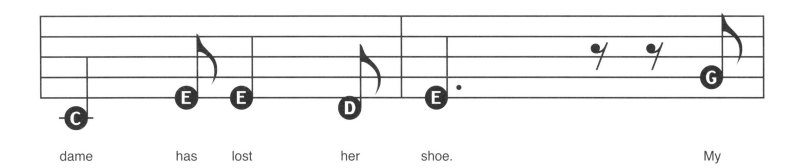

dame   has   lost   her   shoe.   My

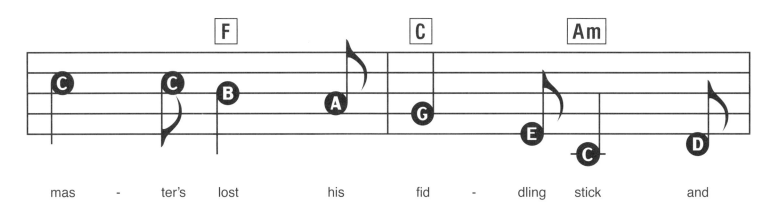

mas - ter's   lost   his   fid - dling   stick   and

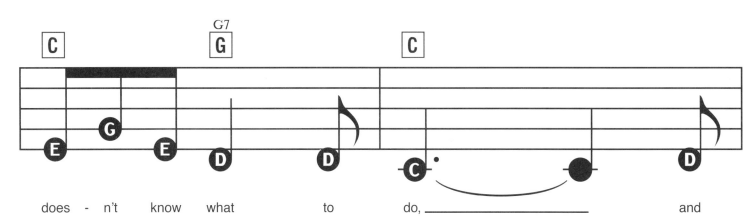

does - n't   know   what   to   do, _____   and

does - n't know what to do, _____ and

does - n't know what to do. _____ My

mas - ter's lost his fid - dling stick and

does - n't know what to do. _____

Additional Lyrics

2. Cock-a-doodle doo, what is my dame to do?
   'Til master finds his fiddling stick,
   She'll dance without her shoe.
   She'll dance without her shoe,
   She'll dance without her shoe.
   'Til master finds his fiddling stick,
   She'll dance without her shoe.

Curly Locks

Registration 1
Rhythm: 6/8 March

Traditional

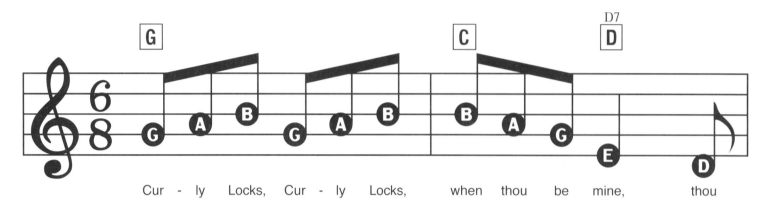

Cur - ly Locks, Cur - ly Locks, when thou be mine, thou

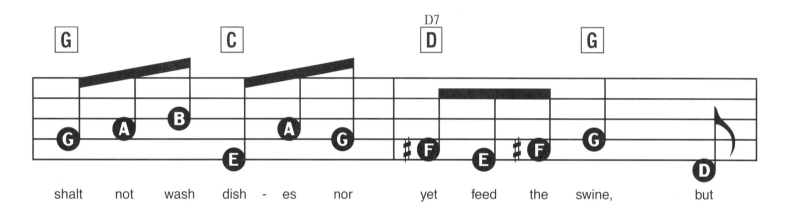

shalt not wash dish - es nor yet feed the swine, but

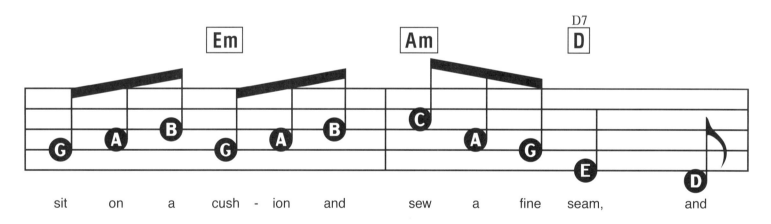

sit on a cush - ion and sew a fine seam, and

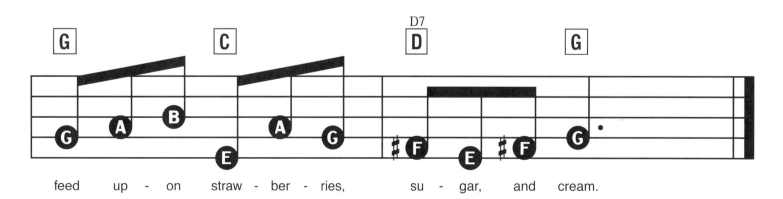

feed up - on straw - ber - ries, su - gar, and cream.

Diddle, Diddle Dumpling, My Son John

Registration 10
Rhythm: March or Polka

Traditional

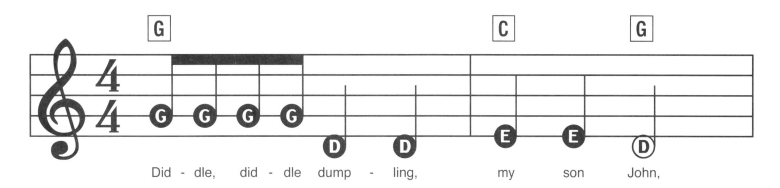

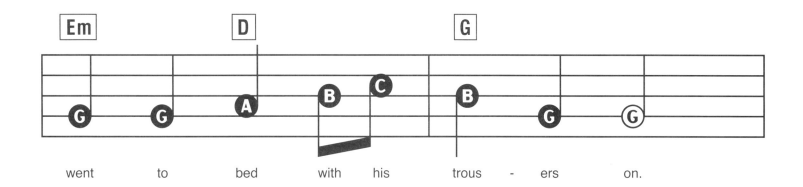

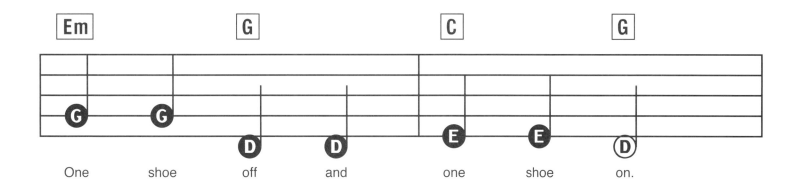

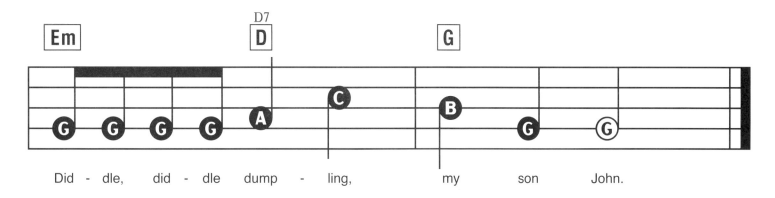

Daddy Fox

Registration 7
Rhythm: Fox Trot or March

Traditional

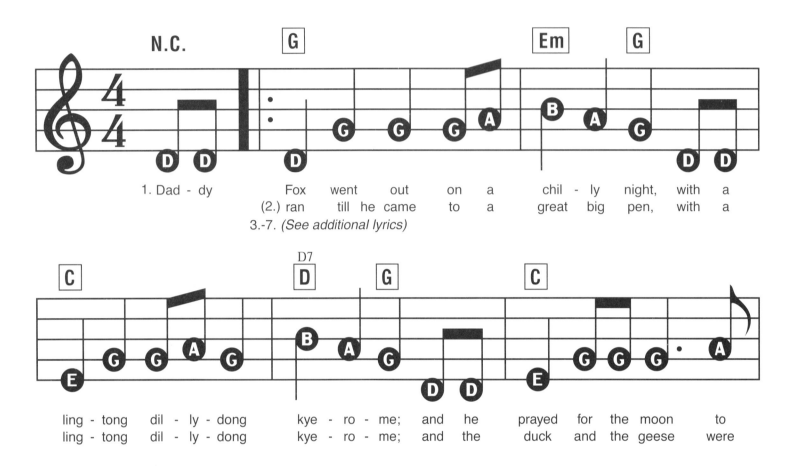

1. Dad - dy   Fox went out   on   a   chil - ly night, with a
(2.) ran   till he came   to   a   great big pen, with a

3.-7. *(See additional lyrics)*

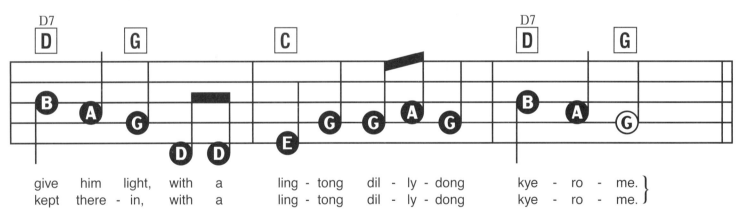

ling - tong dil - ly - dong   kye - ro - me; and he   prayed for the moon to
ling - tong dil - ly - dong   kye - ro - me; and the   duck and the geese were

give him light, with a   ling - tong dil - ly - dong   kye - ro - me. }
kept there - in, with a   ling - tong dil - ly - dong   kye - ro - me. }

Chorus

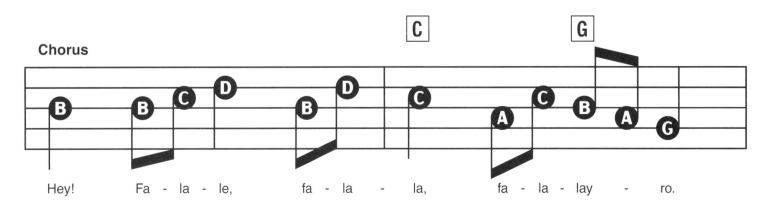

Hey! Fa - la - le,   fa - la - la,   fa - la - lay - ro.

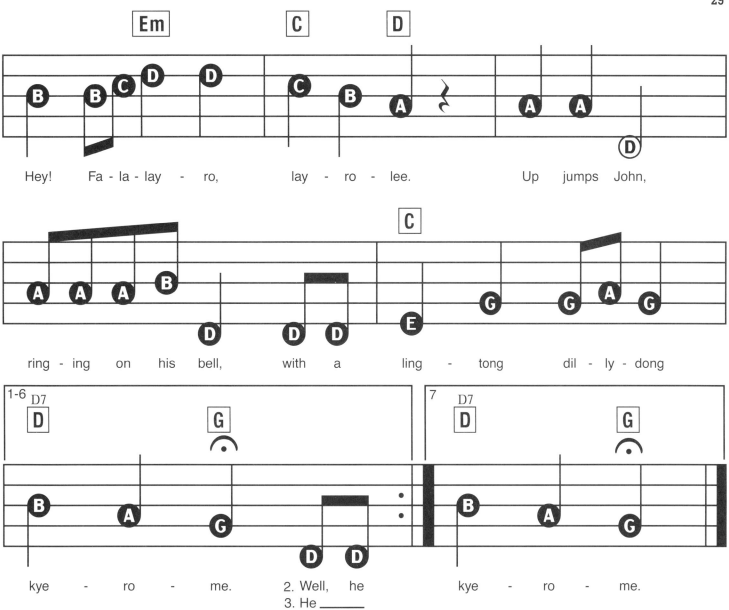

Additional Lyrics

3. He grabbed the grey goose by the neck,
   With a ling-tong dilly-dong kye-ro-me;
   And up with the little ones over his back,
   With a ling-tong dilly-dong kye-ro-me.
   Chorus

4. Old Mother Flipper-Flopper jumped out of bed,
   With a ling-tong dilly-dong kye-ro-me;
   Out of the window she stuck her little head,
   With a ling-tong dilly-dong kye-ro-me.
   Chorus

5. John, he ran to the top hill,
   With a ling-tong dilly-dong kye-ro-me;
   And he blew his little horn both loud and shrill,
   With a ling-tong dilly-dong kye-ro-me.
   Chorus

6. The fox, he ran to his cosy din,
   With a ling-tong dilly-dong kye-ro-me;
   And there were the little ones, eight, nine, ten,
   With a ling-tong dilly-dong kye-ro-me.
   Chorus

7. Then the fox and his wife, without any strife,
   With a ling-tong dilly-dong kye-ro-me;
   They cut up the goose with a carving knife,
   With a ling-tong dilly-dong kye-ro-me.
   Chorus

Ding Dong Bell

Registration 9
Rhythm: March

Traditional

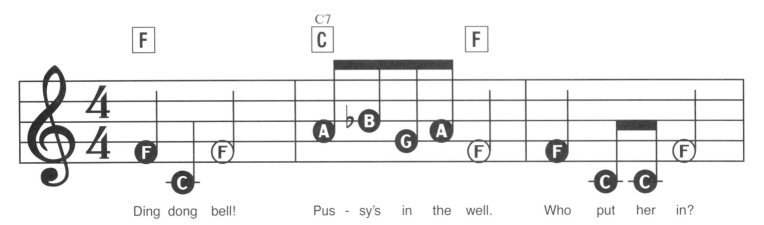

Ding dong bell! Pus - sy's in the well. Who put her in?

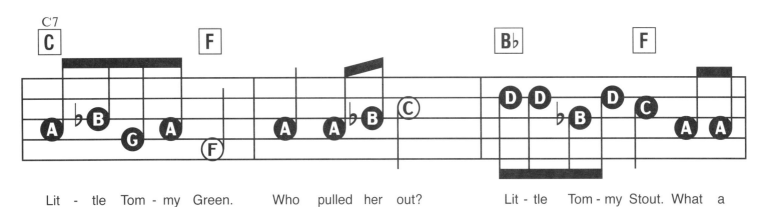

Lit - tle Tom - my Green. Who pulled her out? Lit - tle Tom - my Stout. What a

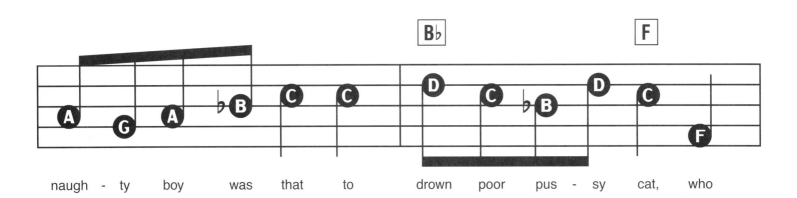

naugh - ty boy was that to drown poor pus - sy cat, who

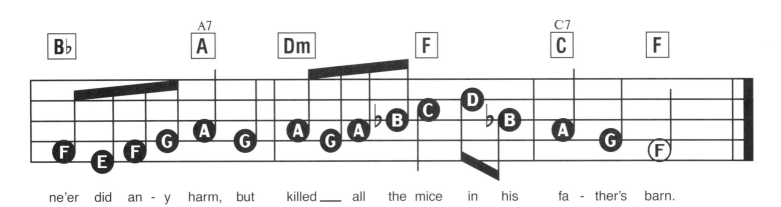

ne'er did an - y harm, but killed ___ all the mice in his fa - ther's barn.

Doctor Foster

Registration 1
Rhythm: 6/8 March

Traditional

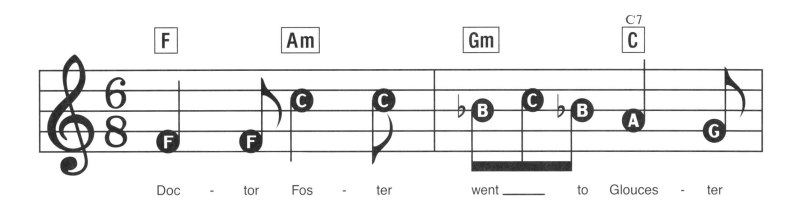

Doc - tor Fos - ter   went _____ to Glouces - ter

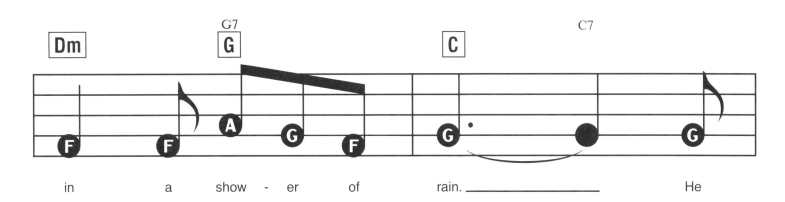

in   a   show - er   of   rain. _____   He

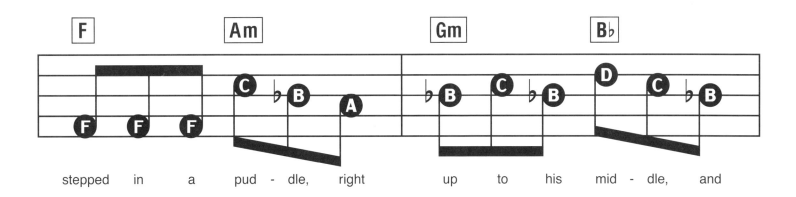

stepped   in   a   pud - dle,   right   up   to   his   mid - dle,   and

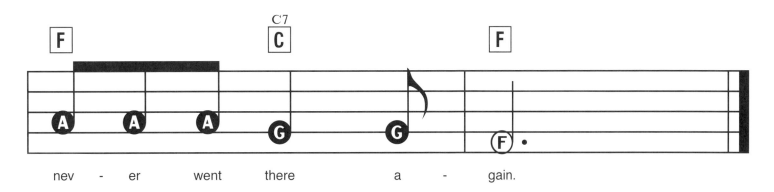

nev - er   went   there   a - gain.

Do Your Ears Hang Low?

Registration 4
Rhythm: Fox Trot or Swing

Traditional

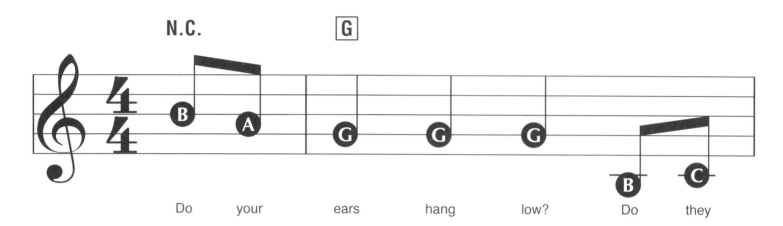

Do your ears hang low? Do they

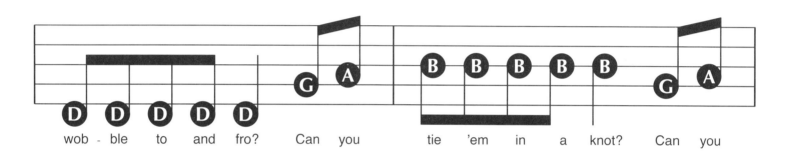

wob - ble to and fro? Can you tie 'em in a knot? Can you

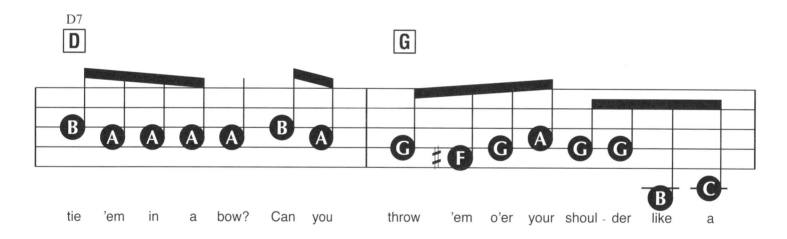

tie 'em in a bow? Can you throw 'em o'er your shoul - der like a

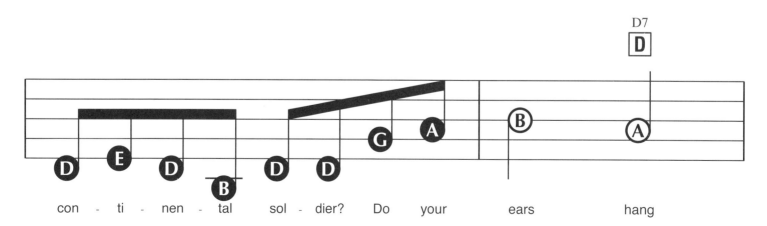

con - ti - nen - tal sol - dier? Do your ears hang

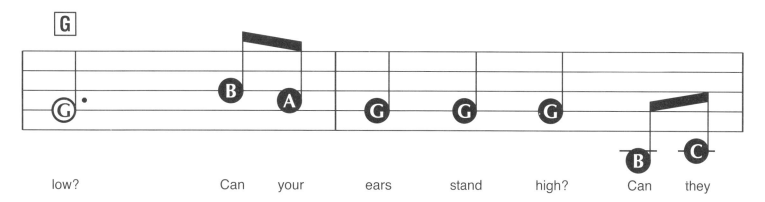

low? Can your ears stand high? Can they

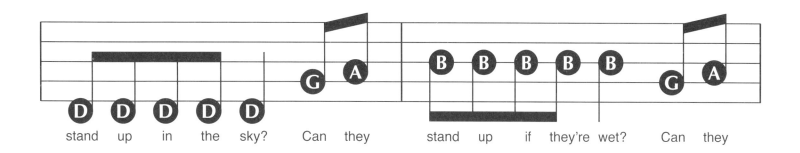

stand up in the sky? Can they stand up if they're wet? Can they

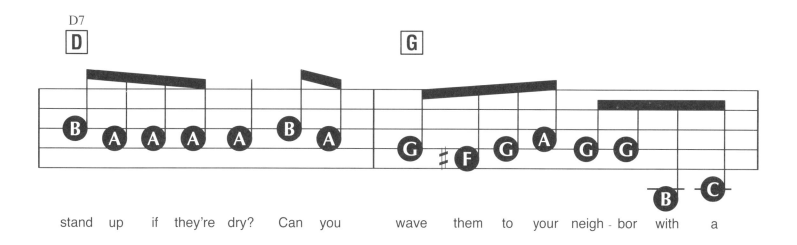

stand up if they're dry? Can you wave them to your neigh-bor with a

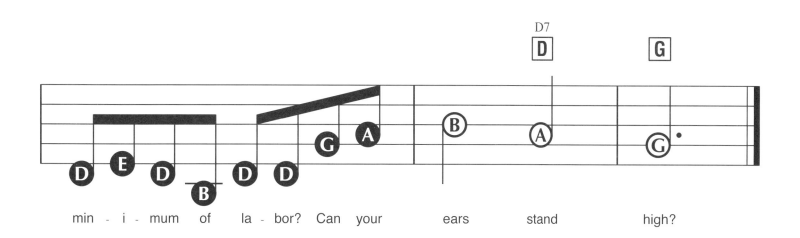

min-i-mum of la-bor? Can your ears stand high?

The Drunken Sailor

Registration 4
Rhythm: Fox Trot

American Sea Chantey

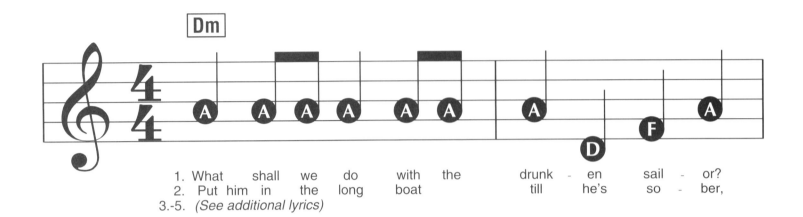

1. What shall we do with the drunk - en sail - or?
2. Put him in the long boat till he's so - ber,
3.-5. (See additional lyrics)

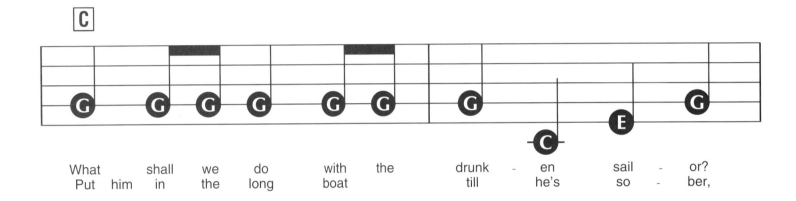

What shall we do with the drunk - en sail - or?
Put him in the long boat till he's so - ber,

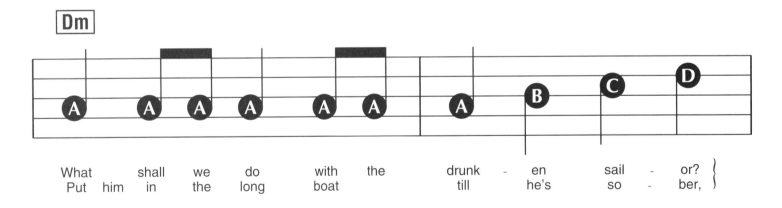

What shall we do with the drunk - en sail - or?
Put him in the long boat till he's so - ber,

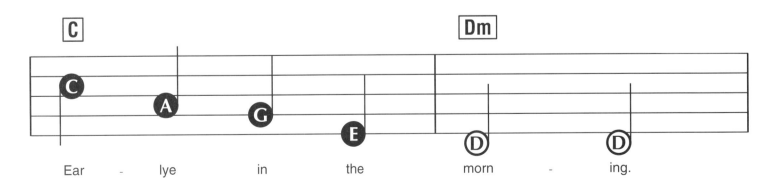

Ear - lye in the morn - ing.

Chorus

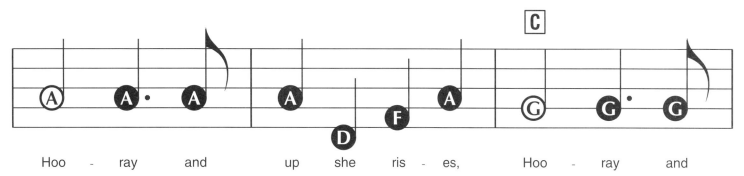

Hoo - ray and up she ris - es, Hoo - ray and

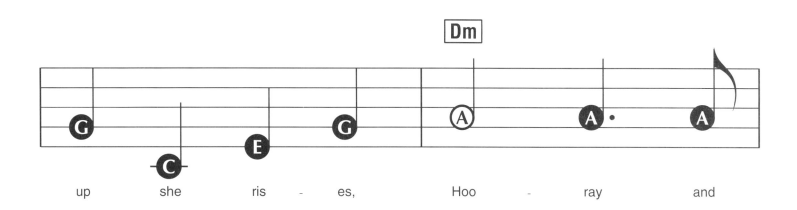

up she ris - es, Hoo - ray and

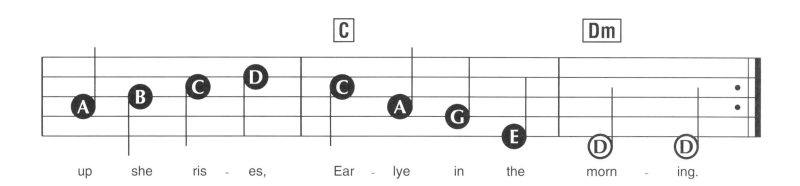

up she ris - es, Ear - lye in the morn - ing.

Additional Lyrics

3. Pull out the plug and wet him all over,
   Pull out the plug and wet him all over,
   Pull out the plug and wet him all over,
   Earlye in the morning.
   Chorus

4. Tie him to the top mast when she's under,
   Tie him to the top mast when she's under,
   Tie him to the top mast when she's under,
   Earlye in the morning.
   Chorus

5. Put him in the scuppers with the hosepipe on him,
   Put him in the scuppers with the hosepipe on him,
   Put him in the scuppers with the hosepipe on him,
   Earlye in the morning.
   Chorus

Dry Bones

Registration 5
Rhythm: Swing

Traditional

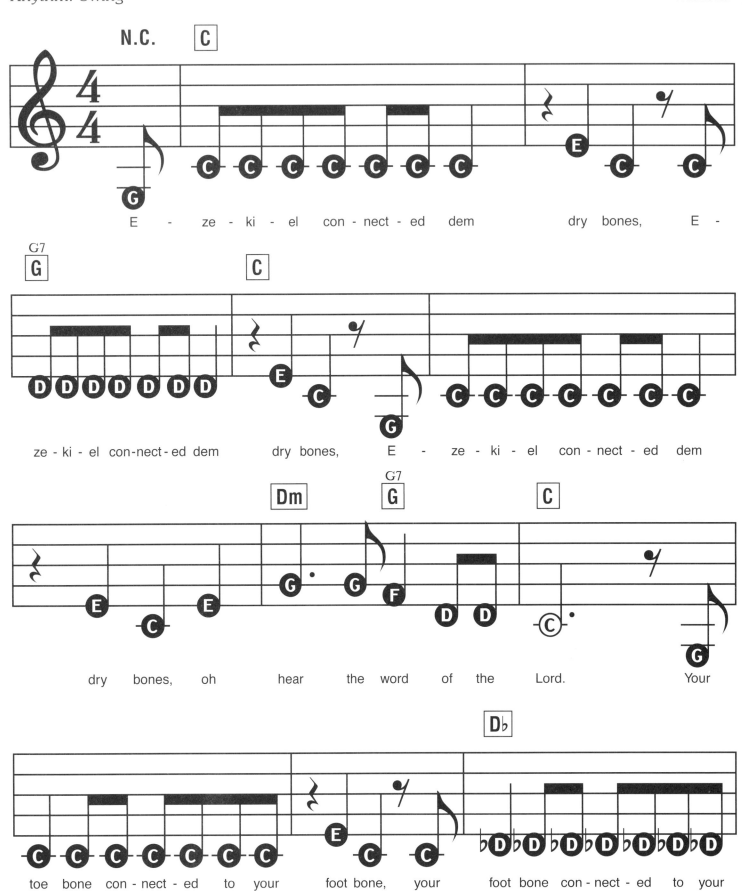

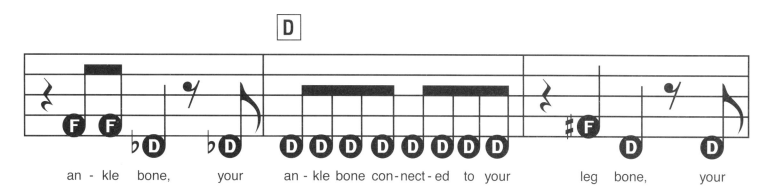

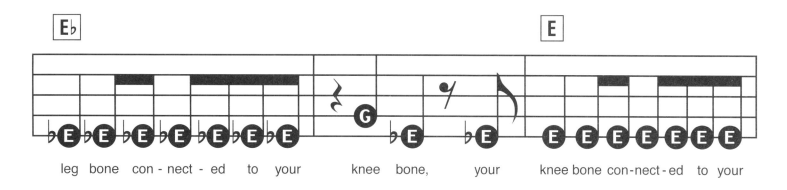

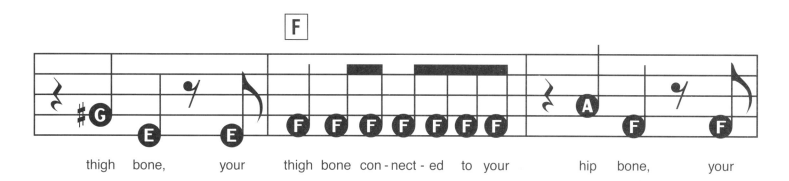

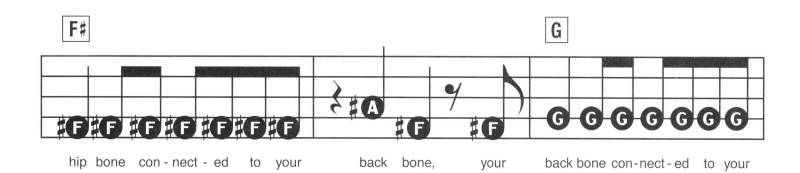

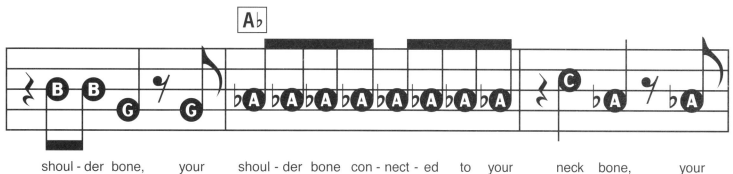

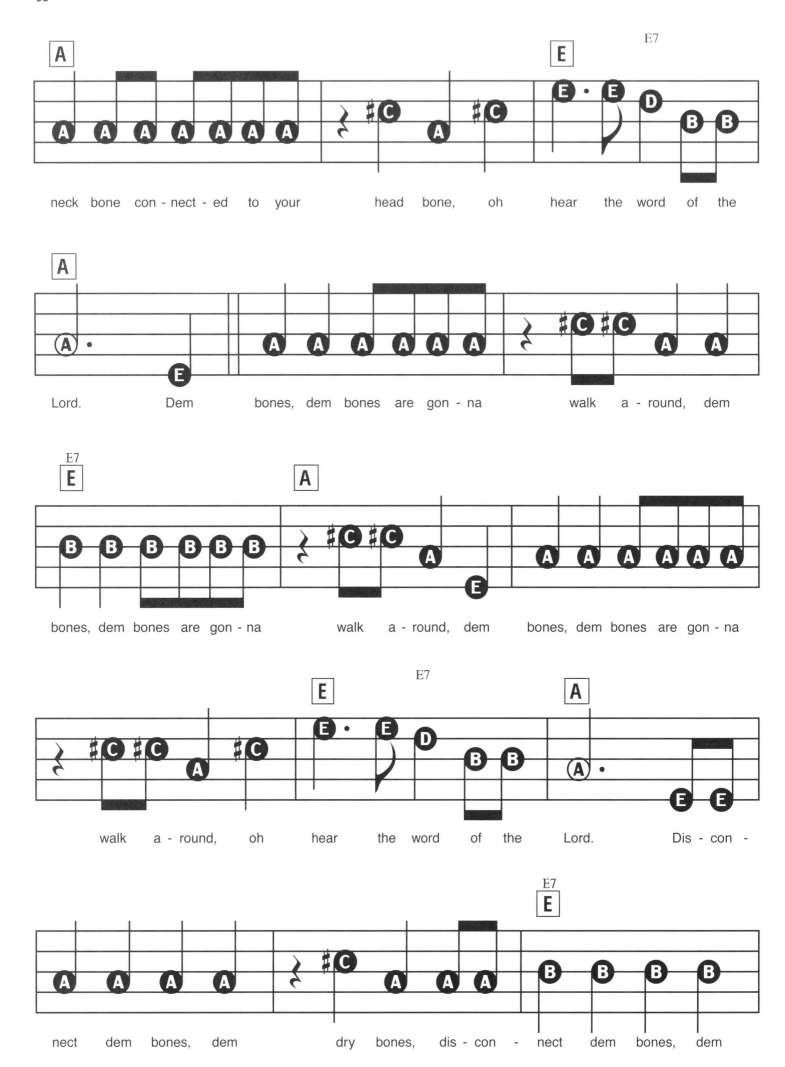

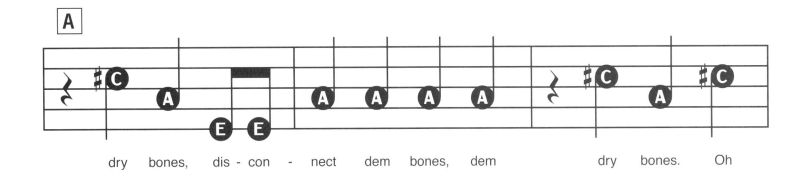

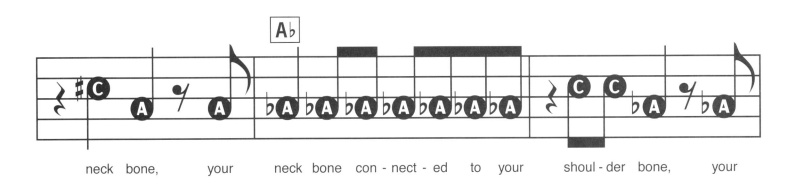

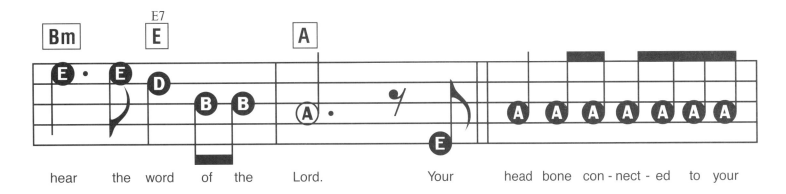

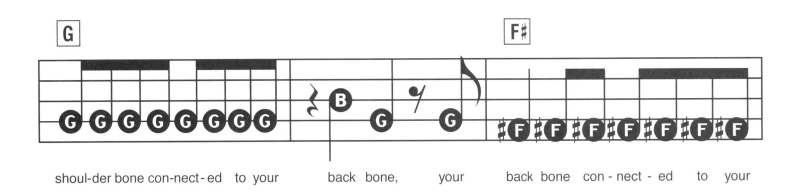

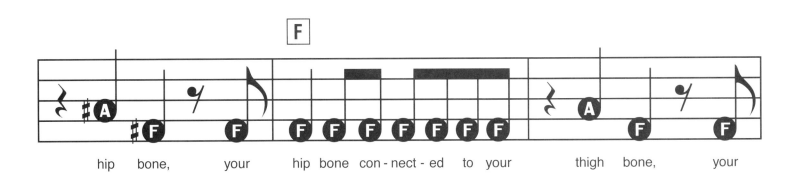

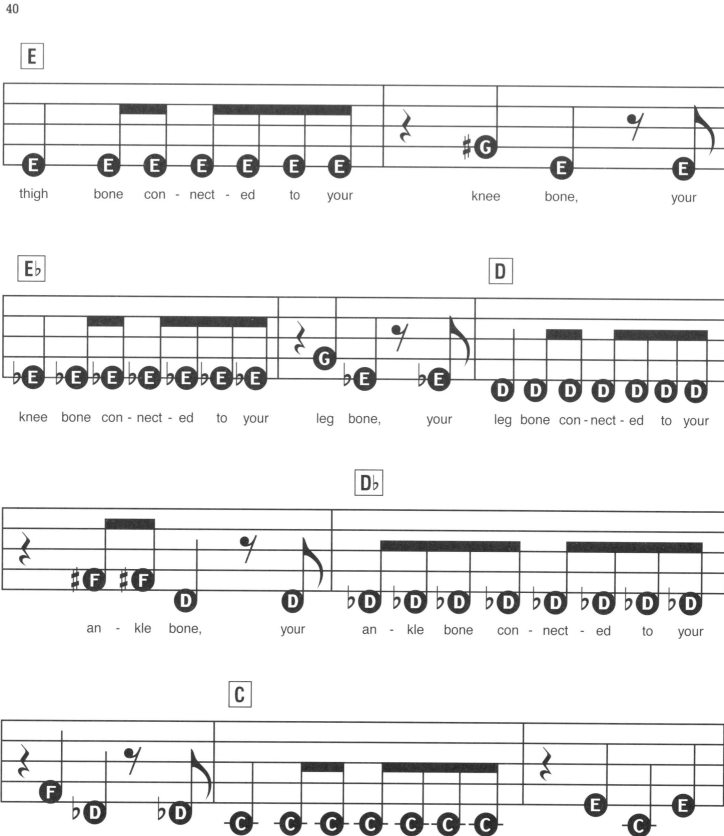

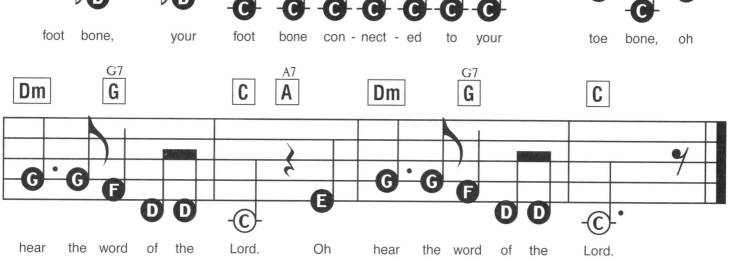

The Farmer in the Dell

Registration 3
Rhythm: Waltz

Traditional

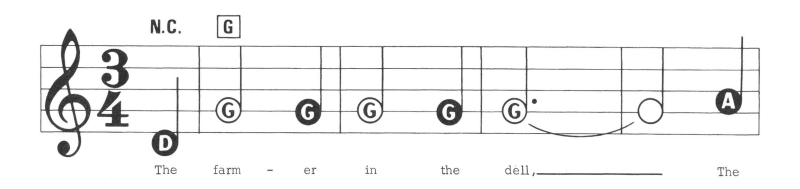

The farm - er in the dell,_____ The

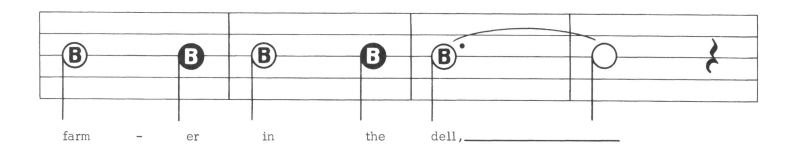

farm - er in the dell,_____

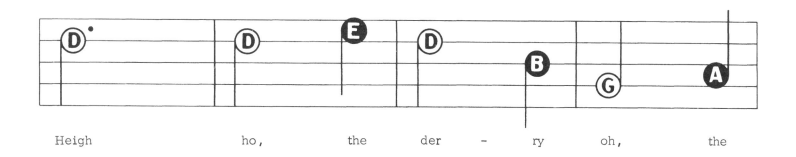

Heigh ho, the der - ry oh, the

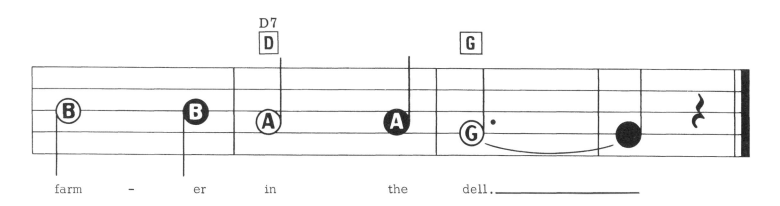

farm - er in the dell._____

Eensy Weensy Spider

Registration 8
Rhythm: Waltz

Traditional

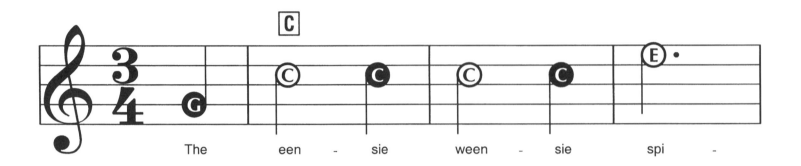

The een - sie ween - sie spi -

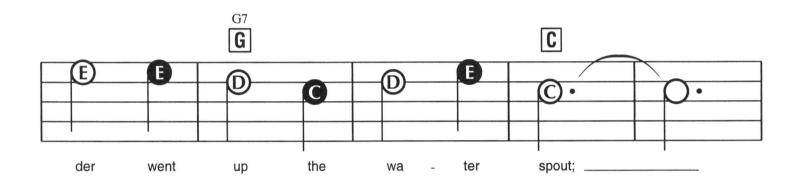

der went up the wa - ter spout; _____

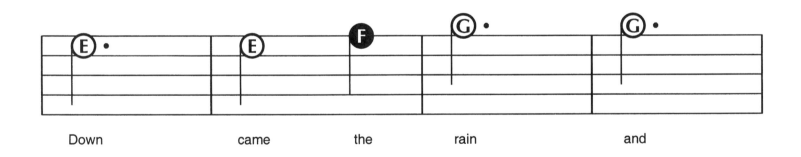

Down came the rain and

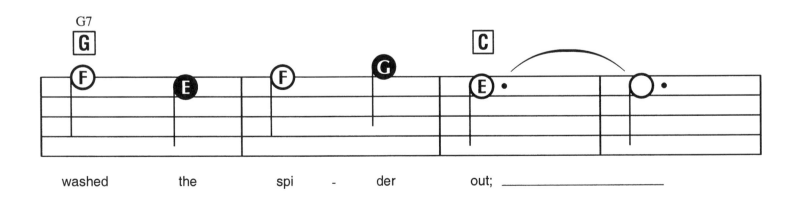

washed the spi - der out; _____

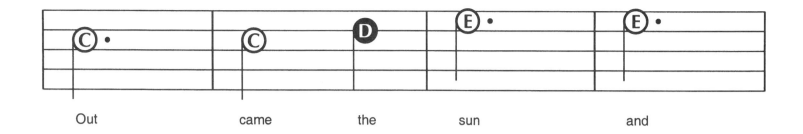

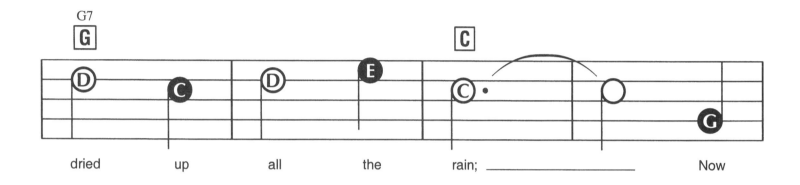

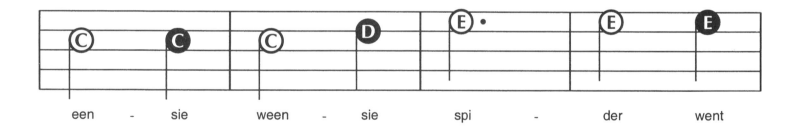

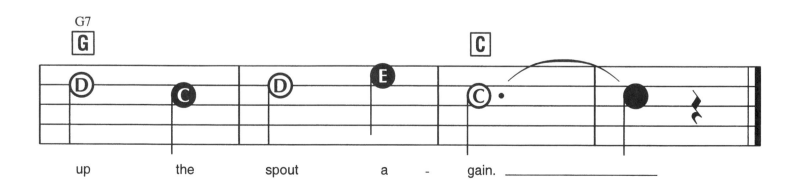

Fee! Fi! Foe! Fum!

Registration 2
Rhythm: March

Traditional

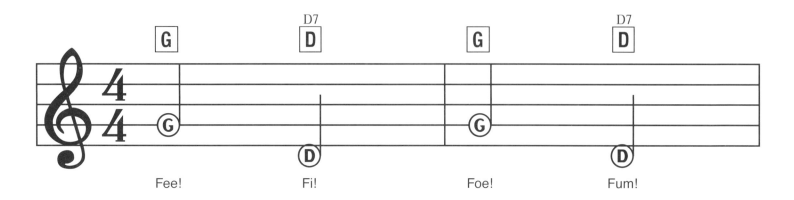

Fee!   Fi!   Foe!   Fum!

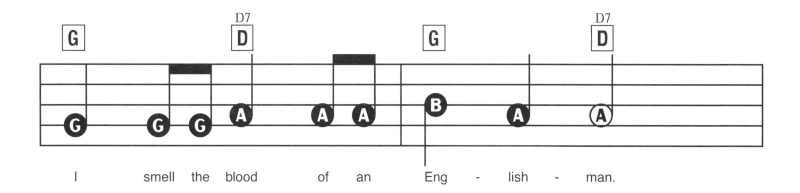

I   smell   the   blood   of   an   Eng - lish - man.

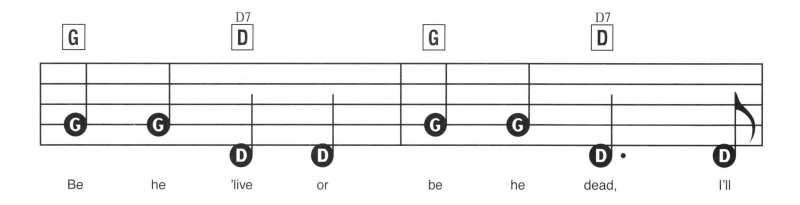

Be   he   'live   or   be   he   dead,   I'll

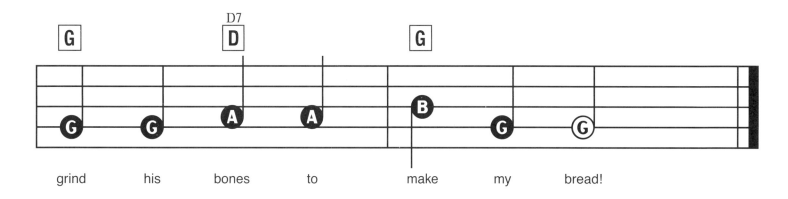

grind   his   bones   to   make   my   bread!

Five Little Ducks

Registration 7
Rhythm: March

Traditional

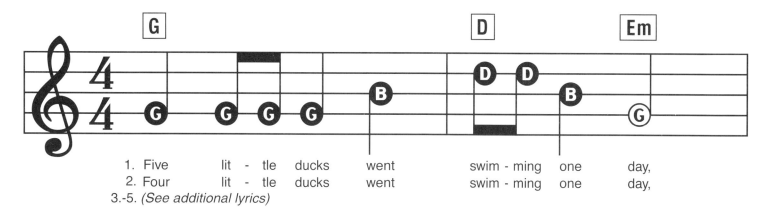

1. Five lit - tle ducks went swim - ming one day,
2. Four lit - tle ducks went swim - ming one day,
3.-5. *(See additional lyrics)*

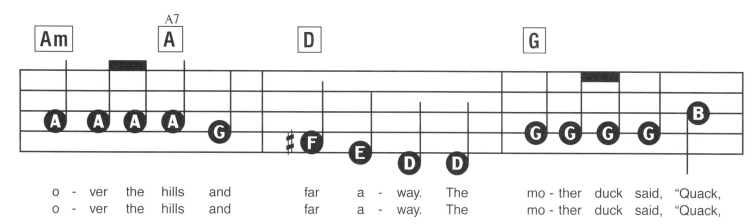

o - ver the hills and far a - way. The mo - ther duck said, "Quack,
o - ver the hills and far a - way. The mo - ther duck said, "Quack,

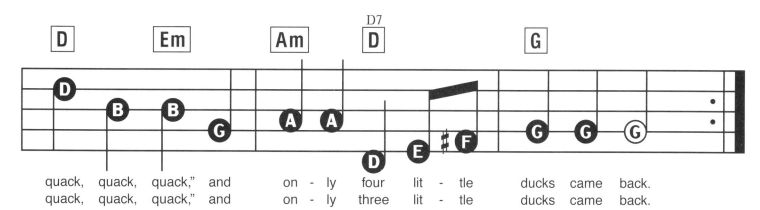

quack, quack, quack," and on - ly four lit - tle ducks came back.
quack, quack, quack," and on - ly three lit - tle ducks came back.

Additional Lyrics

3. Three little ducks went swimming one day,
over the hills and far away.
The mother duck said, "Quack, quack, quack, quack,"
and only two little ducks came swimming back.

4. Two little ducks went swimming one day,
over the hills and far away.
The mother duck said, "Quack, quack, quack, quack,"
and only one little duck came swimming back.

5. One little duck went swimming one day,
over the hills and far away.
The mother duck said, "Quack, quack, quack, quack,"
and five little ducks came swimming right back.

Fiddle-De-Dee

Registration 5
Rhythm: 6/8 March

Traditional

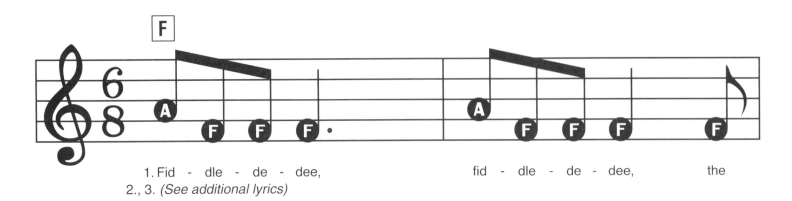

1. Fid - dle - de - dee,   fid - dle - de - dee,   the
2., 3. *(See additional lyrics)*

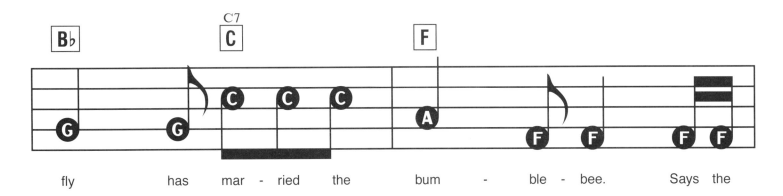

fly   has   mar - ried   the   bum - ble - bee.   Says the

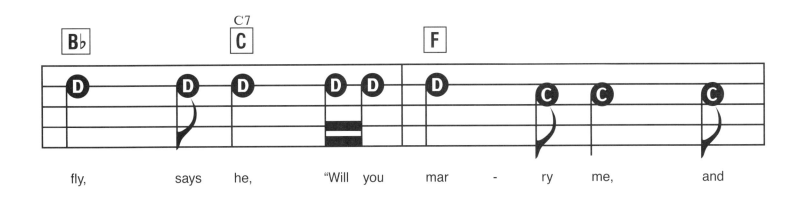

fly,   says   he,   "Will   you   mar - ry   me,   and

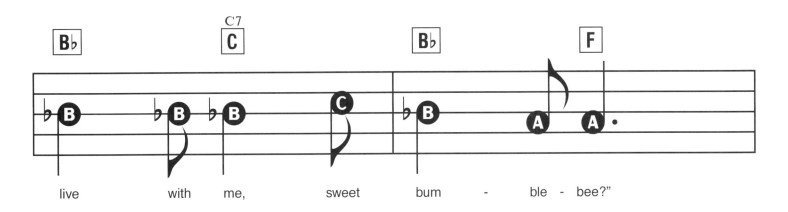

live   with   me,   sweet   bum - ble - bee?"

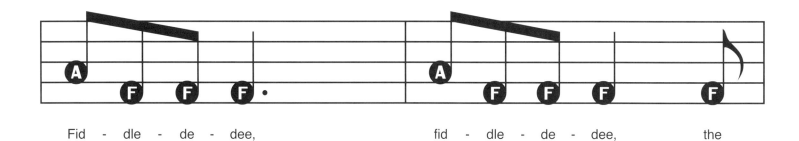

Fid - dle - de - dee,　　fid - dle - de - dee,　　the

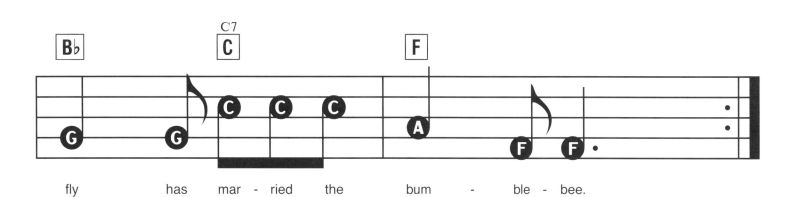

fly　　has　mar - ried　the　　bum - ble - bee.

Additional Lyrics

2. Fiddle-de-dee, fiddle-de-dee,
The fly has married the bumblebee.
Says the bee, says she, "I'll live under your wing,
And you'll never know I carry a sting."
Fiddle-de-dee, fiddle-de-dee,
the fly has married the bumblebee.

3. Fiddle-de-dee, fiddle-de-dee,
The fly has married the bumblebee.
And when parson beetle had married the pair,
They both went out to take the air.
Fiddle-de-dee, fiddle-de-dee,
the fly has married the bumblebee.

Five Little Speckled Frogs

Registration 9
Rhythm: Fox Trot or Polka

Traditional

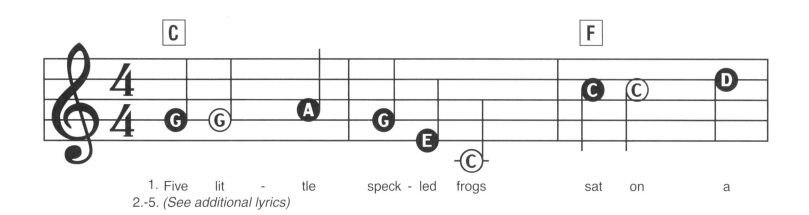

1. Five lit - tle speck - led frogs sat on a
2.-5. *(See additional lyrics)*

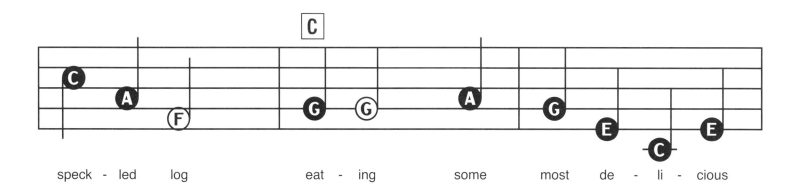

speck - led log eat - ing some most de - li - cious

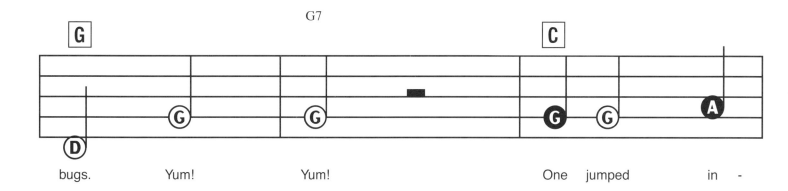

bugs. Yum! Yum! One jumped in -

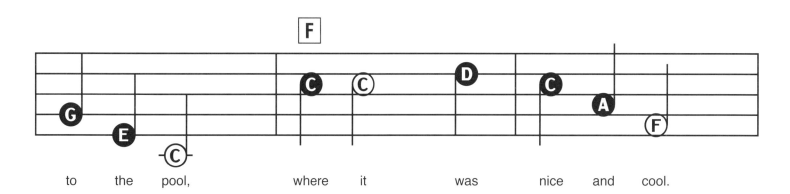

to the pool, where it was nice and cool.

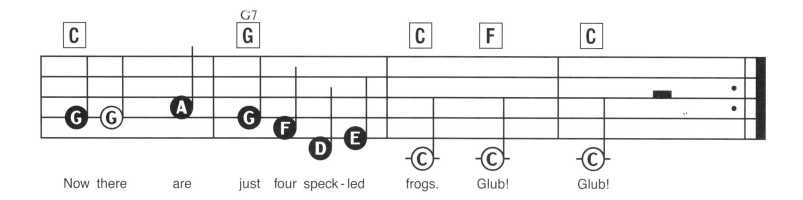

Now there   are   just four speck-led   frogs.   Glub!   Glub!

Additional Lyrics

2. Four little speckled frogs *etc.*

3. Three little speckled frogs *etc.*

4. Two little speckled frogs *etc.*

5. One little speckled frog
   Sat on a speckled log,
   Eating some most delicious bugs,
   Yum! Yum!
   One jumped into the pool,
   Where it was nice and cool,
   Now there are no more speckled frogs,
   Glub! Glub!

Found a Peanut

Registration 9
Rhythm: Waltz

Traditional

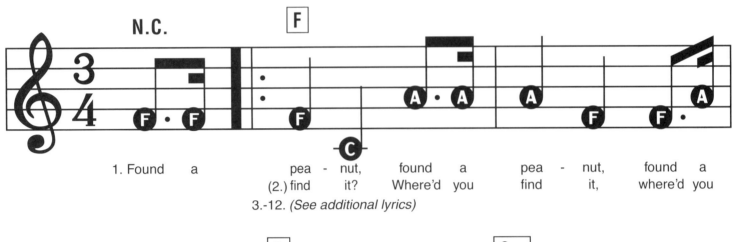

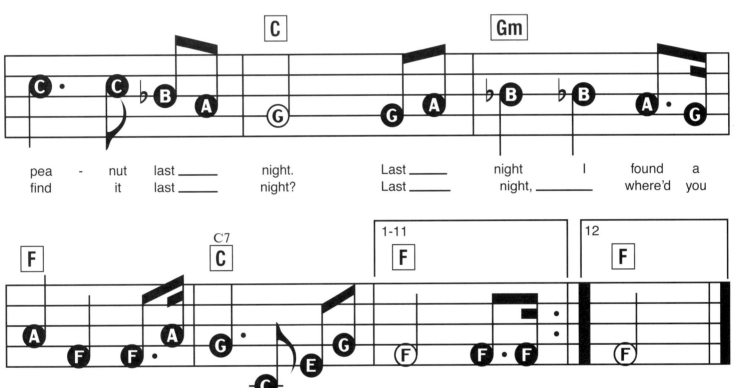

Additional Lyrics

3. In a dustbin, *etc.*

4. Cracked it open, *etc.*

5. Found it rotten, *etc.*

6. Ate it anyway, *etc.*

7. I felt sick, *etc.*

8. Called the doctor, *etc.*

9. Went to heaven, *etc.*

10. Didn't want me, *etc.*

11. Went the other way, *etc.*

12. Shoveling coal, *etc.*

Georgie Porgie

Registration 4
Rhythm: 6/8 March

Traditional

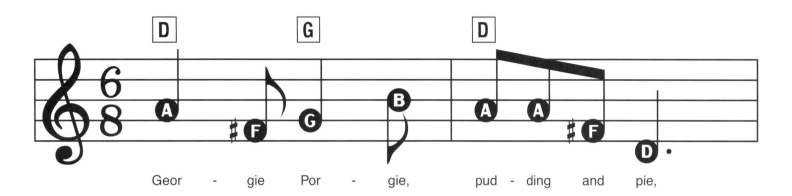

Geor - gie Por - gie, pud - ding and pie,

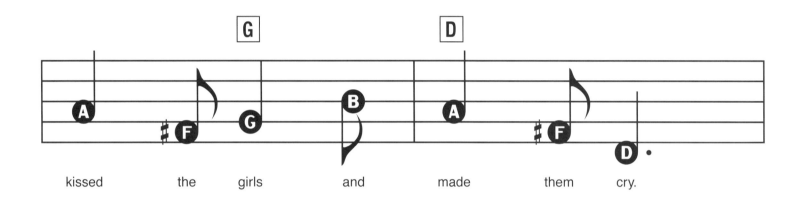

kissed the girls and made them cry.

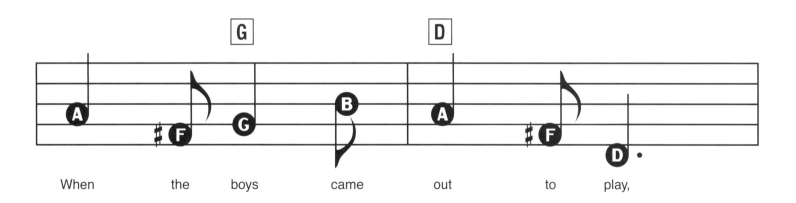

When the boys came out to play,

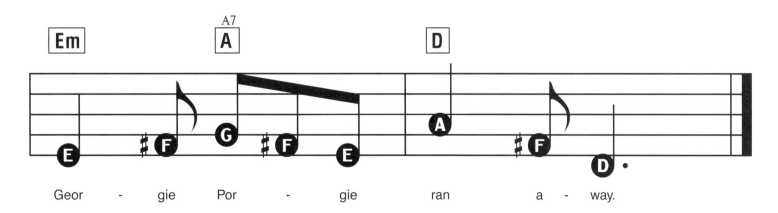

Geor - gie Por - gie ran a - way.

Frère Jacques
(Are You Sleeping?)

Registration 8
Rhythm: Fox Trot

Traditional French

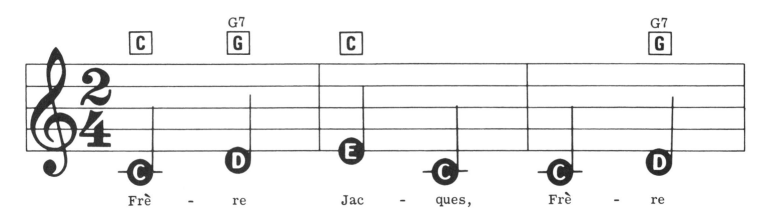

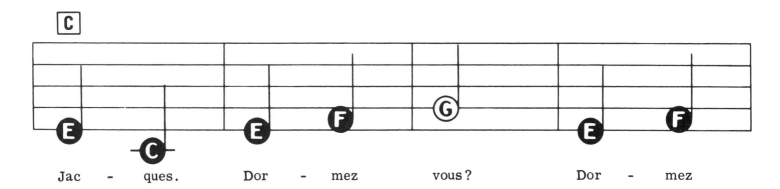

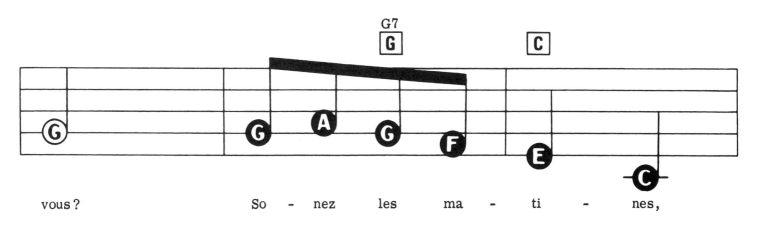

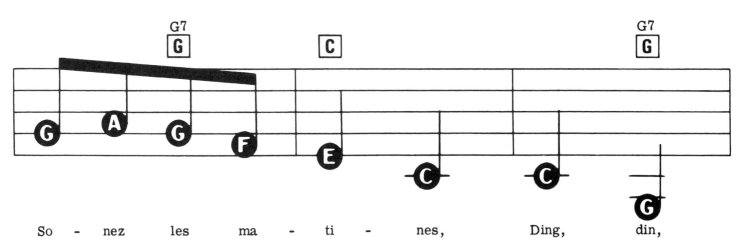

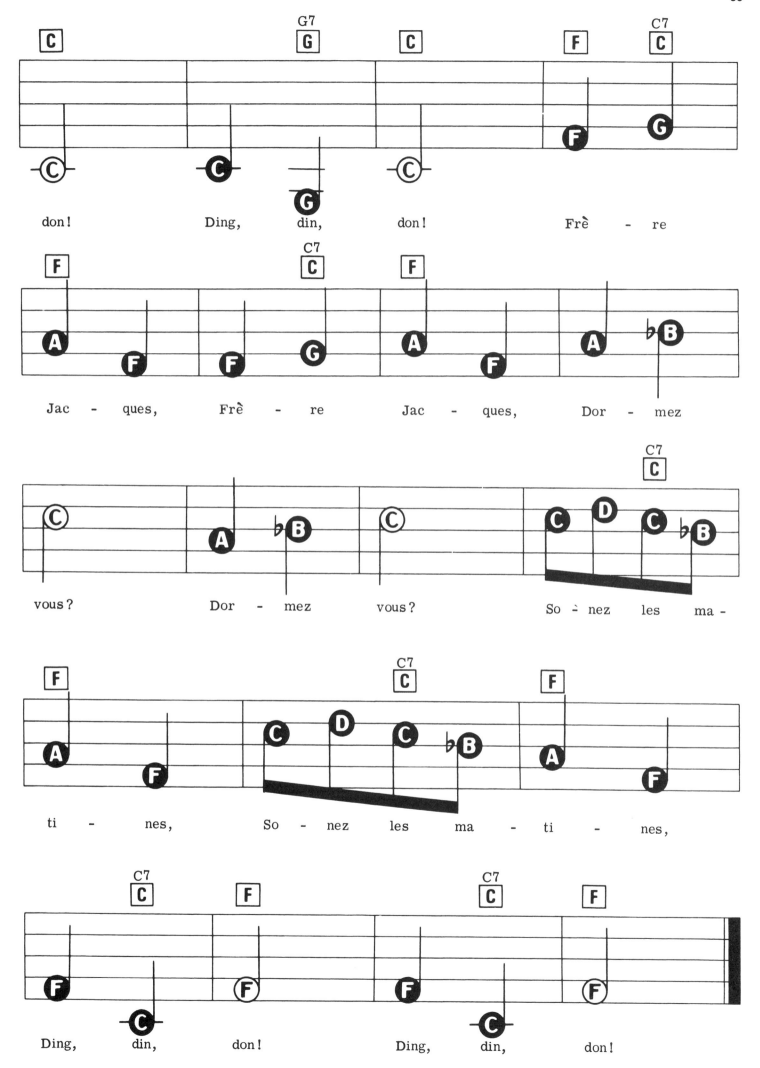

Frog Went A-Courtin'

Registration 2
Rhythm: March, Polka or Pops

Traditional

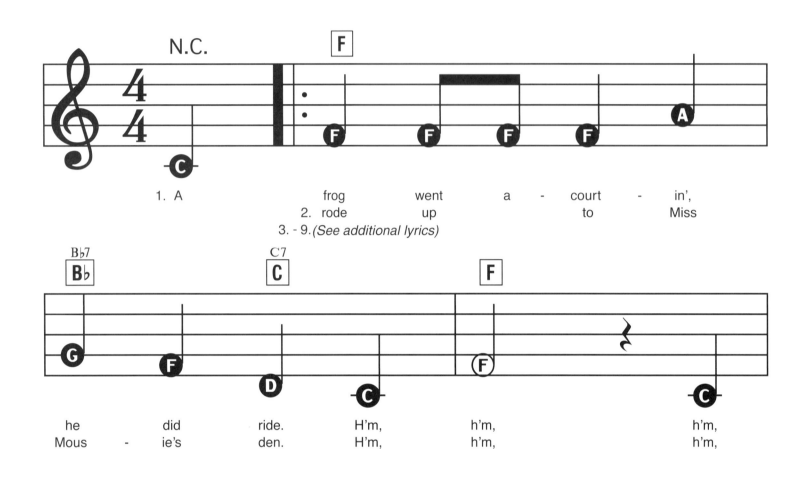

1. A frog went a - court - in',
2. rode up to Miss
3. - 9. *(See additional lyrics)*

he did ride. H'm, h'm, h'm,
Mous - ie's den. H'm, h'm, h'm,

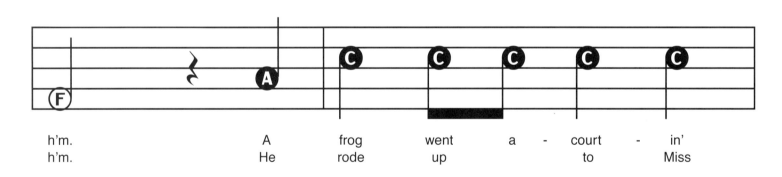

h'm. A frog went a - court - in'
h'm. He rode up to in' Miss

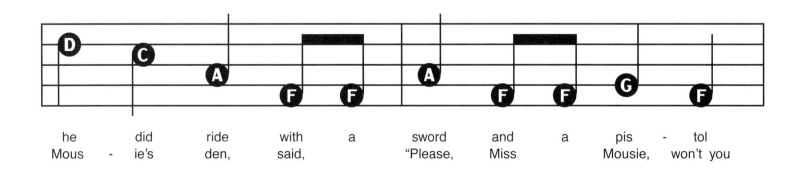

he did ride with a sword and a pis - tol
Mous - ie's den, said, "Please, Miss Mousie, won't you

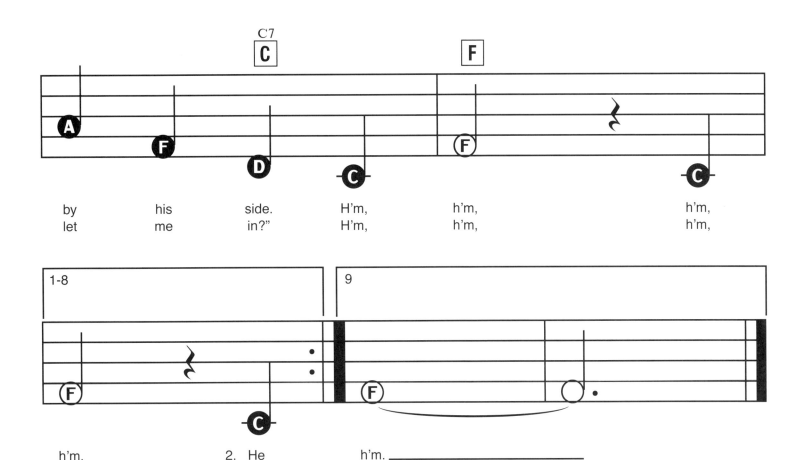

by   his   side.   H'm,   h'm,   h'm,
let   me   in?"   H'm,   h'm,   h'm,

h'm.   2. He   h'm. _____
h'm.

Additional Lyrics

3. "Yes, Sir Frog, I sit and spin."
   H'm, h'm, H'm, h'm.
   "Yes, Sir Frog, I sit and spin;
   Pray Mister Froggie, won't you walk in?"
   H'm, h'm, H'm, h'm.

4. The frog said, "My dear, I've come to see."
   H'm, h'm, H'm, h'm.
   The frog said, "My dear, I've come to see
   If you, Miss Mousie, will marry me."
   H'm, h'm, H'm, h'm.

5. "I don't know what to say to that."
   H'm, h'm, H'm, h'm.
   "I don't know what to say to that
   Till I speak with my Uncle Rat."
   H'm, h'm, H'm, h'm.

6. When Uncle Rat came riding home,
   H'm, h'm, H'm, h'm.
   When Uncle Rat came riding home,
   Said he, "Who's been here since I've been gone?"
   H'm, h'm, H'm, h'm.

7. "A fine young froggie has been here."
   H'm, h'm, H'm, h'm.
   "A fine young froggie has been here;
   He means to marry me, it's clear."
   H'm, h'm, H'm, h'm.

8. So Uncle Rat, he rode to town.
   H'm, h'm, H'm, h'm.
   So Uncle Rat, he rode to town
   And bought his niece a wedding gown.
   H'm, h'm, H'm, h'm.

9. The frog and mouse they went to France.
   H'm, h'm, H'm, h'm.
   The frog and mouse they went to France,
   And that's the end of my romance.
   H'm, h'm, H'm, h'm.

Ging Gang Gooli

Registration 5
Rhythm: Fox Trot or Polka

Traditional

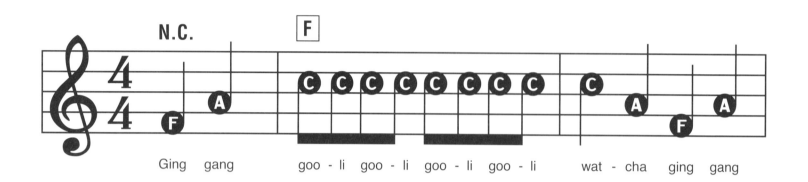

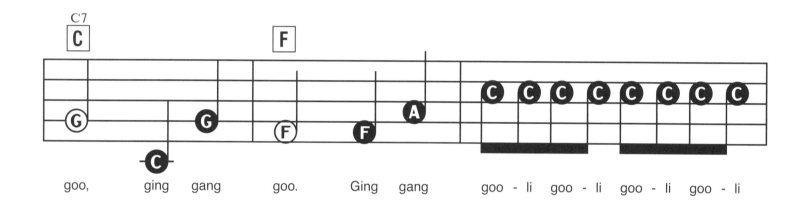

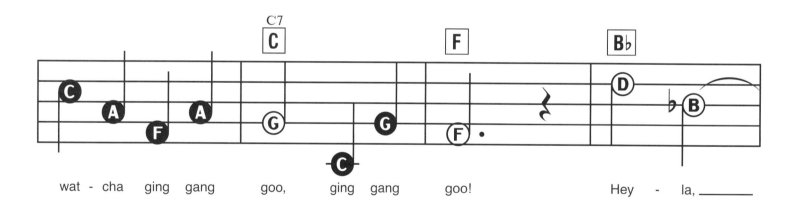

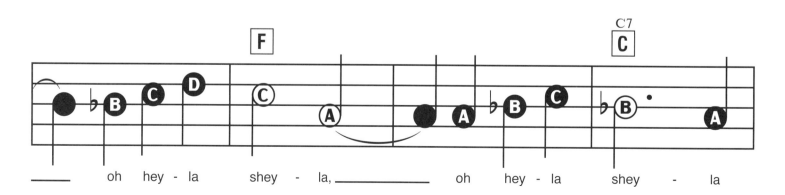

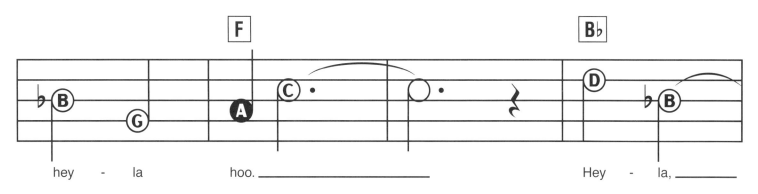

hey - la   hoo. _____   Hey - la, _____

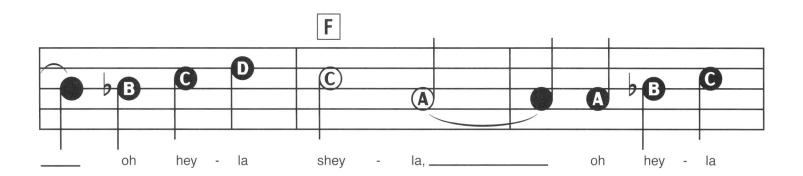

_____   oh hey - la   shey - la, _____   oh hey - la

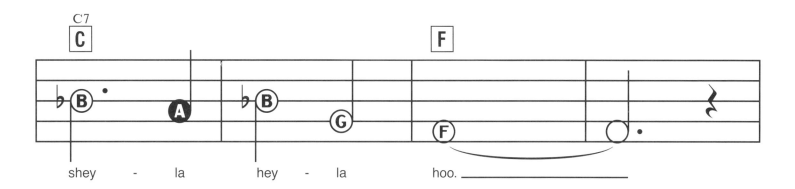

shey - la   hey - la   hoo. _____

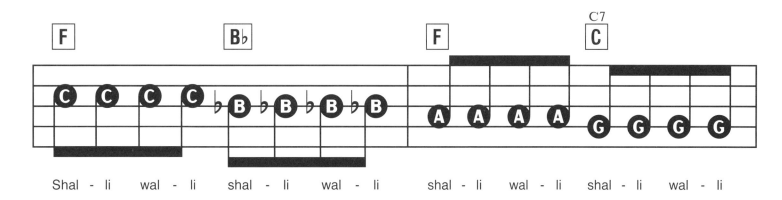

Shal - li wal - li shal - li wal - li shal - li wal - li shal - li wal - li

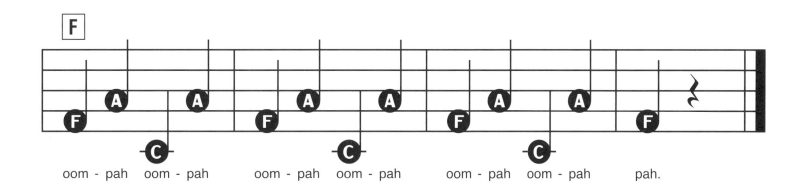

oom - pah oom - pah   oom - pah oom - pah   oom - pah oom - pah pah.

Going Over the Sea

Registration 9
Rhythm: 6/8 March

Traditional

1. When I was one I played a drum,
(2.) I was two I played ka - zoo,
3.-5. *(See additional lyrics)*

go - ing o - ver the sea.
go - ing o - ver the sea. I jumped a - board a

pi - rate's ship and the cap - tain said _____ to

me: "We're go - ing this way, that way,

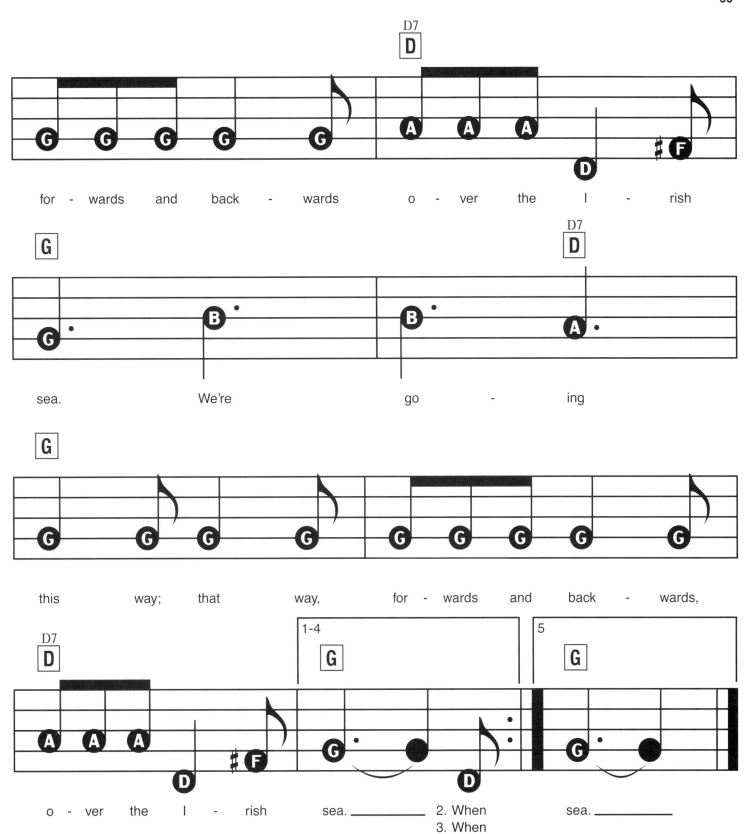

Additional Lyrics

3. When I was three I sang merrily,
   Going over the sea. *etc.*

4. When I was four I danced on the floor,
   Going over the sea. *etc.*

5. When I was five I did a jive,
   Going over the sea. *etc.*

Goosey, Goosey Gander

Registration 8
Rhythm: Fox Trot

Traditional

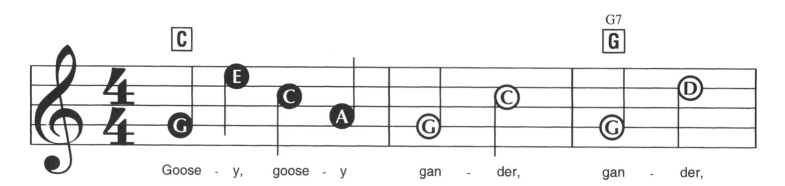

Goose - y, goose - y gan - der, gan - der,

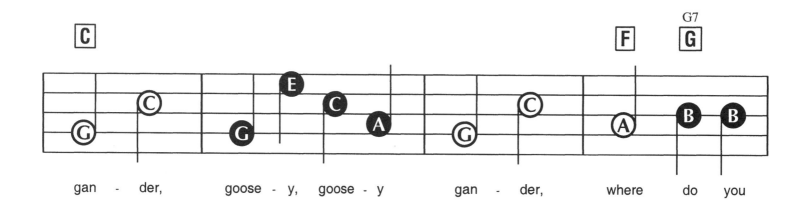

gan - der, goose - y, goose - y gan - der, where do you

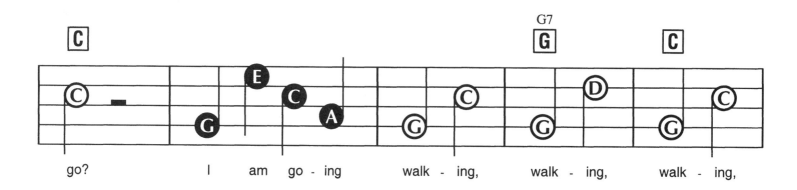

go? I am go - ing walk - ing, walk - ing, walk - ing,

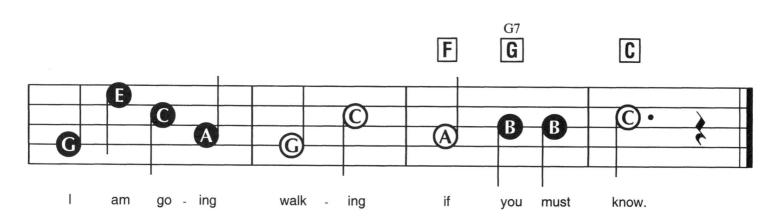

I am go - ing walk - ing if you must know.

The Grand Old Duke of York

Registration 2
Rhythm: March

Traditional

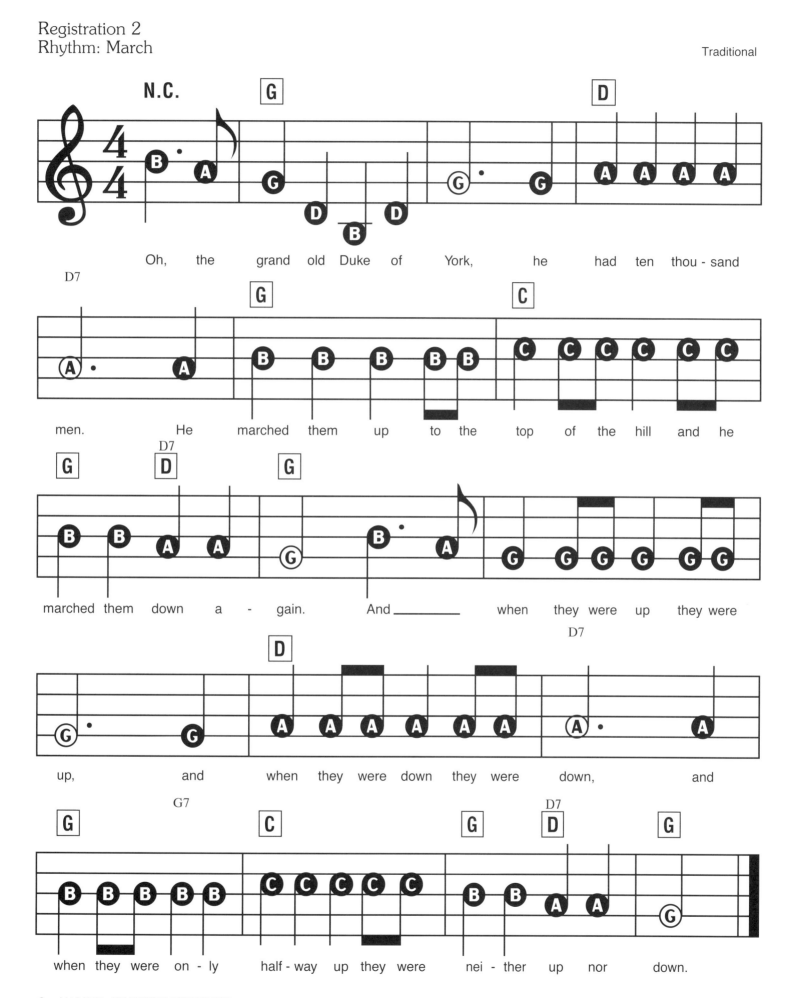

Grandfather's Clock

Registration 7
Rhythm: 8-Beat or Pops

By Henry Clay Work

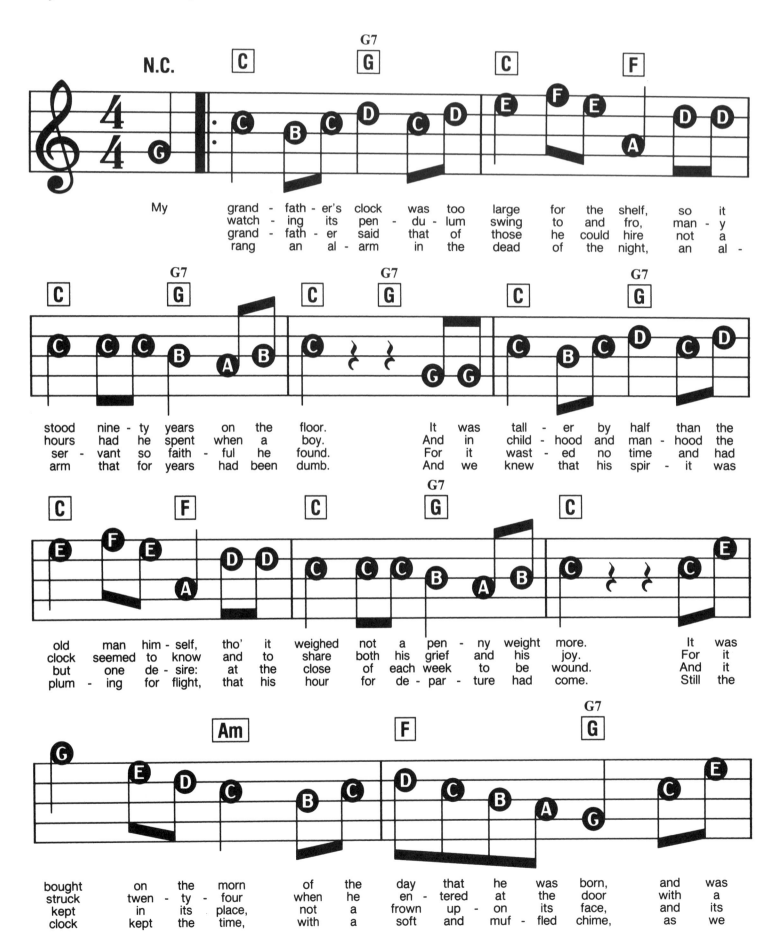

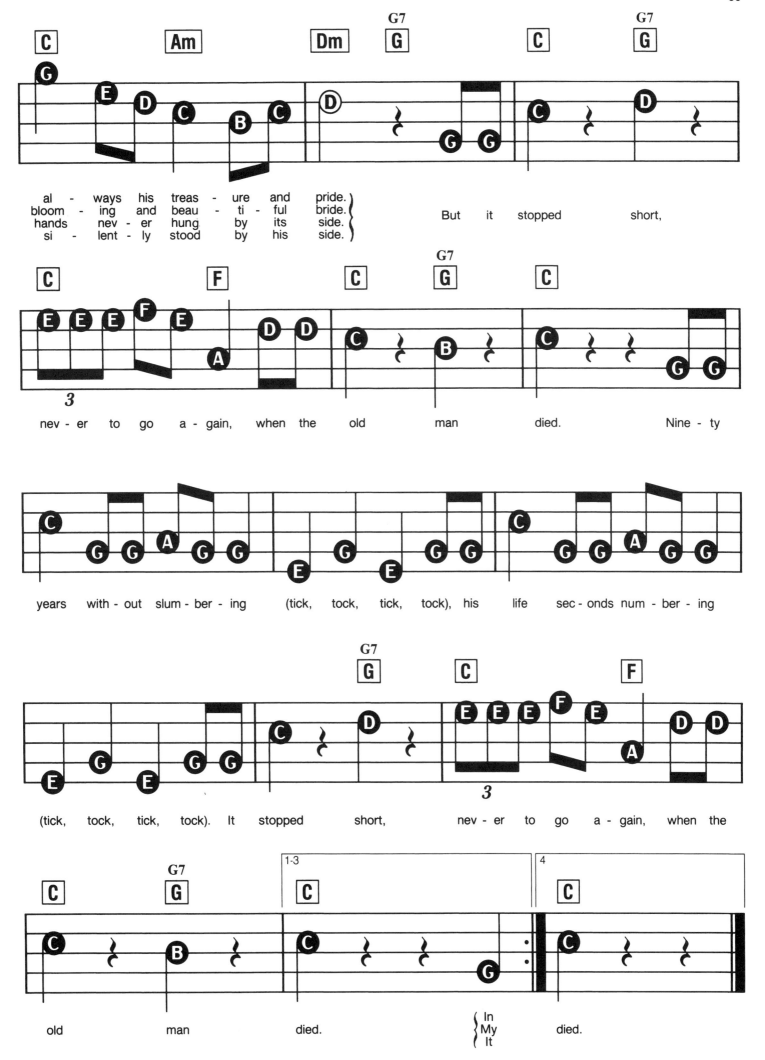

Green Grow the Rushes, O

Registration 1
Rhythm: March

Traditional Irish Folksong

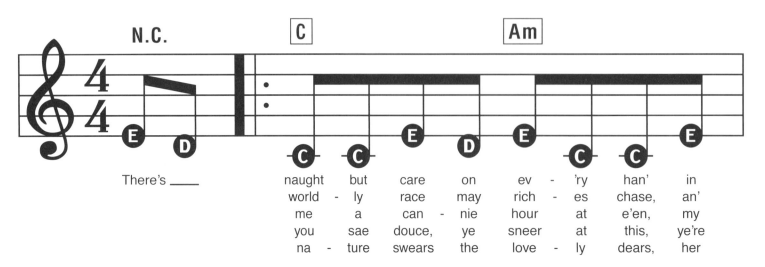

There's ___	naught	but	care	on	ev -	'ry	han'	in
	world -	ly	race	may	rich -	es	chase,	an'
	me	a	can -	nie	hour	at	e'en,	my
	you	sae	douce,	ye	sneer	at	this,	ye're
	na -	ture	swears	the	love -	ly	dears,	her

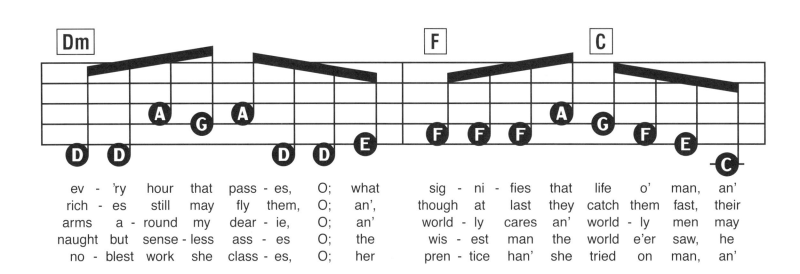

ev -	'ry	hour	that	pass -	es,	O;	what	sig -	ni -	fies	that	life	o' man, an'
rich -	es	still	may	fly	them,	O;	an',	though	at	last	they	catch	them fast, their
arms	a -	round	my	dear -	ie,	O;	an'	world -	ly	cares	an'	world -	ly men may
naught	but	sense -	less	ass -	es,	O;	the	wis -	est	man	the	world	e'er saw, he
no -	blest	work	she	class -	es,	O;	her	pren -	tice	han'	she	tried	on man, an'

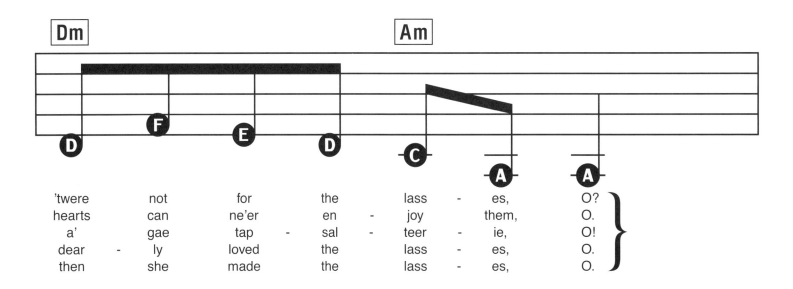

'twere	not	for	the	lass -	es,	O?
hearts	can	ne'er	en -	joy	them,	O.
a'	gae	tap -	sal -	teer -	ie,	O!
dear -	ly	loved	the	lass -	es,	O.
then	she	made	the	lass -	es,	O.

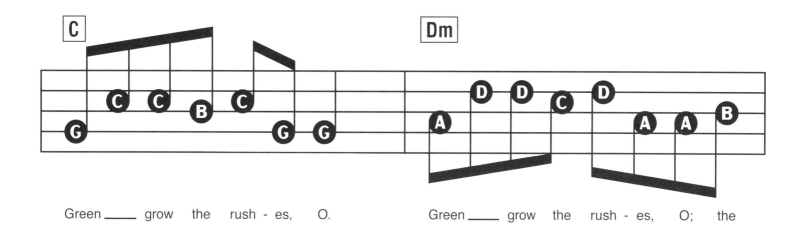

Green _____ grow the rush - es, O.   Green _____ grow the rush - es, O; the

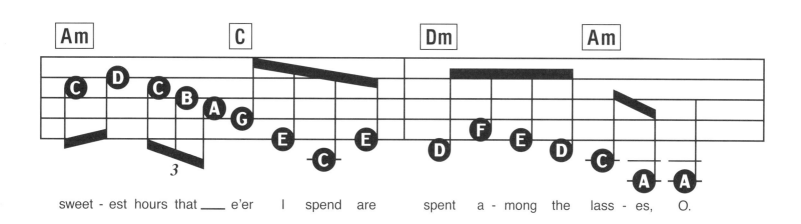

sweet - est hours that _____ e'er   I   spend are   spent a - mong the lass - es, O.

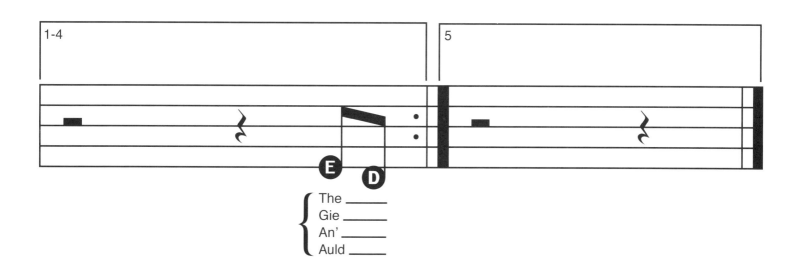

The _____
Gie _____
An' _____
Auld _____

Hark, Hark, the Dogs Do Bark

Registration 2
Rhythm: Waltz

Traditional

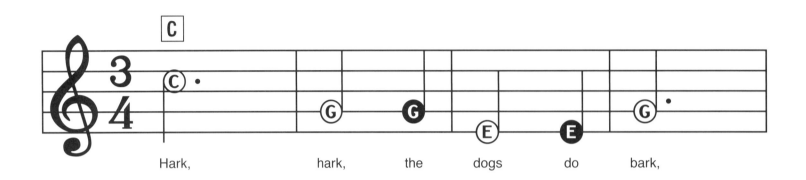

Hark, hark, the dogs do bark,

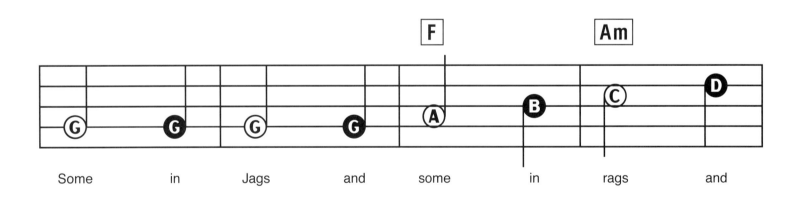

beg - gars are com - ing to town. _____

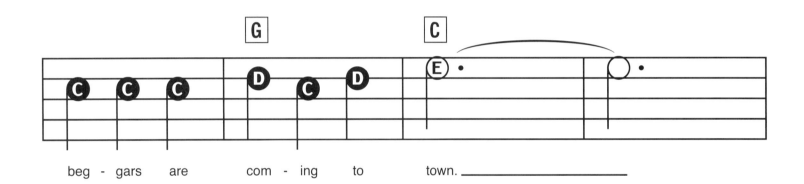

Some in Jags and some in rags and

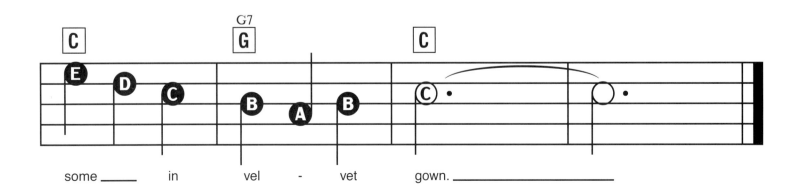

some _____ in vel - vet gown. _____

Head, Shoulders, Knees and Toes

Registration 9
Rhythm: March or Polka

Traditional

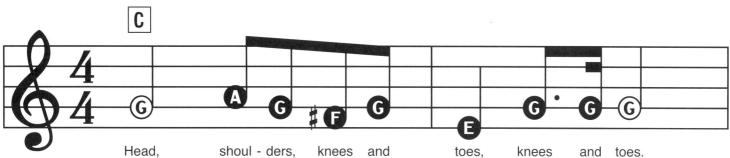

Head, shoul - ders, knees and toes, knees and toes.

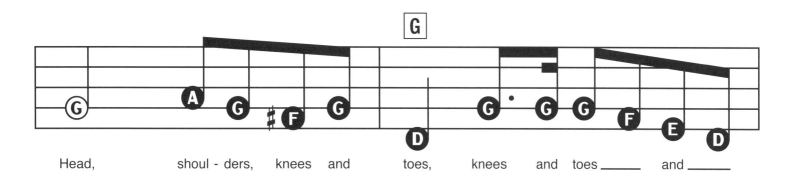

Head, shoul - ders, knees and toes, knees and toes _____ and _____

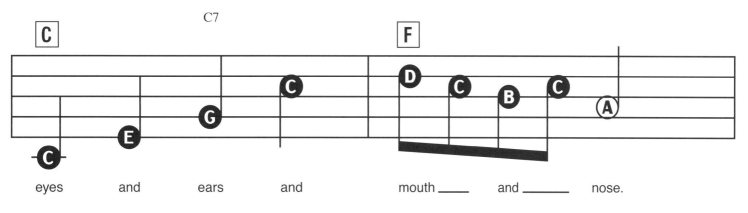

eyes and ears and mouth ____ and _____ nose.

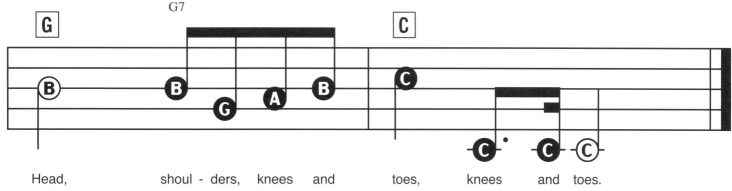

Head, shoul - ders, knees and toes, knees and toes.

Activity

Repeat the song, each time omitting a body part, in the order that they are sung. For example, the second time around you would point at your head but not actually say the word "head" out loud. The third time around you would leave out "head" and "shoulder" but still point to them. Keep doing this until you are not saying anything – just pointing at the body parts. You could also try getting faster and faster for an extra challenge!

Have a Little Dog

Registration 4
Rhythm: Fox Trot

Traditional

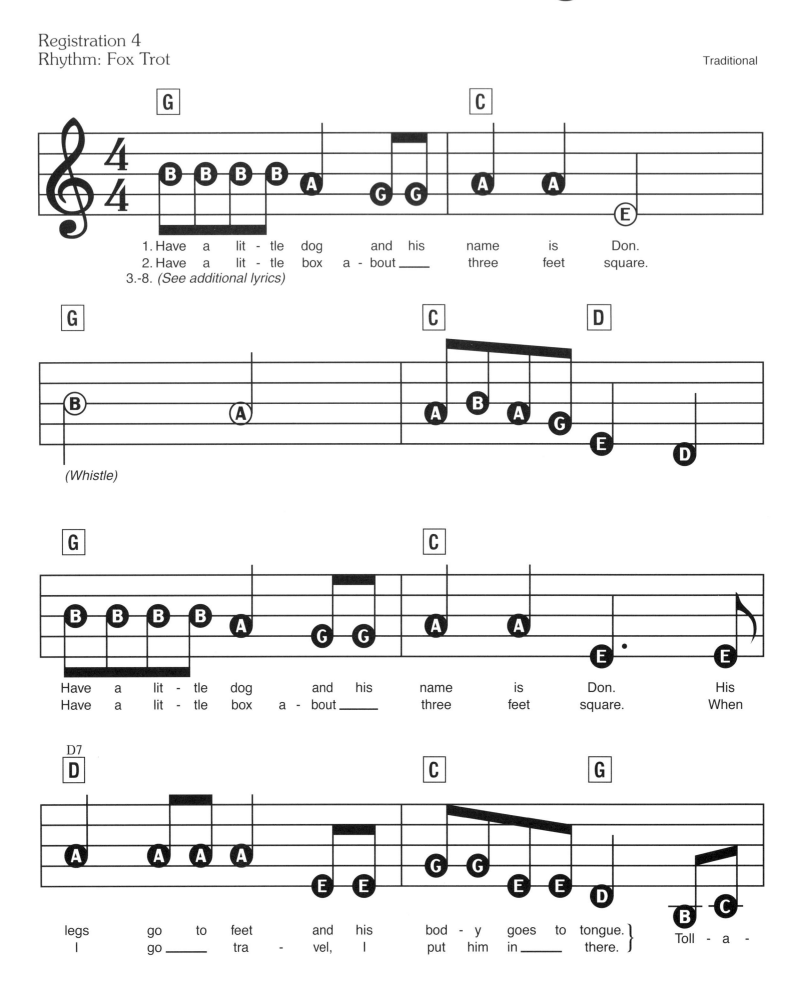

1. Have a lit - tle dog   and his   name   is   Don.
2. Have a lit - tle box a - bout ____ three   feet   square.
3.-8. *(See additional lyrics)*

(Whistle)

Have a lit - tle dog   and his   name   is   Don.   His
Have a lit - tle box a - bout ____ three   feet   square.   When

legs   go to feet   and his   bod - y   goes to tongue.
I   go ____ tra - vel, I   put him in ____ there.

Toll - a -

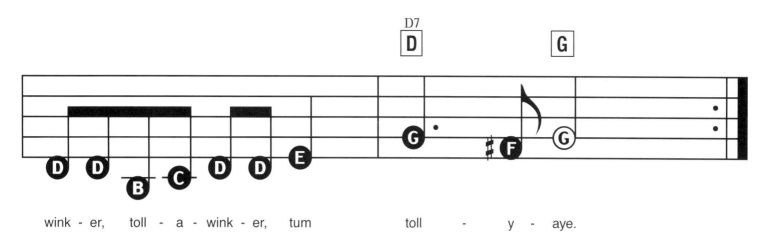

winker, toll-a-winker, tum toll-y-aye.

Additional Lyrics

3. When I go to travel, I travel like an ox. *(whistle)*
   When I go to travel, I travel like an ox.
   And in that vest pocket I carry that box.
   Toll-a-winker, toll-a-winker, tum-toll-aye.

4. Had a little hen and her color was fair. *(whistle)*
   Had a little hen and her color was fair.
   Sat her on a bomb and she hatched me a hare.
   Toll-a-winker, toll-a-winker, tum-toll-aye.

5. The hare turned a horse about six feet high. *(whistle)*
   The hare turned a horse about six feet high.
   If you want to beat this, you'll have to tell a lie.
   Toll-a-winker, toll-a-winker, tum-toll-aye.

6. I had a little mule and his name was Jack. *(whistle)*
   I had a little mule and his name was Jack.
   I rode him on his tail to save his back.
   Toll-a-winker, toll-a-winker, tum-toll-aye.

7. I had a little mule and his name was Jay. *(whistle)*
   I had a little mule and his name was Jay.
   I pulled his tail to hear him bray.
   Toll-a-winker, toll-a-winker, tum-toll-aye.

8. I had a little mule, he was made of hay. *(whistle)*
   I had a little mule, he was made of hay.
   First big wind come along and blew him away.
   Toll-a-winker, toll-a-winker, tum-toll-aye.

Here We Go Gathering Nuts in May

Registration 7
Rhythm: Waltz

Traditional

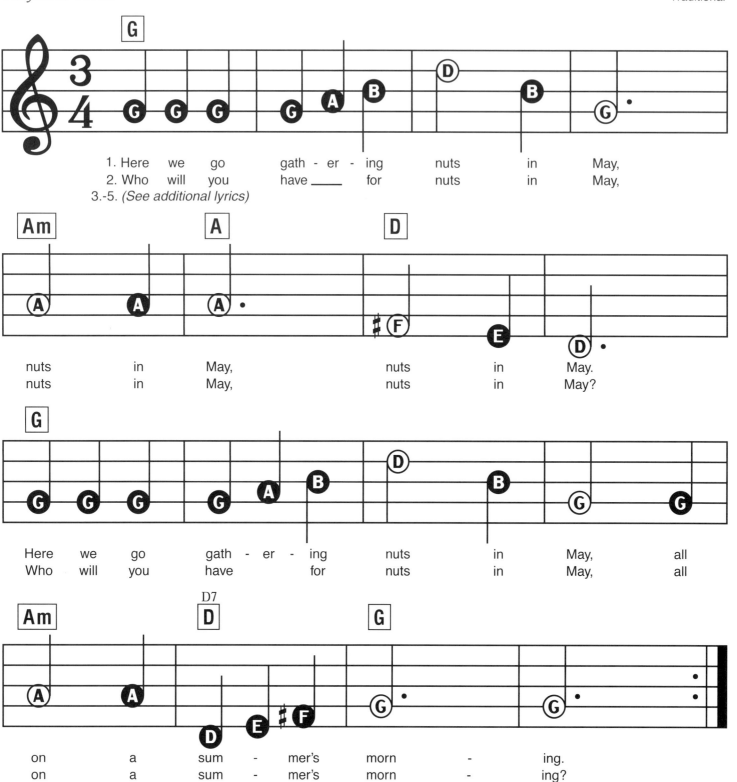

1. Here   we   go   gath - er - ing   nuts   in   May,
2. Who   will   you   have _____   for   nuts   in   May,
3.-5. *(See additional lyrics)*

nuts   in   May,   nuts   in   May.
nuts   in   May,   nuts   in   May?

Here   we   go   gath - er - ing   nuts   in   May,   all
Who   will   you   have   for   nuts   in   May,   all

on   a   sum - mer's   morn   -   ing.
on   a   sum - mer's   morn   -   ing?

Additional Lyrics

3. We'll have _____ for nuts in May, *etc.*

4. Who will you send to fetch her/him away? *etc.*

5. We'll send _____ to fetch her/him away, *etc.*

Hey Diddle Diddle

Registration 7
Rhythm: Waltz

Traditional

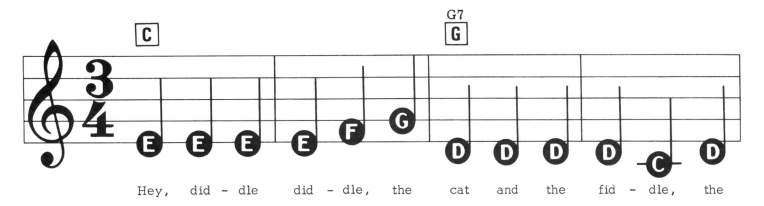

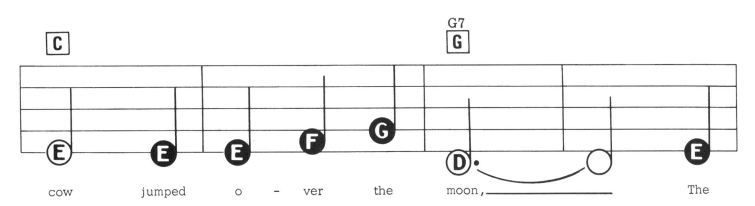

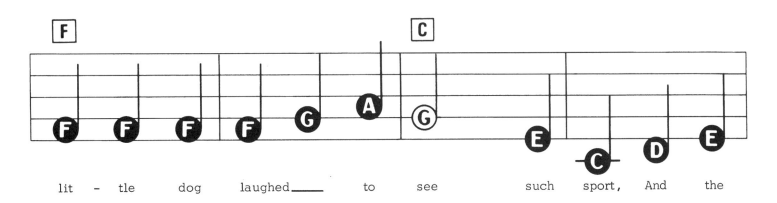

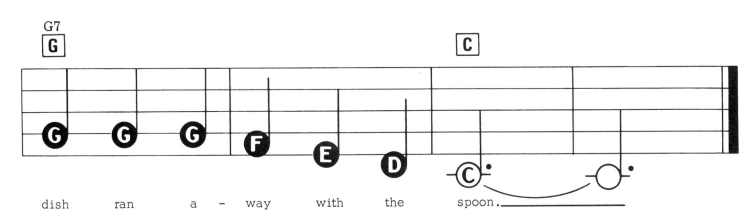

Here We Go Looby Loo

Registration 9
Rhythm: 6/8 March

Traditional

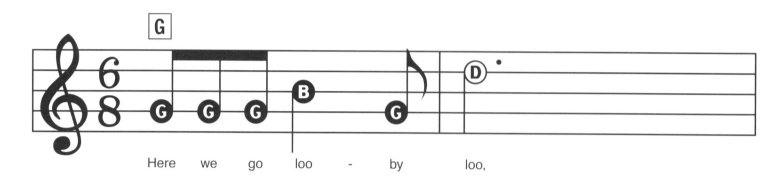

Here we go loo - by loo,

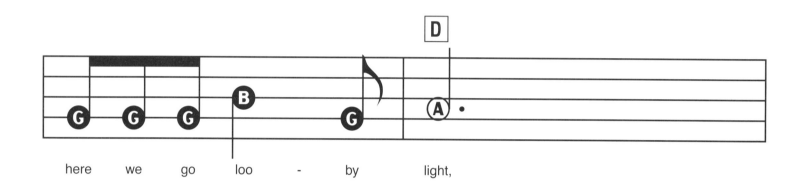

here we go loo - by light,

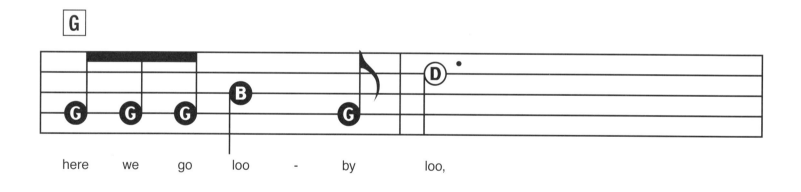

here we go loo - by loo,

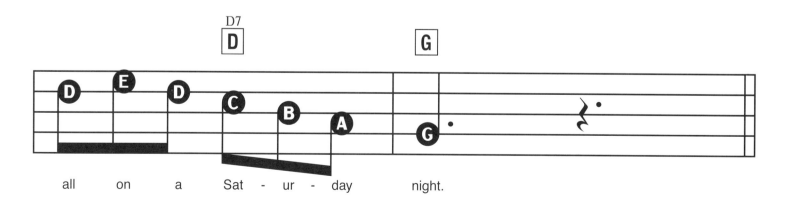

all on a Sat - ur - day night.

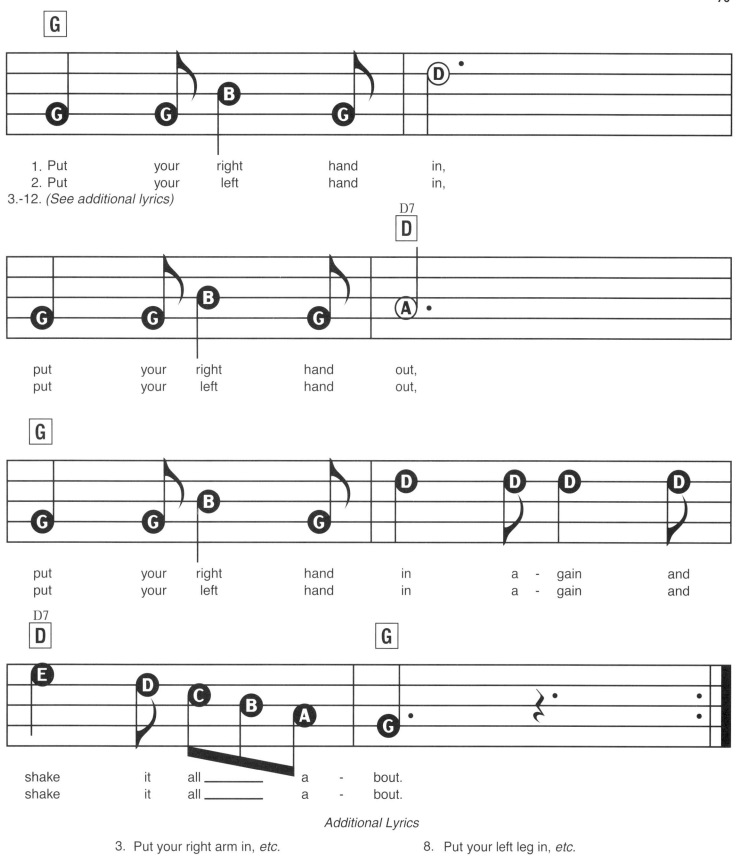

1. Put your right hand in,
2. Put your left hand in,
3.-12. *(See additional lyrics)*

put your right hand out,
put your left hand out,

put your right hand in a - gain and
put your left hand in a - gain and

shake it all_____ a - bout.
shake it all_____ a - bout.

Additional Lyrics

3. Put your right arm in, *etc.*

4. Put your left arm in, *etc.*

5. Put your right foot in, *etc.*

6. Put your left foot in, *etc.*

7. Put your right leg in, *etc.*

8. Put your left leg in, *etc.*

9. Put your back in, *etc.*

10. Put your front in, *etc.*

11. Put your head in, *etc.*

12. Put your whole self in, *etc.*

Hickory Dickory Dock

Registration 8
Rhythm: Waltz

Traditional

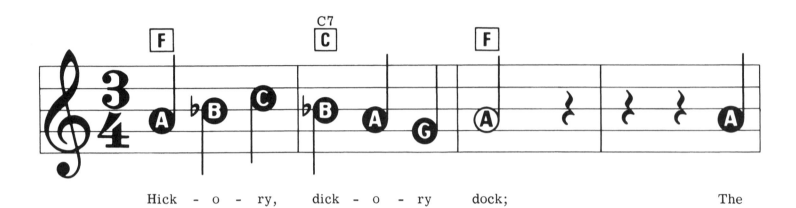

Hick - o - ry,   dick - o - ry   dock;   The

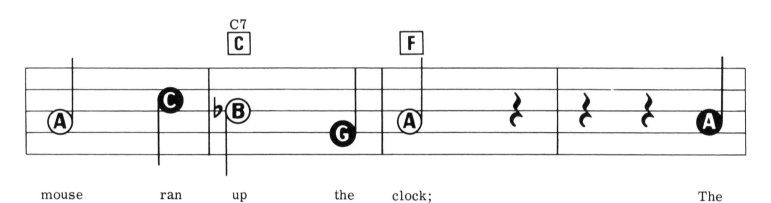

mouse   ran   up   the   clock;   The

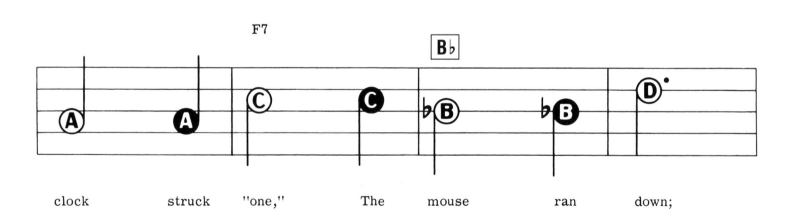

clock   struck   "one,"   The   mouse   ran   down;

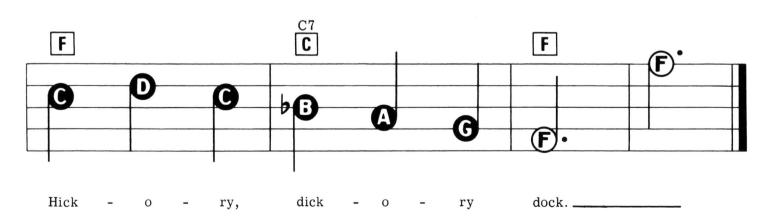

Hick - o - ry,   dick - o - ry   dock. _____

Hob Shoe Hob

Registration 8
Rhythm: March

Traditional

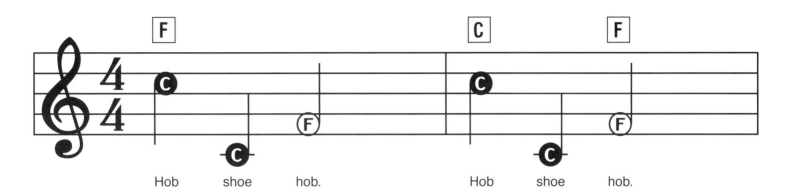

Hob   shoe   hob.   Hob   shoe   hob.

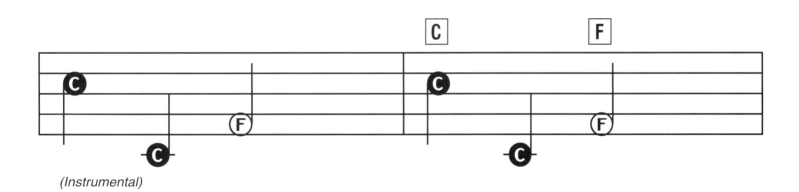

Here a nail and there a nail and   that's   well   shod.

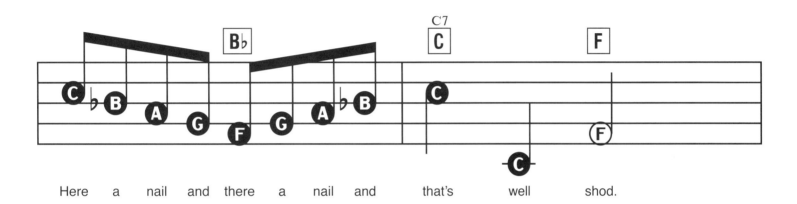

(Instrumental)

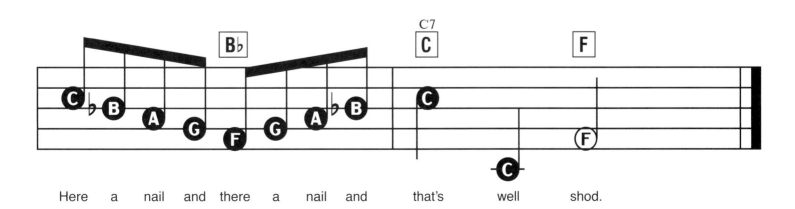

Here a nail and there a nail and   that's   well   shod.

Hot Cross Buns

Registration 5
Rhythm: Fox Trot

Traditional

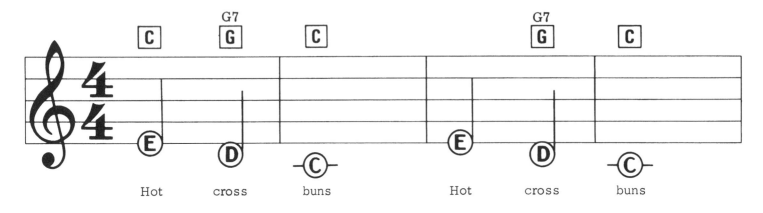

Hot cross buns Hot cross buns

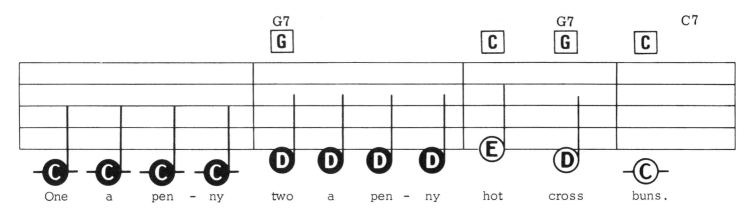

One a pen - ny two a pen - ny hot cross buns.

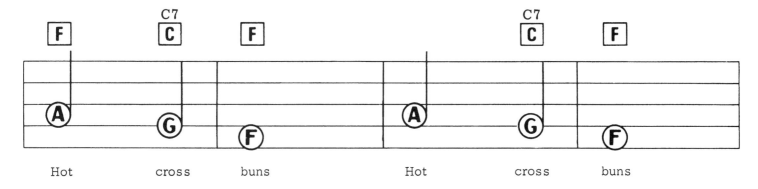

Hot cross buns Hot cross buns

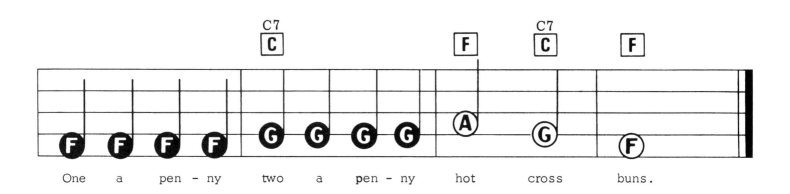

One a pen - ny two a pen - ny hot cross buns.

Humpty Dumpty

Registration 2
Rhythm: Waltz

Traditional

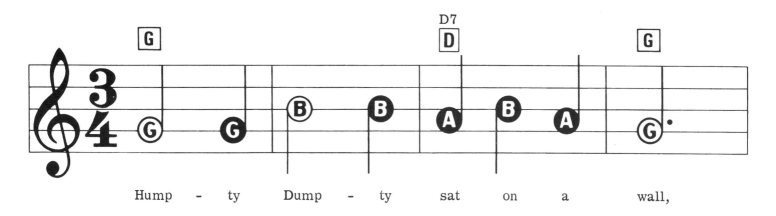

Hump - ty Dump - ty sat on a wall,

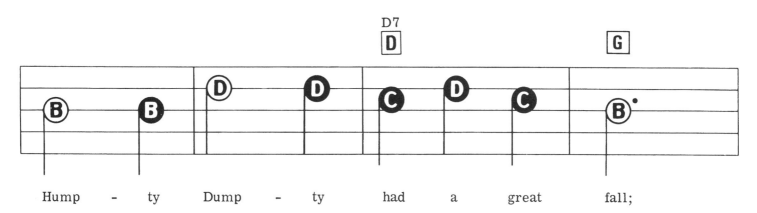

Hump - ty Dump - ty had a great fall;

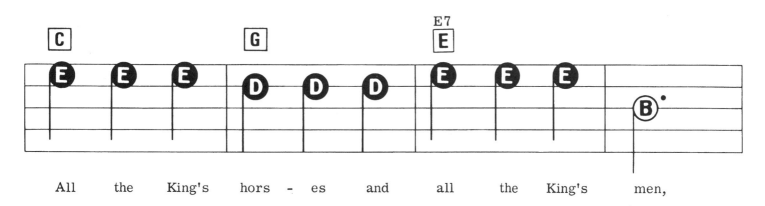

All the King's hors - es and all the King's men,

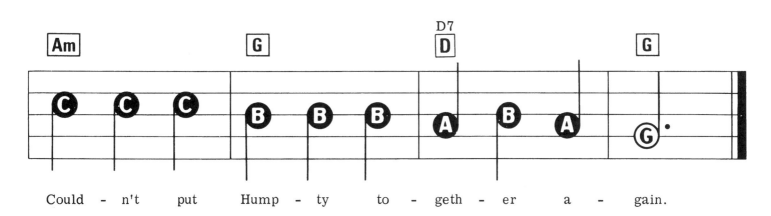

Could - n't put Hump - ty to - geth - er a - gain.

Hush-a-Bye, Baby

Registration 1
Rhythm: 6/8 March

Traditional

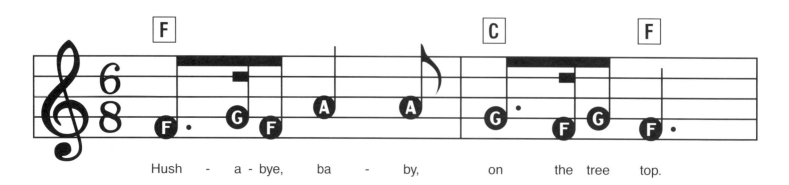

Hush - a - bye, ba - by, on the tree top.

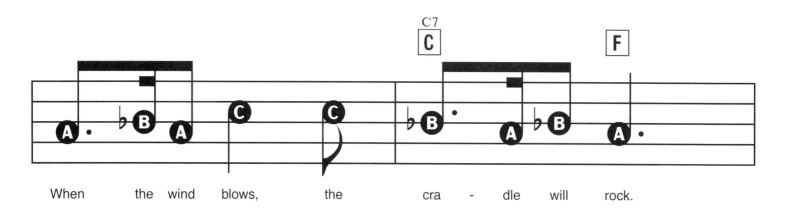

When the wind blows, the cra - dle will rock.

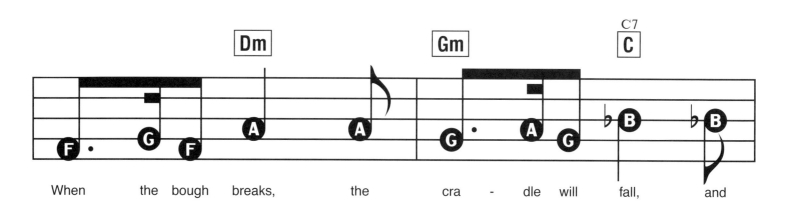

When the bough breaks, the cra - dle will fall, and

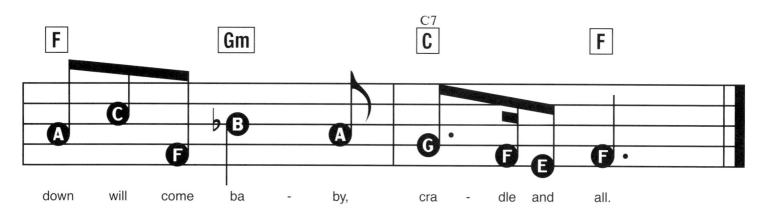

down will come ba - by, cra - dle and all.

Hush, Little Baby

Registration 1
Rhythm: Fox Trot

Traditional

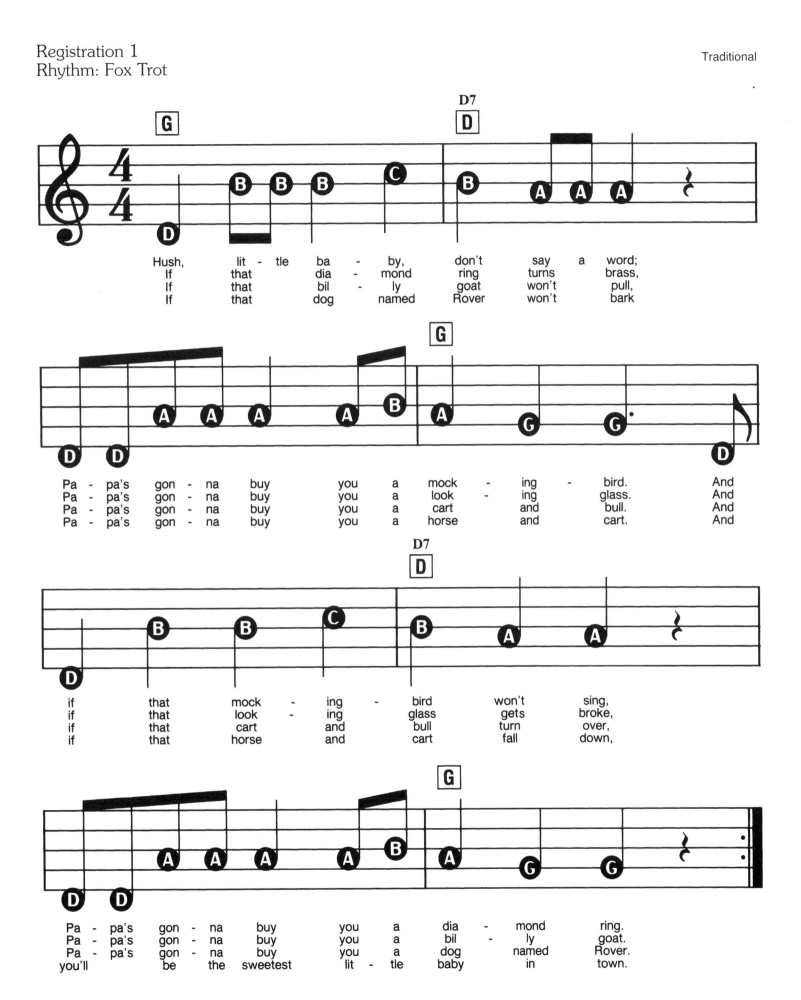

I Had a Little Nut Tree

Registration 1
Rhythm: Fox Trot or March

Traditional

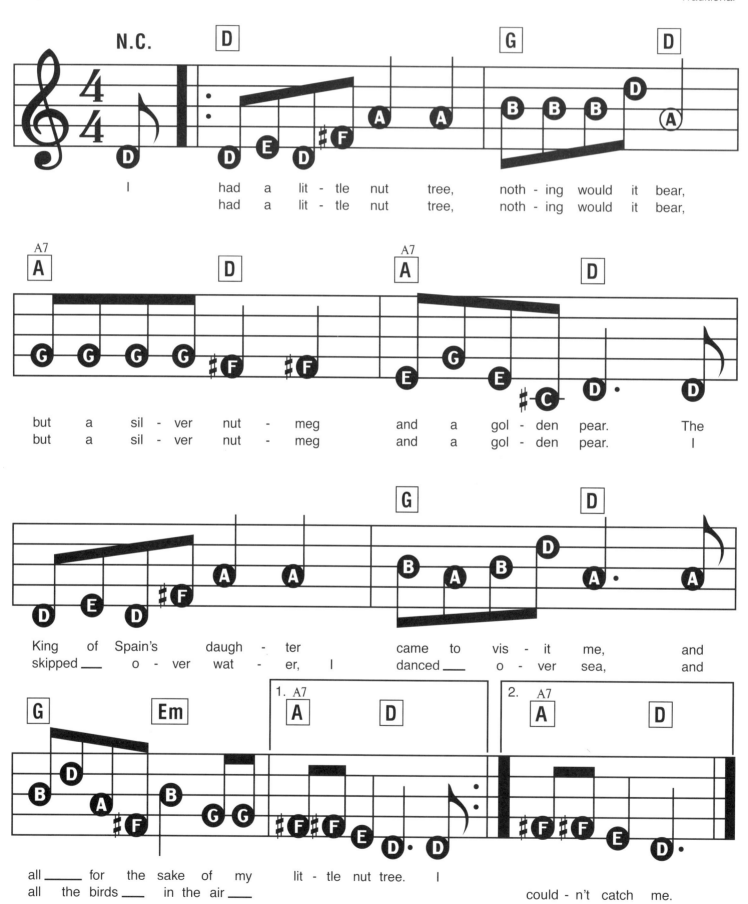

I Know an Old Lady
Who Swallowed a Fly

Registration 4
Rhythm: 6/8 March

Traditional

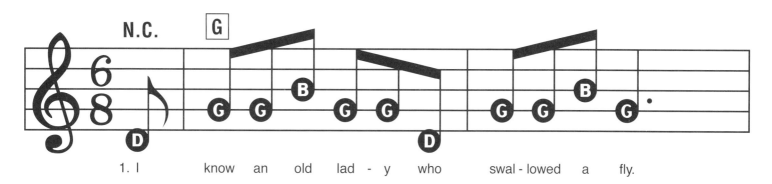

1. I know an old lad-y who swal-lowed a fly.

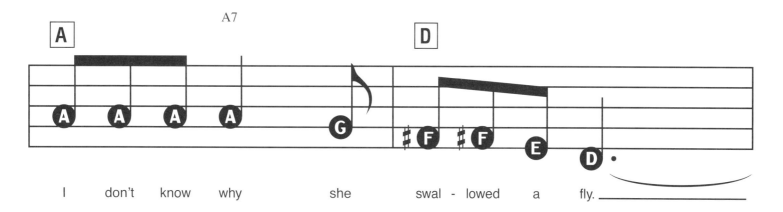

I don't know why she swal-lowed a fly. _____

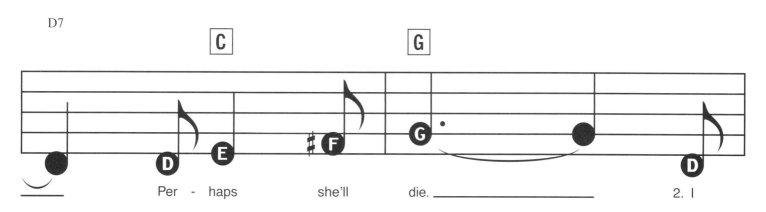

Per-haps she'll die. _____ 2. I

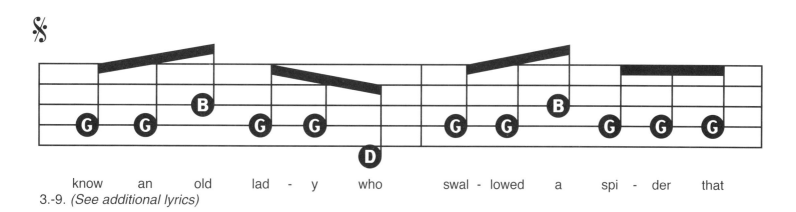

know an old lad-y who swal-lowed a spi-der that

3.-9. *(See additional lyrics)*

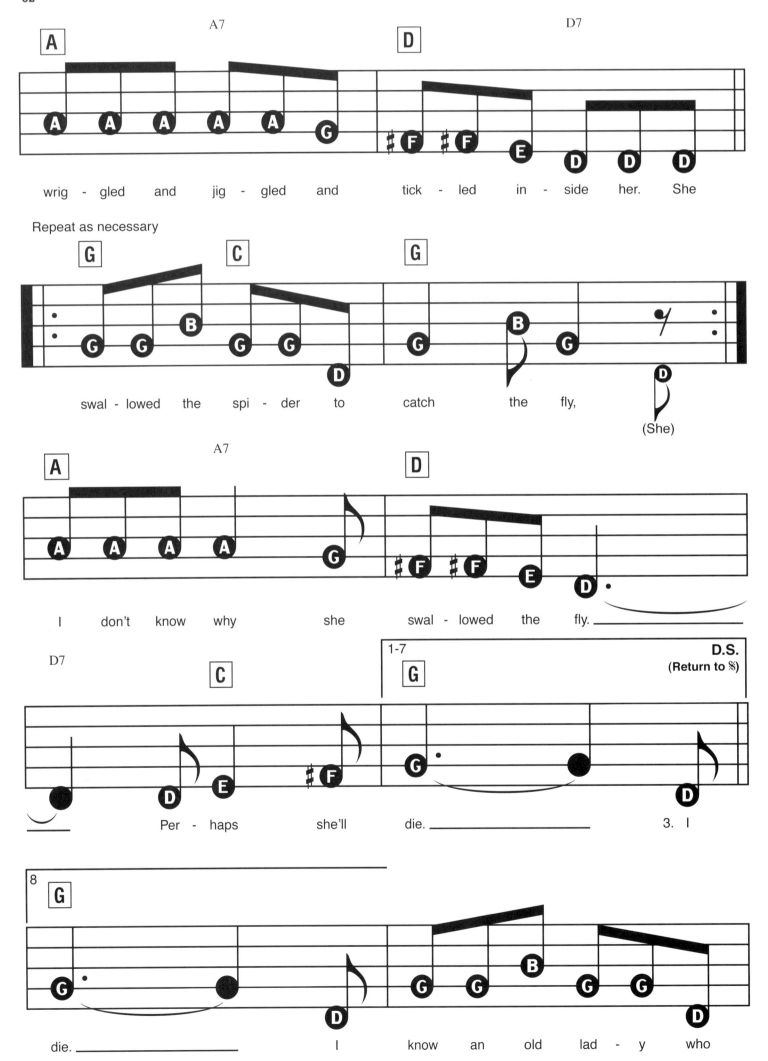

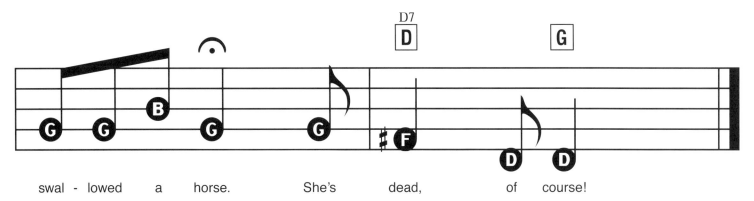

swal - lowed   a   horse.   She's   dead,   of   course!

Additional Lyrics

3. I know an old lady who swallowed a bird.
   How absurd, to swallow a bird!
   She swallowed the bird to catch the spider
   That wriggled and jiggled and tickled inside her.
   She swallowed the spider to catch the fly.
   I don't know why she swallowed the fly.
   Perhaps she'll die!

4. I know an old lady who swallowed a cat.
   Just fancy that, she swallowed a cat!
   She swallowed the cat to catch the bird.
   She swallowed the bird to catch the spider. *etc.*

5. I know an old lady who swallowed a dog.
   What a hog, to swallow the dog!
   She swallowed the dog to catch the cat.
   She swallowed the cat to catch the bird. *etc.*

6. I know an old lady who swallowed a goat.
   She just opened her throat and swallowed the goat!
   She swallowed the goat to catch the dog.
   She swallowed the dog to catch the cat. *etc.*

7. I know an old lady who swallowed a cow.
   I don't know HOW she swallowed a cow.
   She swallowed the cow to catch the goat.
   She swallowed the goat to catch the dog. *etc.*

8. I know an old lady who swallowed a rhinocerous.
   THAT'S PREPOSTEROUS!
   She swallowed the rhino to catch the cow.
   She swallowed the cow to catch the goat. *etc.*

9. I know an old lady who swallowed a horse.
   She's dead, of course!

I Love Little Pussy

Registration 4
Rhythm: Waltz

Traditional

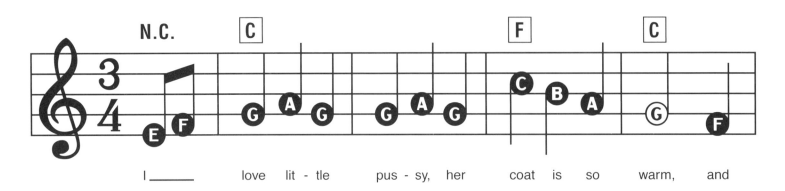

I ____ love lit - tle pus - sy, her coat is so warm, and

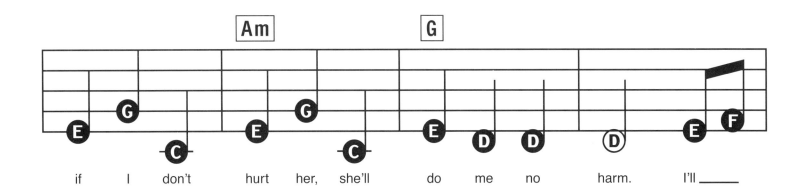

if I don't hurt her, she'll do me no harm. I'll ____

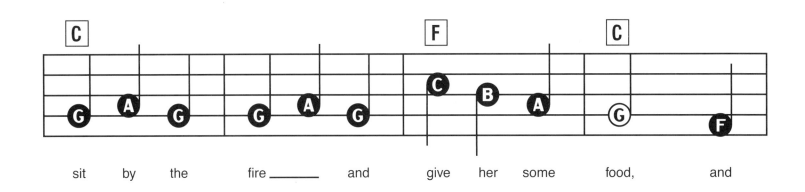

sit by the fire ____ and give her some food, and

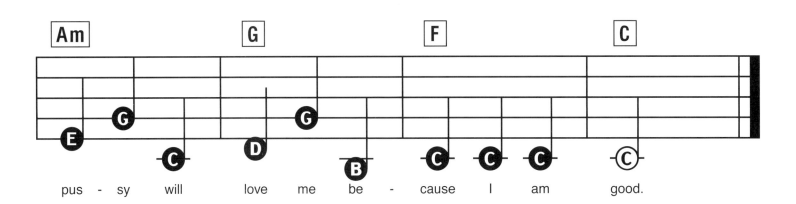

pus - sy will love me be - cause I am good.

It's Raining, It's Pouring

Registration 1
Rhythm: Rock or 8-Beat

Traditional

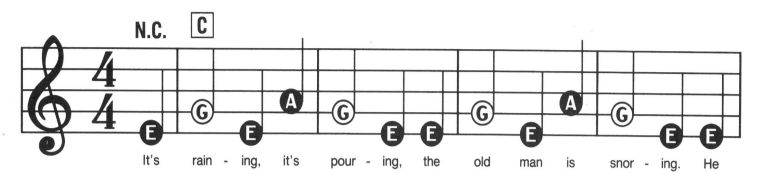

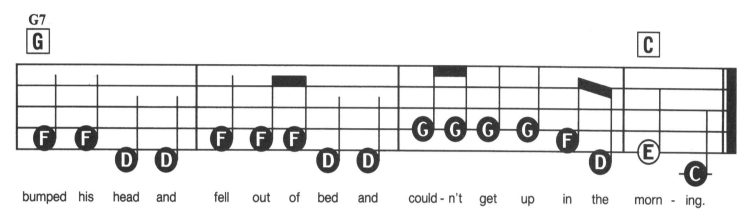

It's rain - ing, it's pour - ing, the old man is snor - ing. He

bumped his head and fell out of bed and could - n't get up in the morn - ing.

Ring Around the Rosie

Registration 2
Rhythm: 6/8 March

Traditional

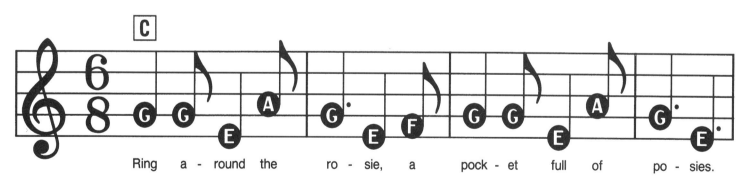

Ring a - round the ro - sie, a pock - et full of po - sies.

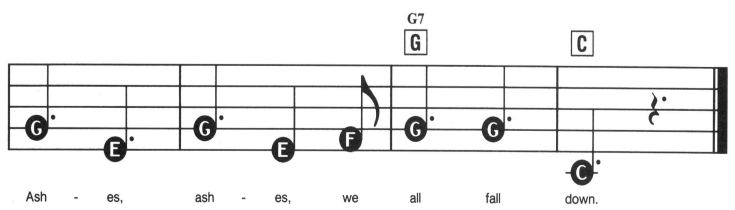

Ash - es, ash - es, we all fall down.

I'm a Nut

Registration 8
Rhythm: Fox Trot or Polka

Traditional

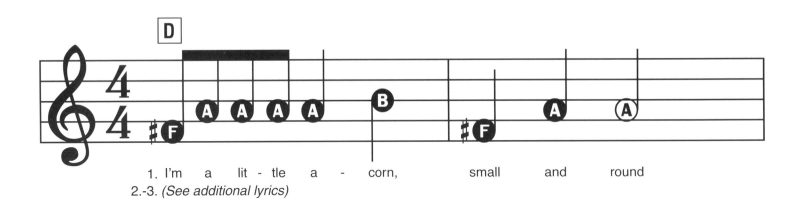

1. I'm a lit - tle a - corn,   small   and   round
2.-3. *(See additional lyrics)*

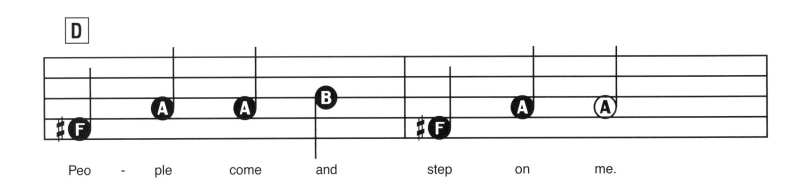

ly - ing   on   the   cold,   cold   ground.

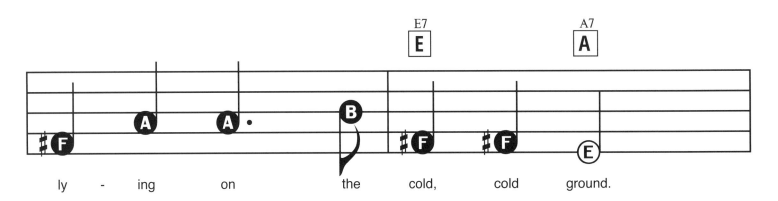

Peo - ple   come   and   step   on   me.

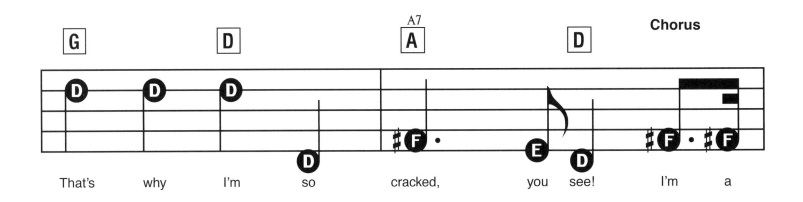

That's   why   I'm   so   cracked,   you   see!   I'm   a

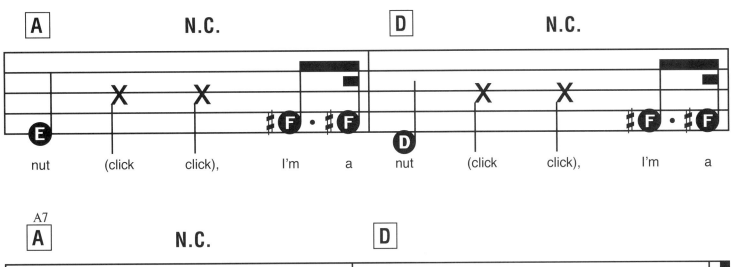

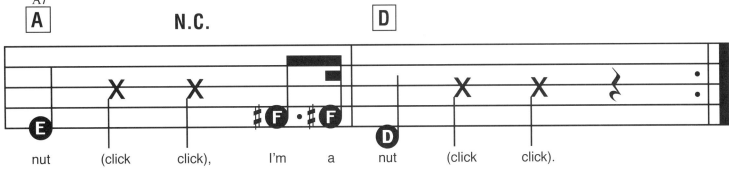

Additional Lyrics

2. I love me, I think I'm grand.
   I sit at the movies and hold my hand.
   I put my arm around my waist
   And when I get fresh, I slap my face.
   Chorus

3. I call myself on the telephone
   Just to hear my golden tone.
   I ask myself for a little date
   And pick myself up about half past eight.
   Chorus

If You're Happy and You Know It

Registration 4
Rhythm: Waltz

Words and Music by
L. Smith

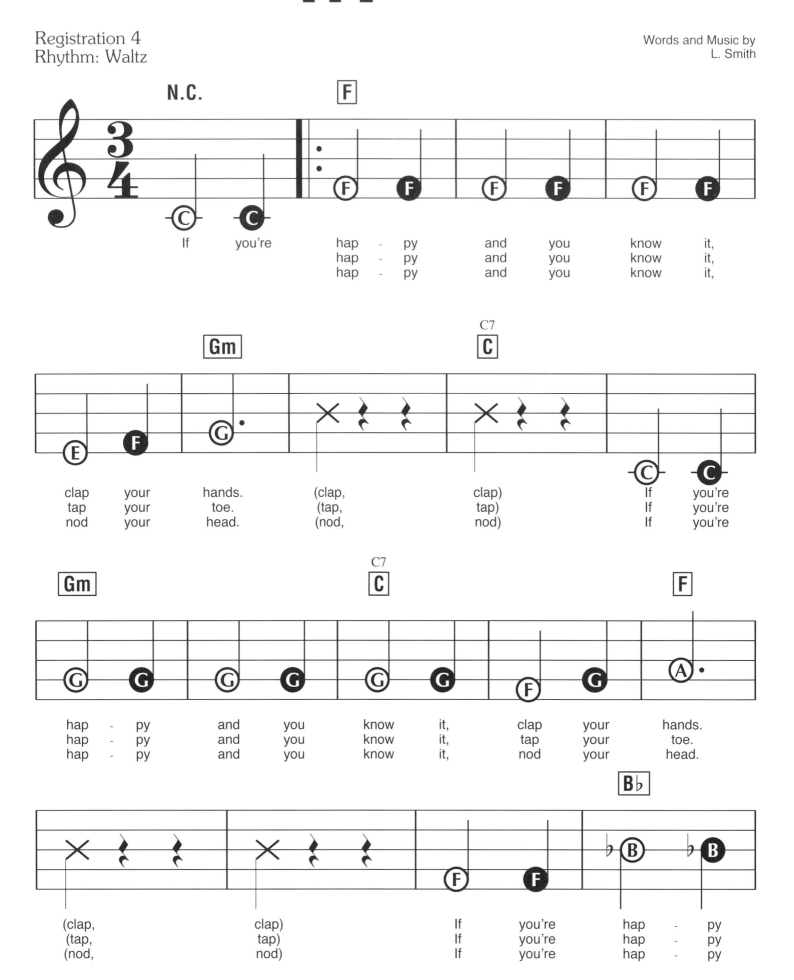

89

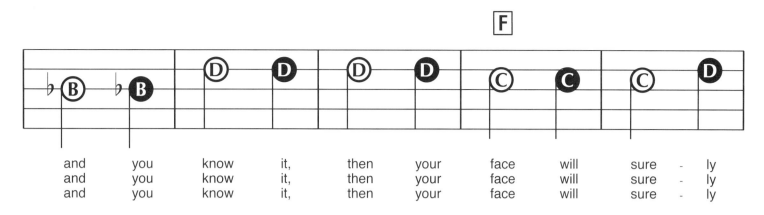

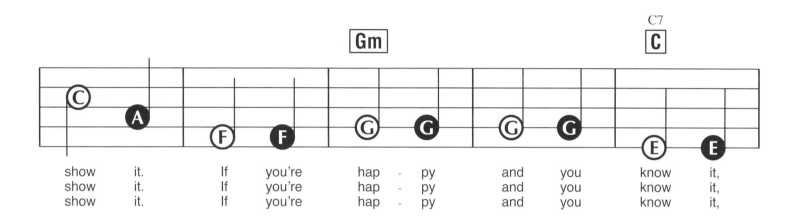

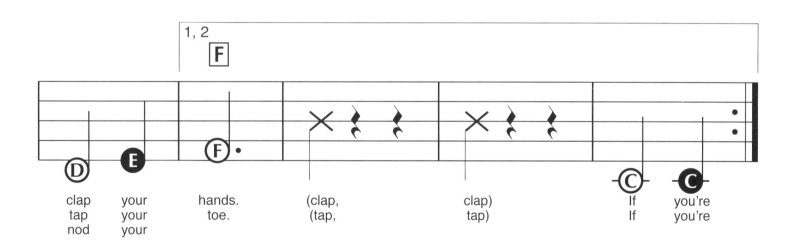

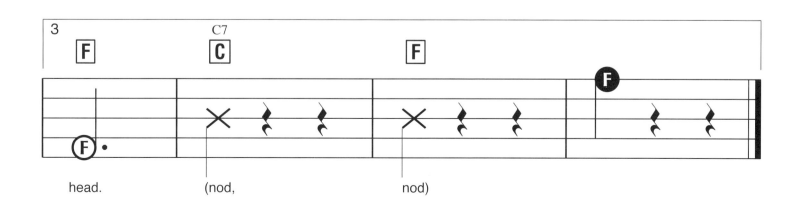

Jack and Jill

Registration 4
Rhythm: Waltz

Traditional

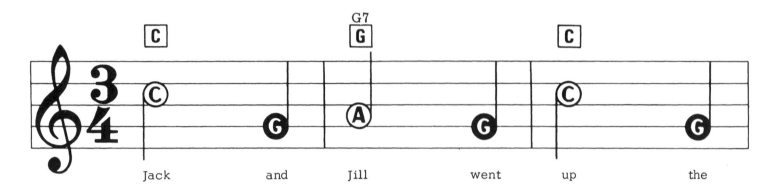

Jack   and   Jill   went   up   the

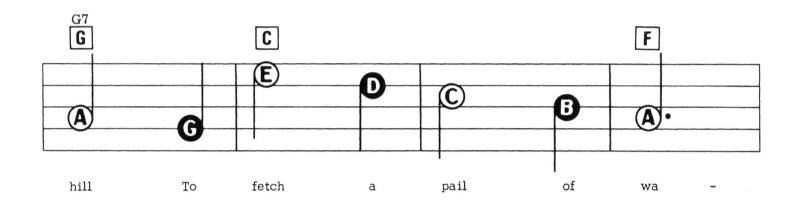

hill   To   fetch   a   pail   of   wa -

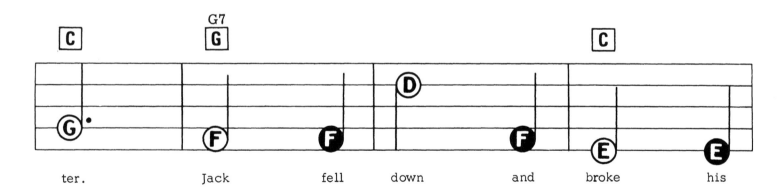

ter.   Jack   fell   down   and   broke   his

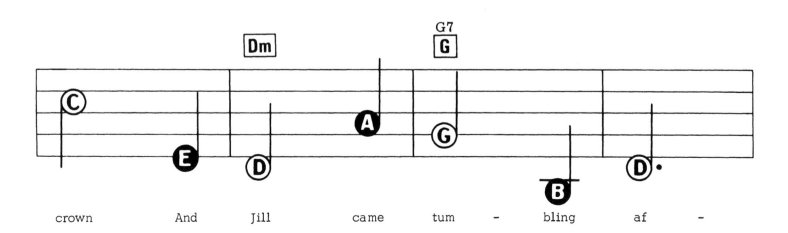

crown   And   Jill   came   tum - bling   af -

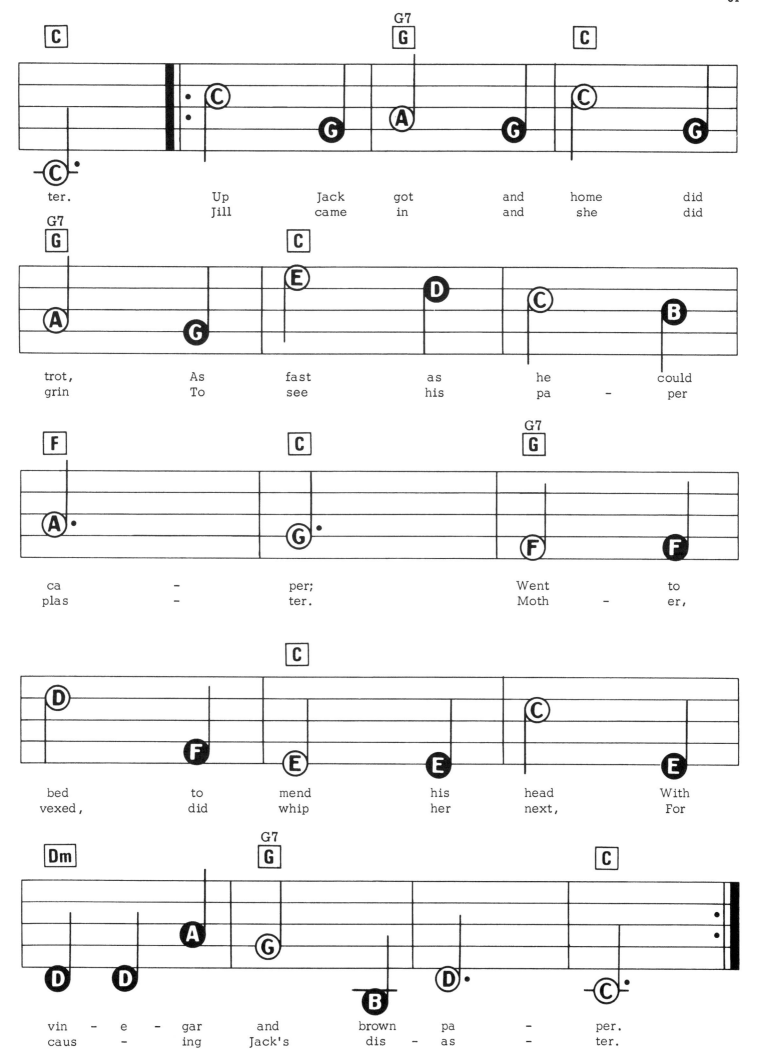

Jack Be Nimble

Registration 9
Rhythm: Fox Trot or March

Traditional

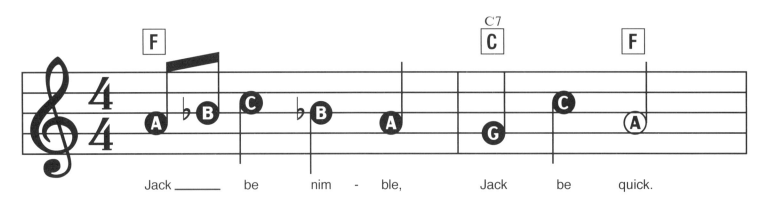

Jack _____ be nim - ble, Jack be quick.

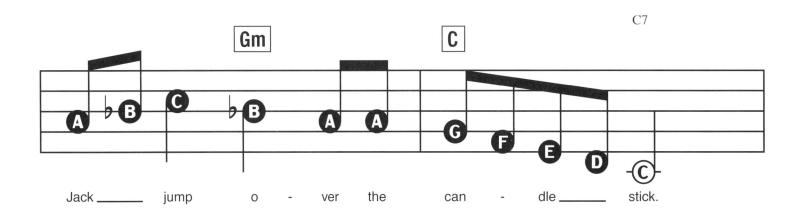

Jack _____ jump o - ver the can - dle _____ stick.

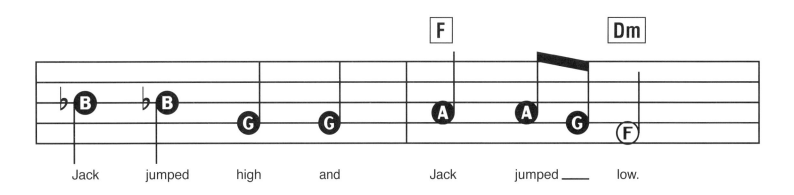

Jack jumped high and Jack jumped _____ low.

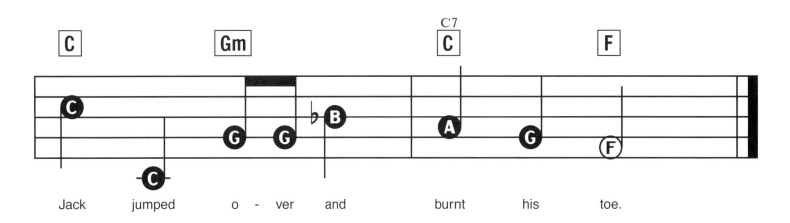

Jack jumped o - ver and burnt his toe.

Ladybird, Ladybird

Registration 3
Rhythm: 6/8 March

Traditional

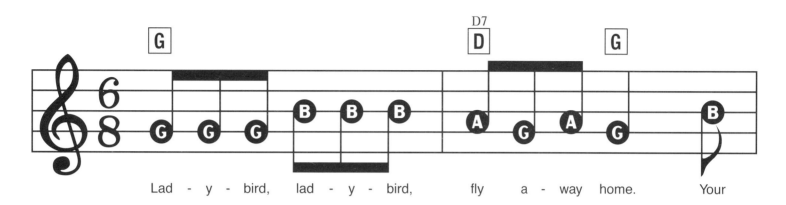

Lad - y - bird, lad - y - bird, fly a - way home. Your

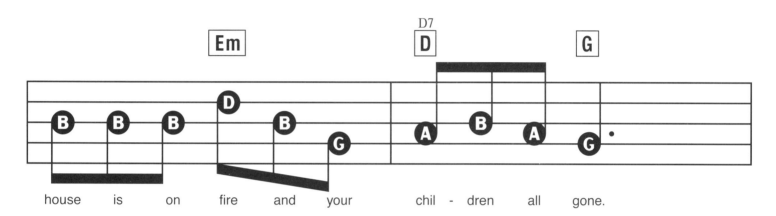

house is on fire and your chil - dren all gone.

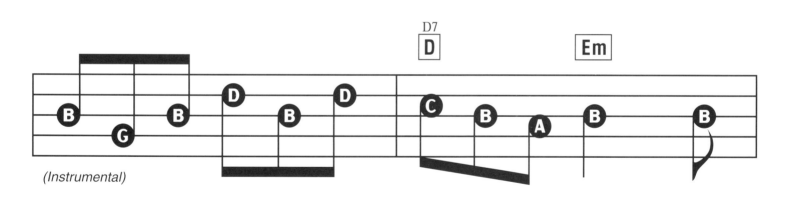

(Instrumental)

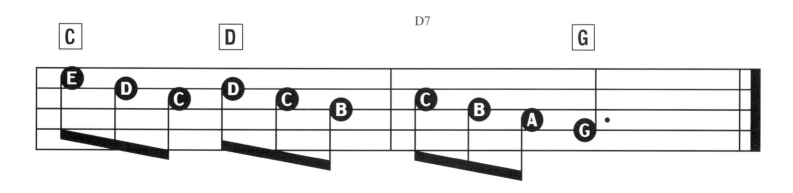

Jesus Loves Me

Registration 2
Rhythm: Gospel or Fox Trot

Traditional

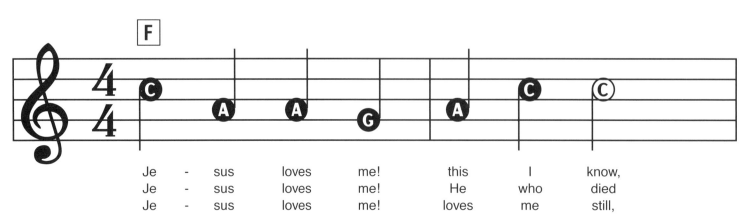

Je - sus loves me! this I know,
Je - sus loves me! He who died
Je - sus loves me! loves me still,

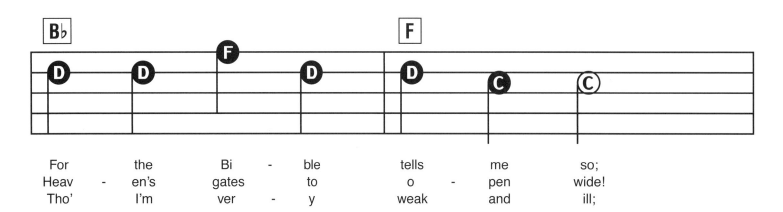

For the Bi - ble tells me so;
Heav - en's gates to o - pen wide!
Tho' I'm ver - y weak and ill;

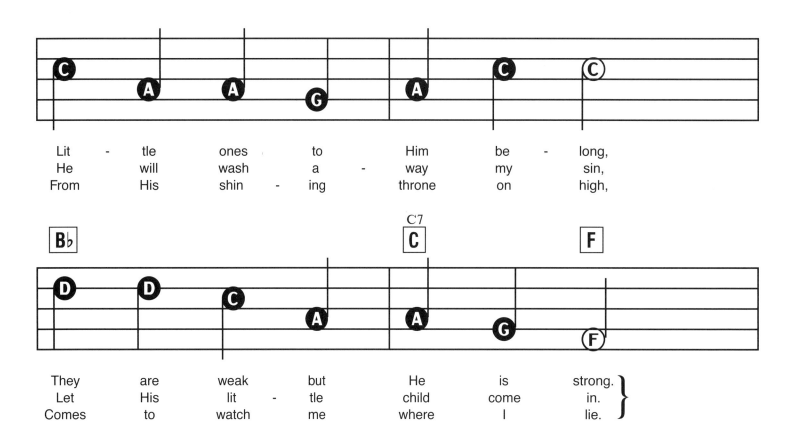

Lit - tle ones to Him be - long,
He will wash a - way my sin,
From His shin - ing throne on high,

They are weak but He is strong. }
Let His lit - tle child come in.
Comes to watch me where I lie.

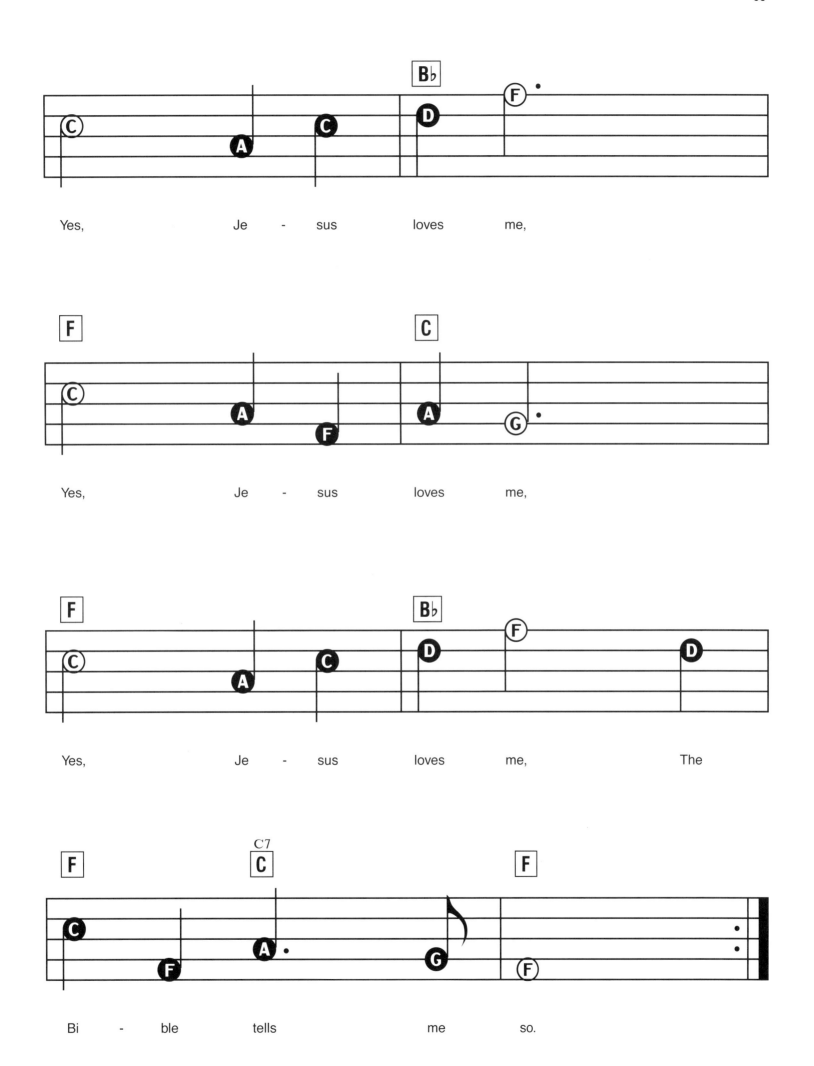

Yes,   Je - sus   loves   me,

Yes,   Je - sus   loves   me,

Yes,   Je - sus   loves   me,   The

Bi - ble   tells   me   so.

Knicky Knacky Knocky Noo

Registration 9
Rhythm: Waltz

Traditional

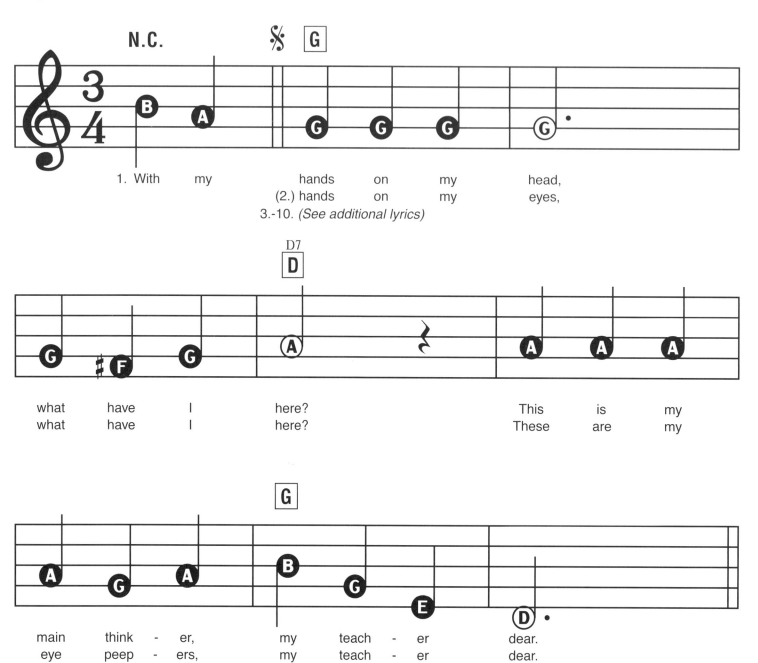

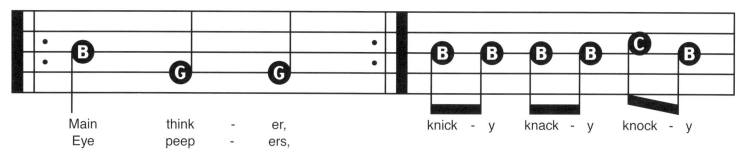

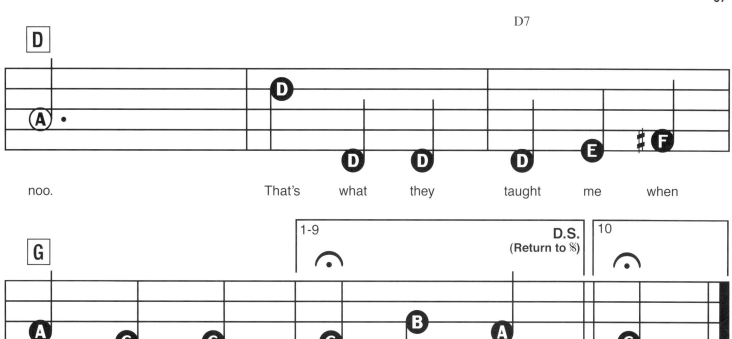

noo.   That's   what   they   taught   me   when

I   went   to   school.   2. With   my   school.
                                3. With   my

Additional Lyrics

3. With my hands on my nose,
   What have I here?
   This is my smell boxer, my teacher dear.
   Main thinker, eye peepers, smell boxer, *etc.*

4. With my hands on my mouth,
   What have I here?
   This is my chatterboxer, *etc.*

5. With my hands on my chin,
   What have I here?
   This is my chin wagger, *etc.*

6. With my hands on my chest,
   What have I here?
   This is my air blower, *etc.*

7. With my hands on my stomach,
   What have I here?
   This is my bread basket, *etc.*

8. With my hands on my lap,
   What have I here?
   This is my lap sitter, *etc.*

9. With my hands on my knees,
   What have I here?
   These are my knee knockers, *etc.*

10. With my hands on my feet,
    What have I here?
    These are my toe tappers, *etc.*

Kum Ba Yah

Registration 3
Rhythm: 8-Beat or Rock

Traditional

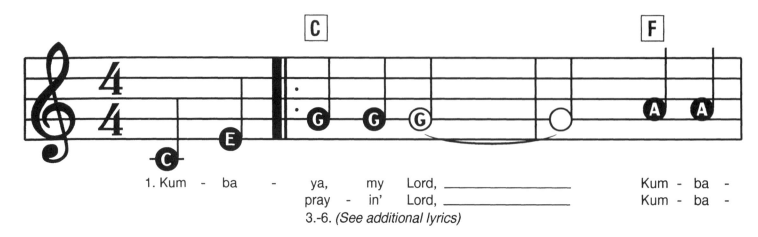

1. Kum - ba - ya, my Lord, _____ Kum - ba -
pray - in' Lord, _____ Kum - ba -
3.-6. *(See additional lyrics)*

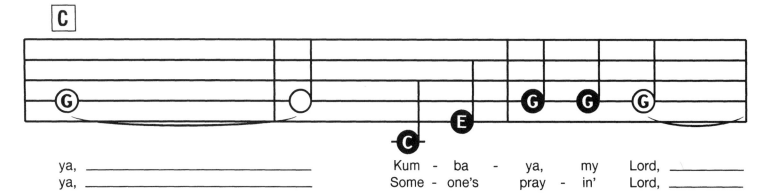

ya, _____
ya, _____
Kum - ba - ya, my Lord, _____
Some - one's pray - in' Lord, _____

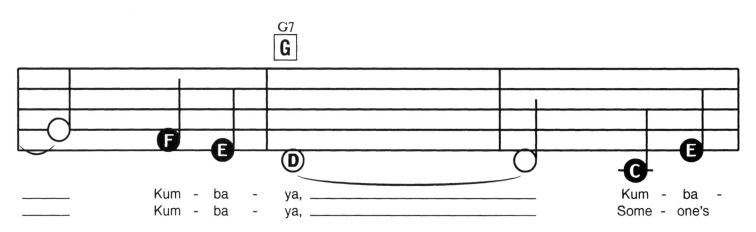

_____ Kum - ba - ya, _____ Kum - ba -
_____ Kum - ba - ya, _____ Some - one's

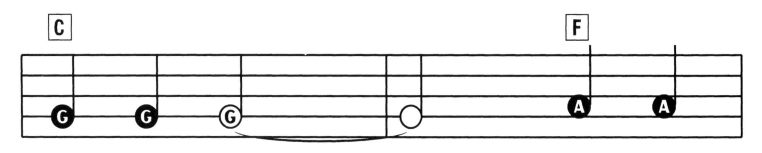

ya, my Lord, _____ Kum - ba -
pray - in' Lord, _____ Kum - ba

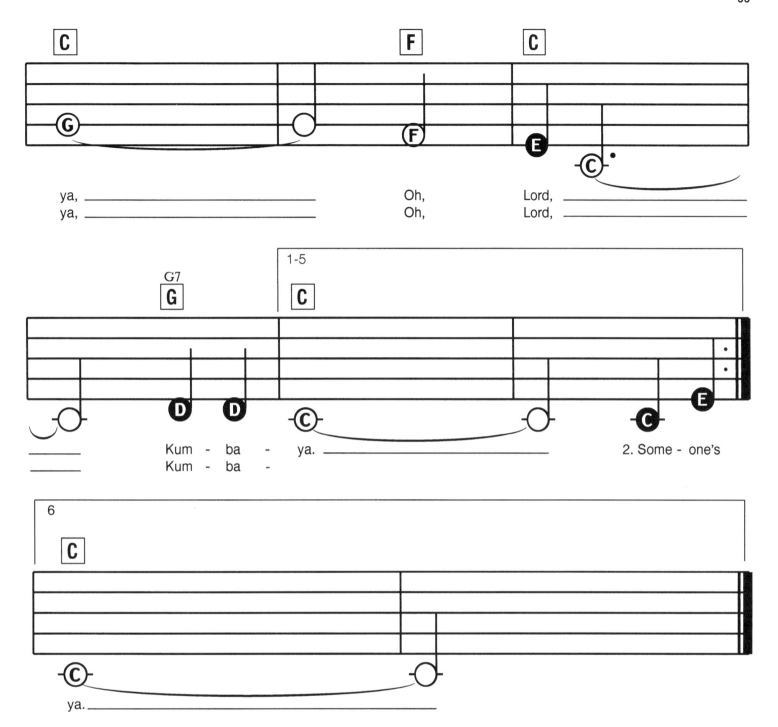

Additional Lyrics

3. Someone's singin', Lord, Kum-bah-ya...
4. Someone's cryin', Lord, Kum-bah-ya...
5. Someone's dancin', Lord, Kum-bah-ya...
6 Someone's shoutin', Lord, Kum-bah-ya...

Lavender's Blue

Registration 3
Rhythm: Fox Trot or Swing

English Folksong

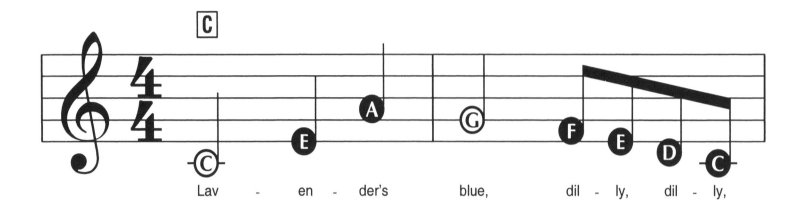

Lav - en - der's blue, dil - ly, dil - ly,

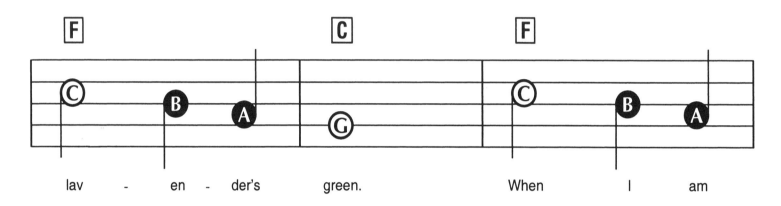

lav - en - der's green. When I am

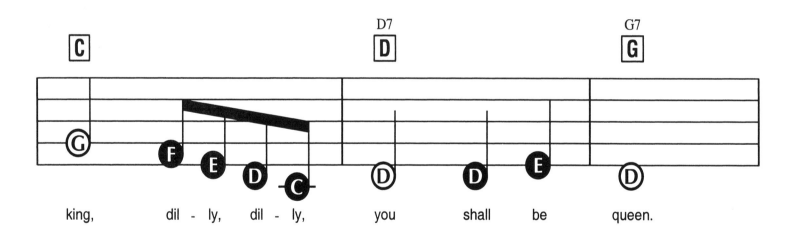

king, dil - ly, dil - ly, you shall be queen.

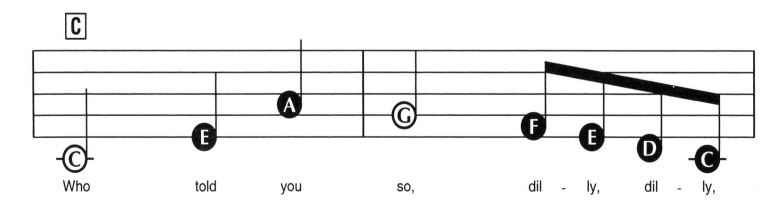

Who told you so, dil - ly, dil - ly,

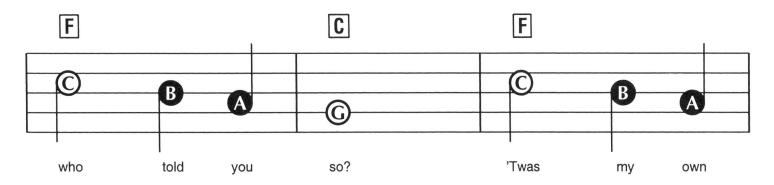

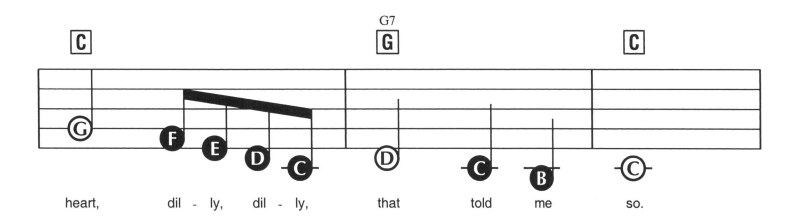

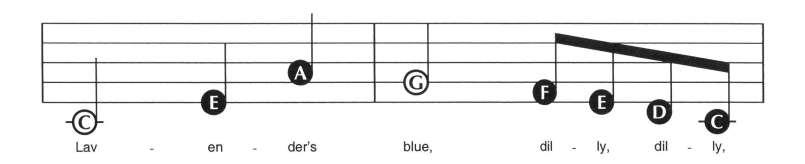

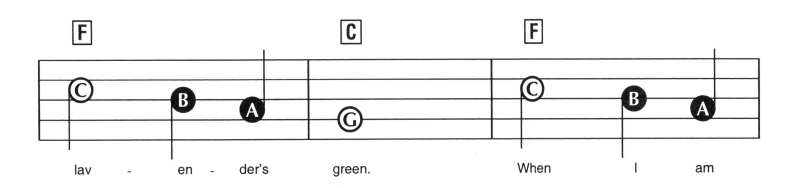

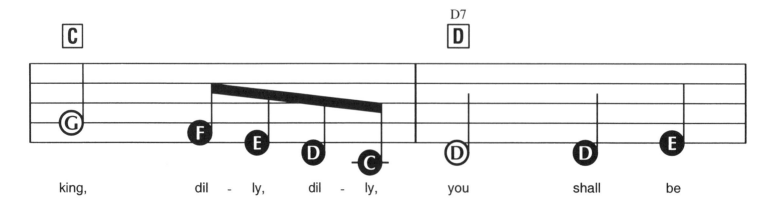

king,   dil - ly,   dil - ly,   you   shall   be

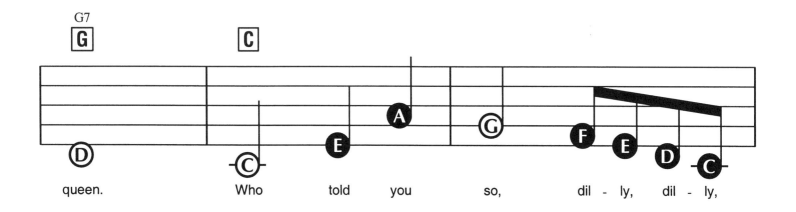

queen.   Who   told   you   so,   dil - ly,   dil - ly,

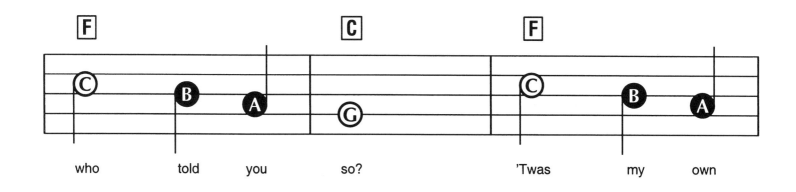

who   told   you   so?   'Twas   my   own

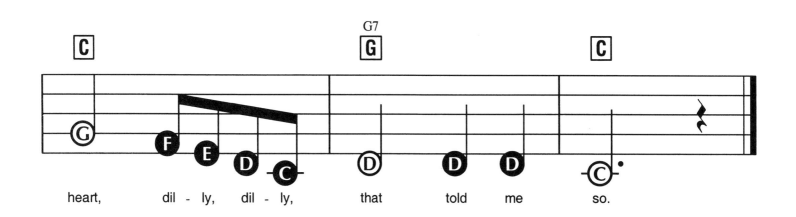

heart,   dil - ly,   dil - ly,   that   told   me   so.

Little Boy Blue

Registration 9
Rhythm: Waltz

Traditional

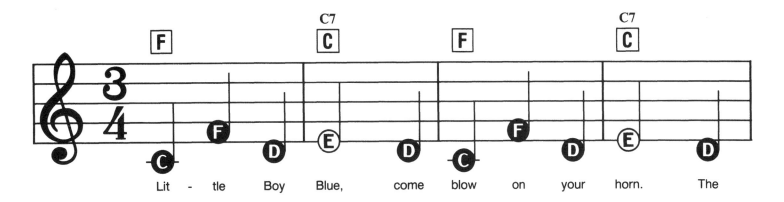

Lit - tle Boy Blue, come blow on your horn. The

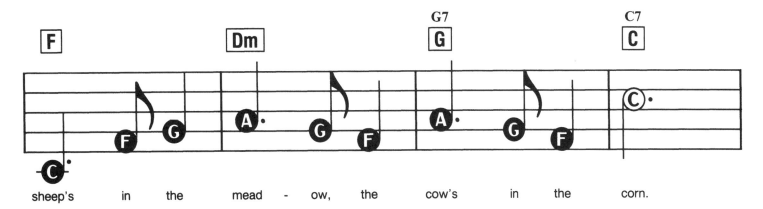

sheep's in the mead - ow, the cow's in the corn.

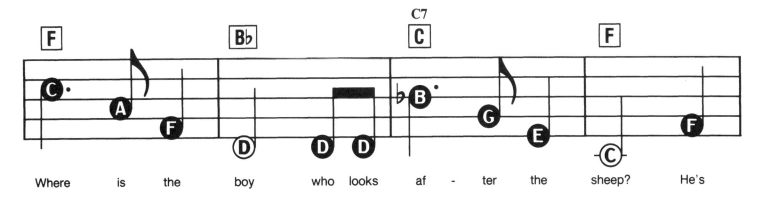

Where is the boy who looks af - ter the sheep? He's

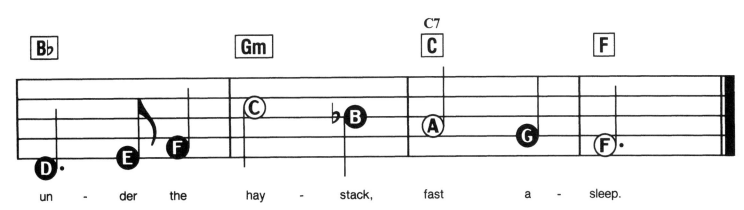

un - der the hay - stack, fast a - sleep.

Lazy Katy, Will You Get Up?

Registration 8
Rhythm: 6/8 March

Traditional

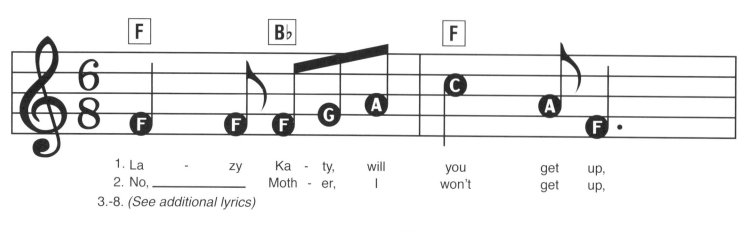

1. La - zy Ka - ty, will you get up,
2. No, _____ Moth - er, I won't get up,
3.-8. *(See additional lyrics)*

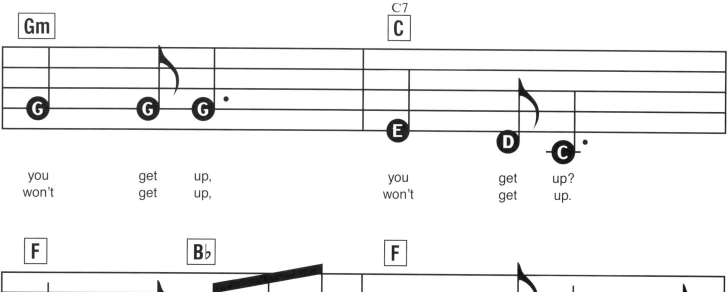

you get up, you get up?
won't get up, won't get up.

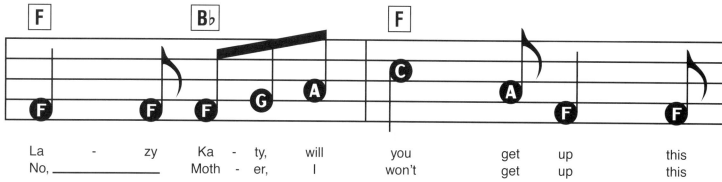

La - zy Ka - ty, will you get up this
No, _____ Moth - er, I won't get up this

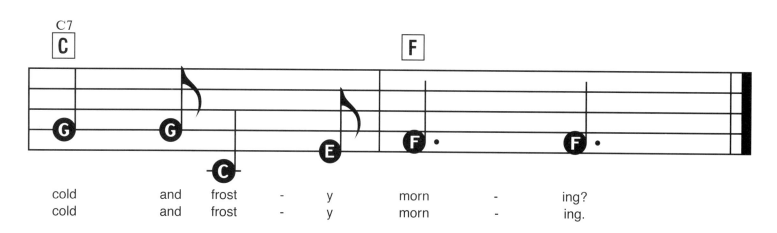

cold and frost - y morn - ing?
cold and frost - y morn - ing.

Additional Lyrics

3. What if I give you some bread and jam,
   Bread and jam, bread and jam?
   What if I give you some bread and jam
   This cold and frosty morning?

4. No, Mother, I won't get up,
   Won't get up, won't get up.
   No, Mother, I won't get up
   This cold and frosty morning?

5. What if I give you some bacon and eggs,
   Bacon and eggs, bacon and eggs?
   What if I give you some bacon and eggs
   This cold and frosty morning?

6. No, Mother, I won't get up,
   Won't get up, won't get up.
   No, Mother, I won't get up,
   This cold and frosty morning?

7. What if I give you a crack on the head,
   Crack on the head, crack on the head?
   What if I give you a crack on the head
   This cold and frosty morning?

8. Yes, Mother, I will get up,
   Will get up, will get up.
   Yes, Mother, I will get up
   This cold and frosty morning?

Little Bird, Little Bird

Registration 3
Rhythm: Fox Trot or Polka

Traditional

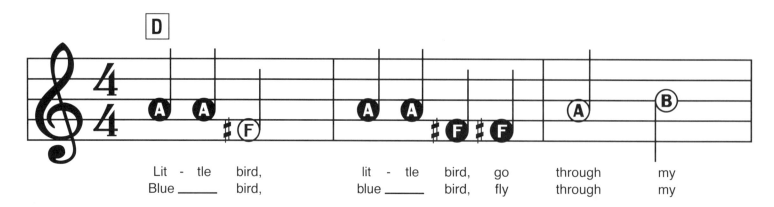

Lit - tle   bird,   lit - tle   bird,   go   through   my
Blue _____ bird,   blue _____ bird,   fly   through   my

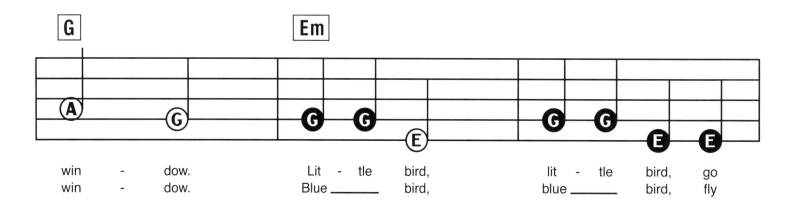

win - dow.   Lit - tle   bird,   lit - tle   bird,   go
win - dow.   Blue _____ bird,   blue _____ bird,   fly

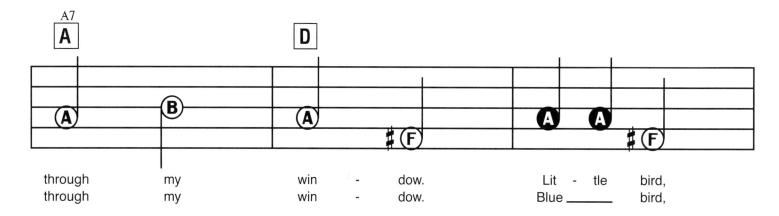

through   my   win - dow.   Lit - tle   bird,
through   my   win - dow.   Blue _____ bird,

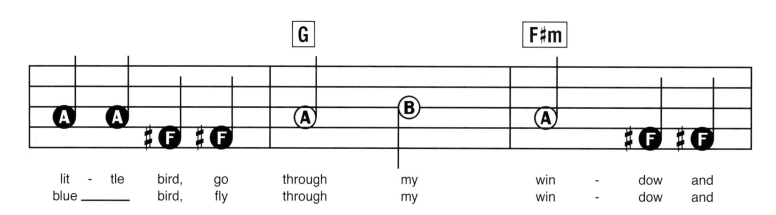

lit - tle   bird,   go   through   my   win - dow   and
blue _____ bird,   fly   through   my   win - dow   and

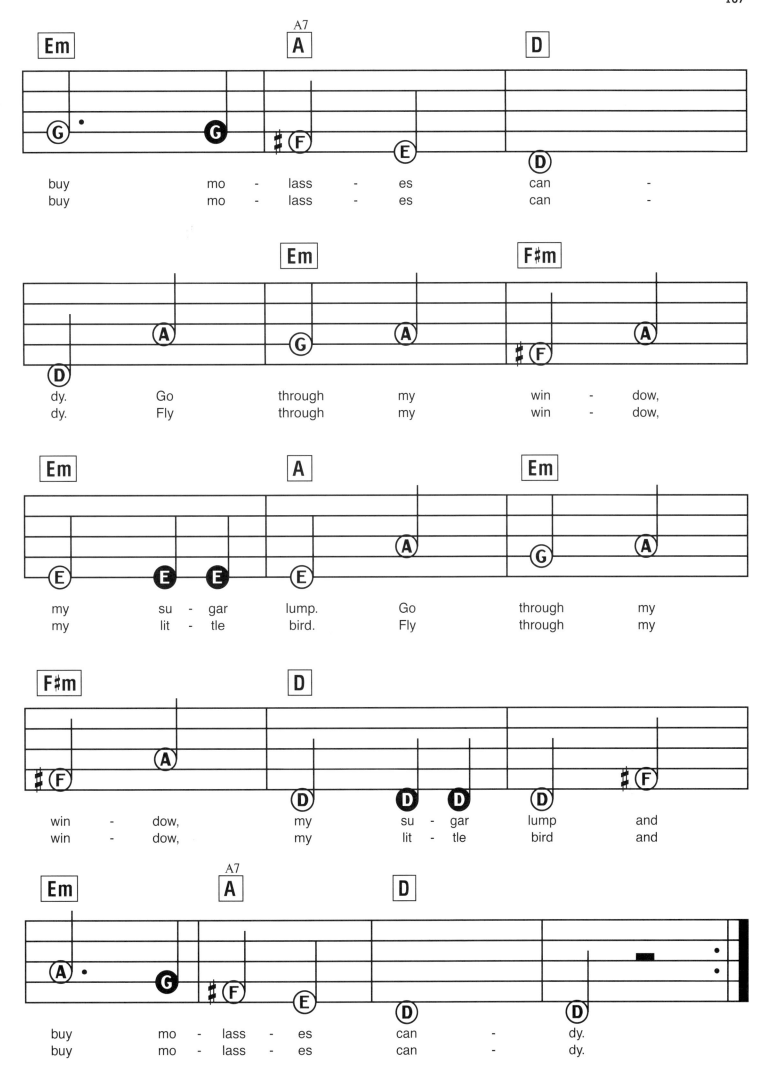

Little Bo-Peep

Registration 2
Rhythm: Waltz

Traditional

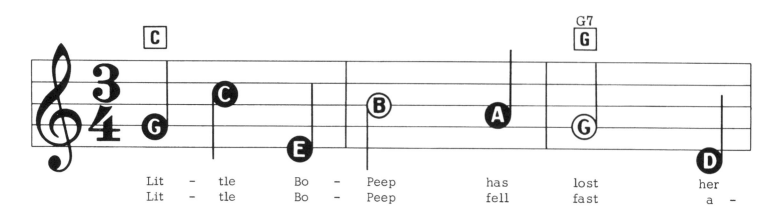

Lit - tle Bo - Peep has lost her
Lit - tle Bo - Peep has fell lost fast a -

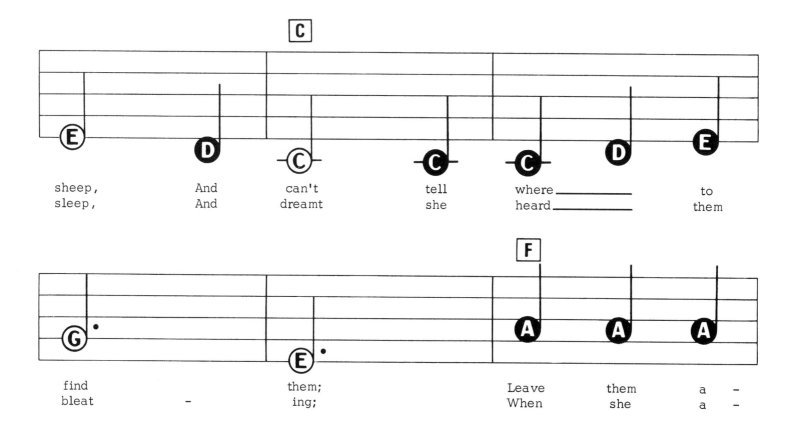

sheep, And can't tell where_____ to
sleep, And dreamt she heard_____ them

find them; Leave them a -
bleat - ing; When she a -

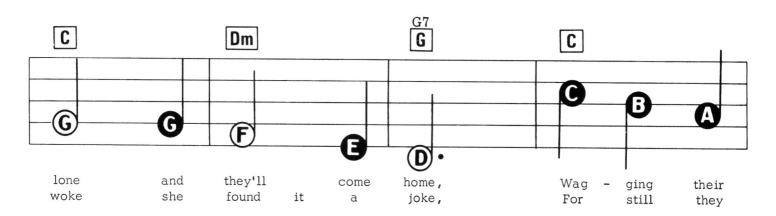

lone and they'll come home, Wag - ging their
woke and she found it a joke, For still they

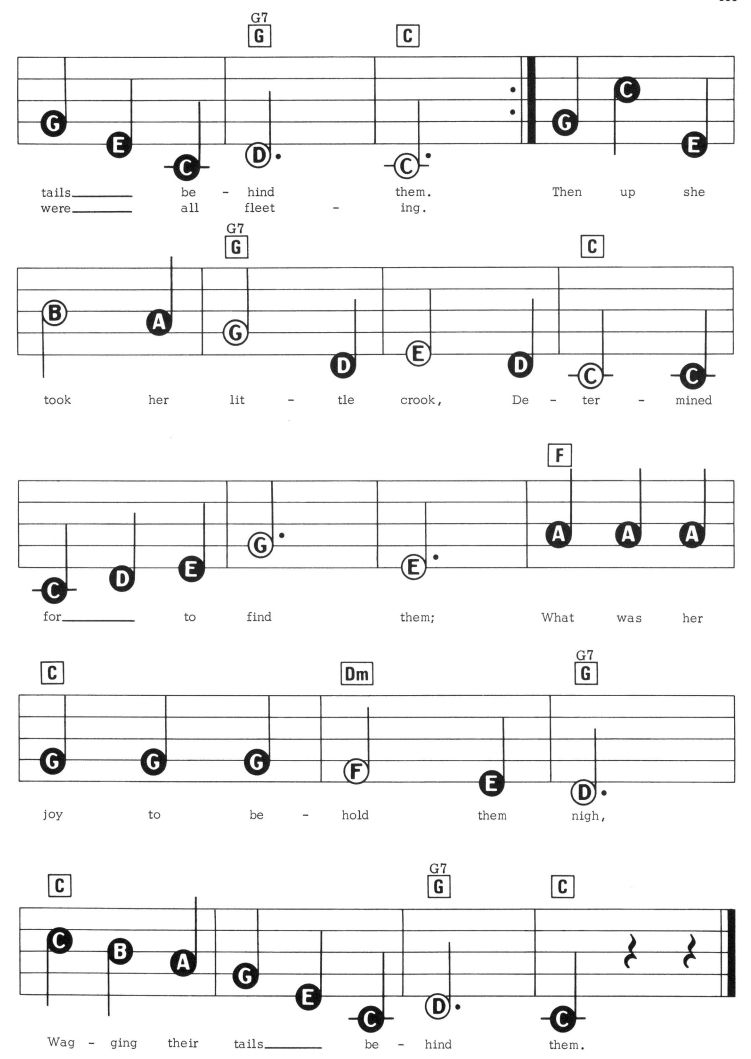

Little Girl

Registration 1
Rhythm: Fox Trot or Polka

Traditional

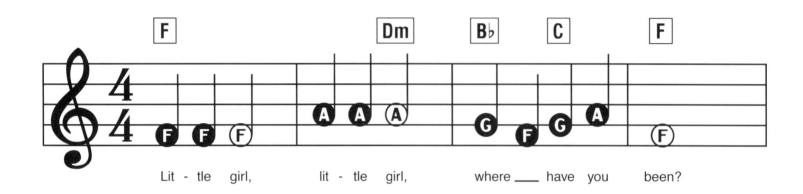

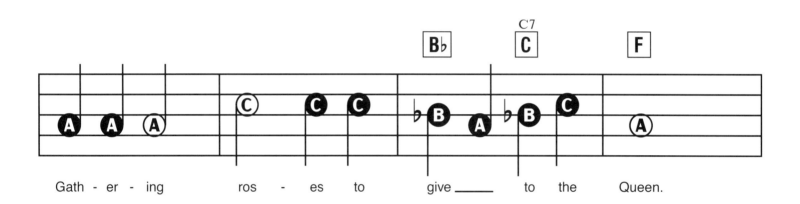

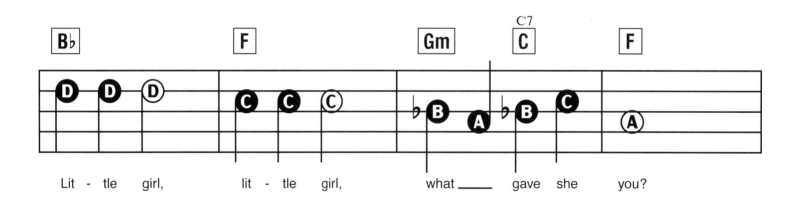

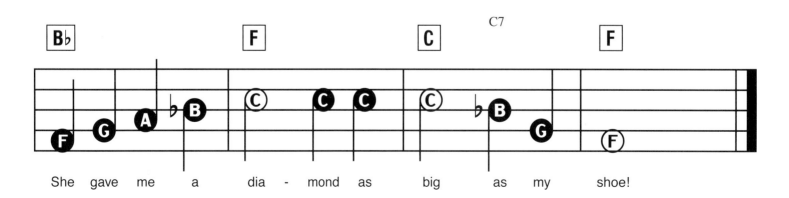

Little Jack Horner

Registration 1
Rhythm: Waltz

Traditional

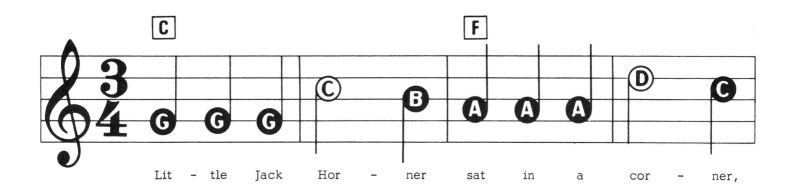

Lit - tle Jack Hor - ner sat in a cor - ner,

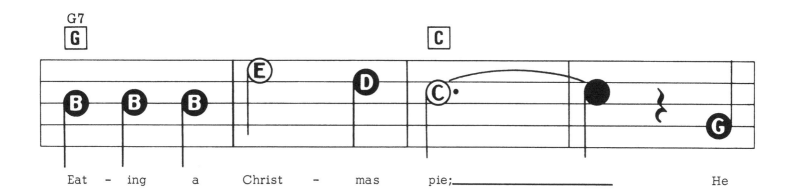

Eat - ing a Christ - mas pie;_____ He

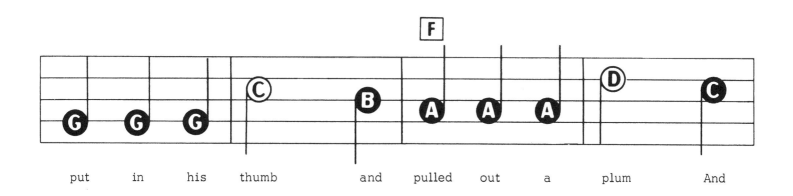

put in his thumb and pulled out a plum And

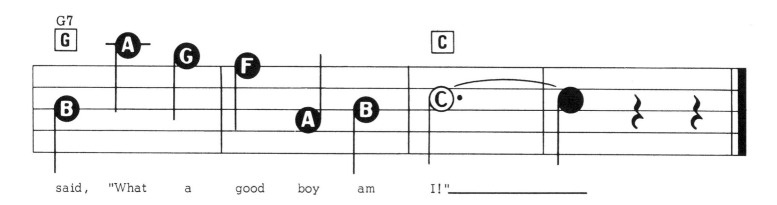

said, "What a good boy am I!"_____

Little Miss Muffet

Registration 8
Rhythm: Waltz

Traditional

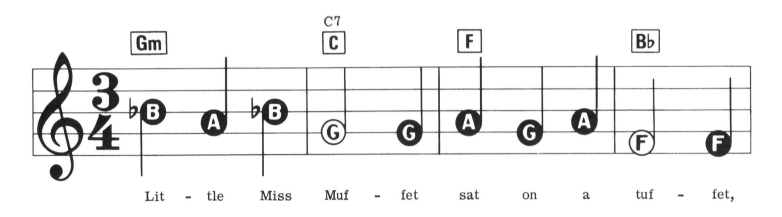

Lit - tle Miss Muf - fet sat on a tuf - fet,

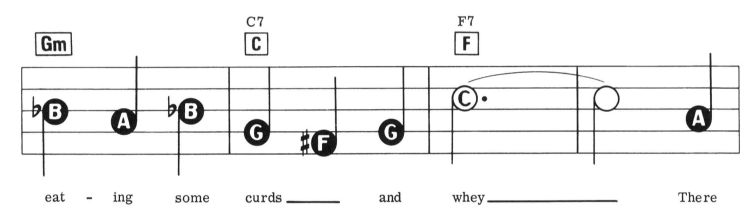

eat - ing some curds _____ and whey _____ There

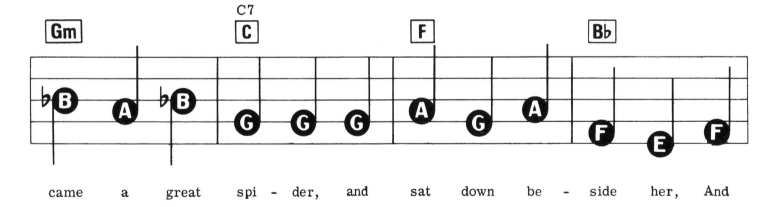

came a great spi - der, and sat down be - side her, And

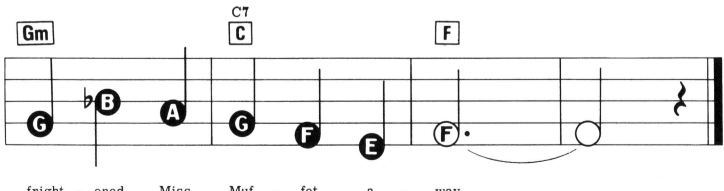

fright - ened Miss Muf - fet a - way. _____

Little Polly Flinders

Registration 4
Rhythm: Fox Trot or March

Traditional

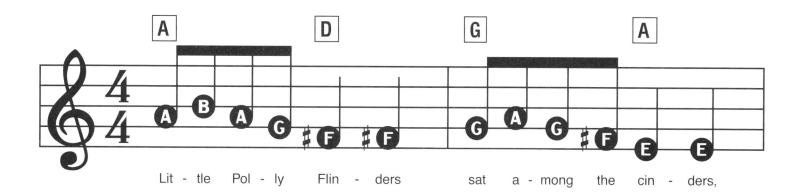

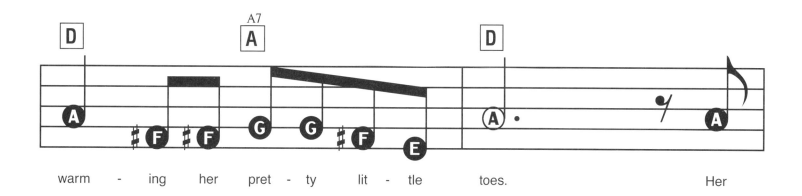

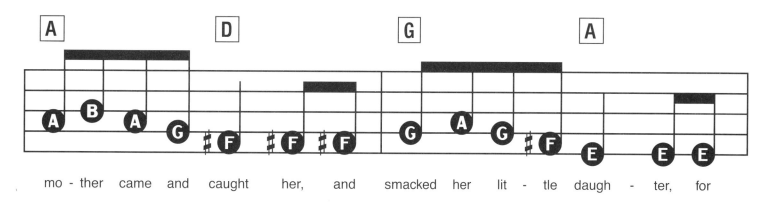

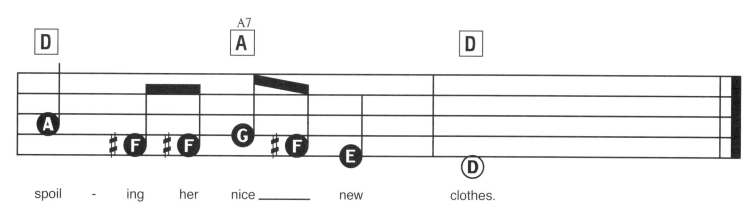

Little Tommy Tucker

Registration 8
Rhythm: Waltz

Traditional

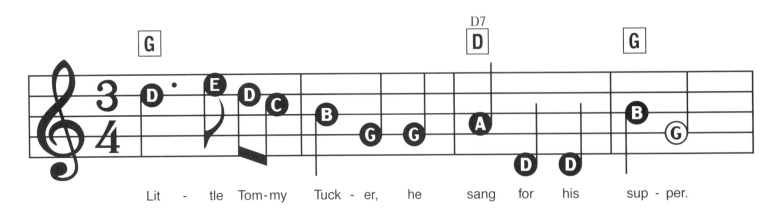

Lit - tle Tom-my Tuck - er, he sang for his sup - per.

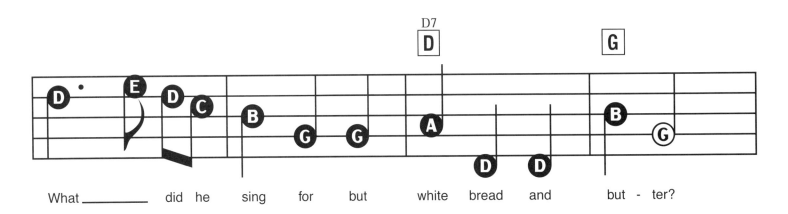

What _____ did he sing for but white bread and but - ter?

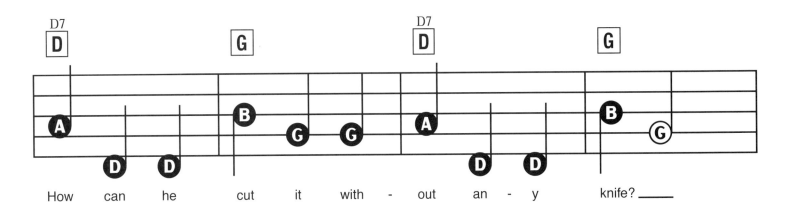

How can he cut it with - out an - y knife? _____

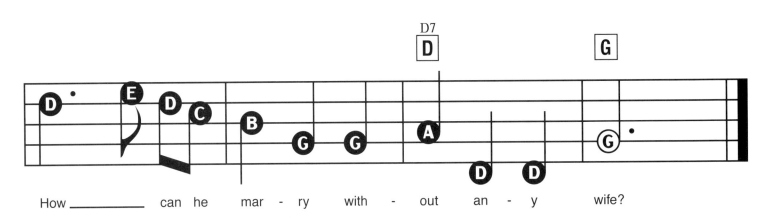

How _____ can he mar - ry with - out an - y wife?

London Bridge Is Falling Down

Registration 8
Rhythm: Fox Trot

Traditional

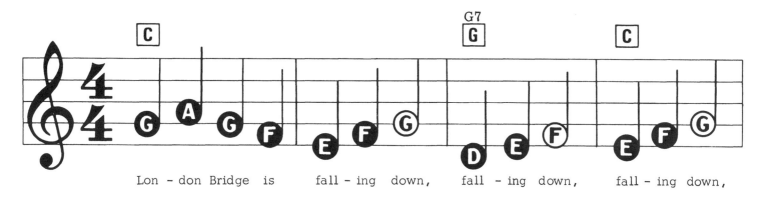

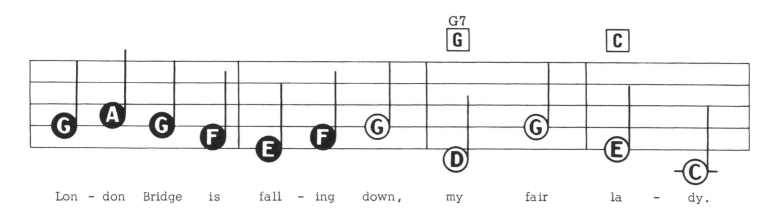

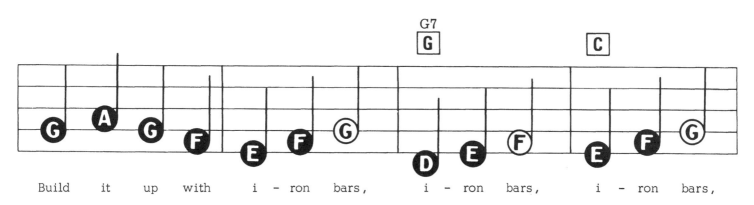

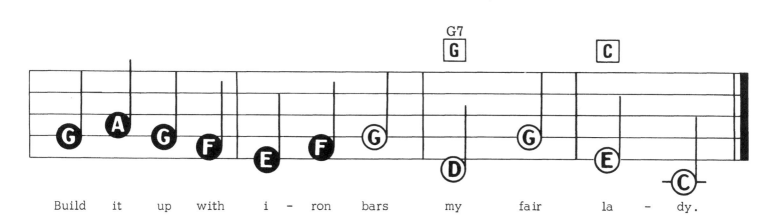

London's Burning

Registration 7
Rhythm: Waltz

Traditional

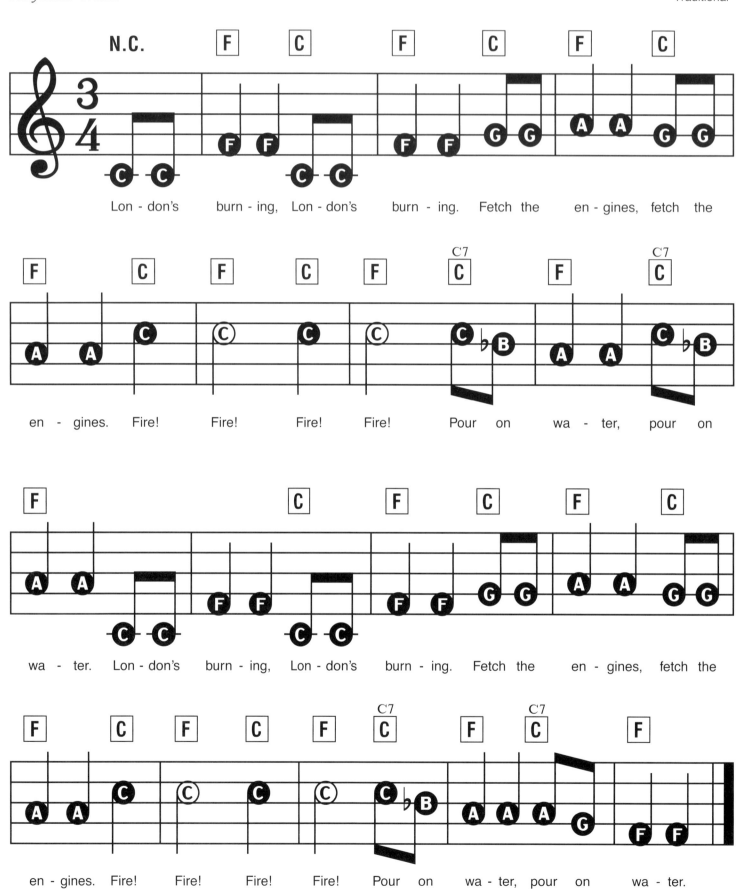

Lucy Locket

Registration 7
Rhythm: March

Traditional

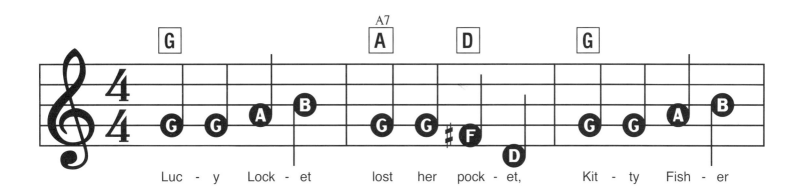

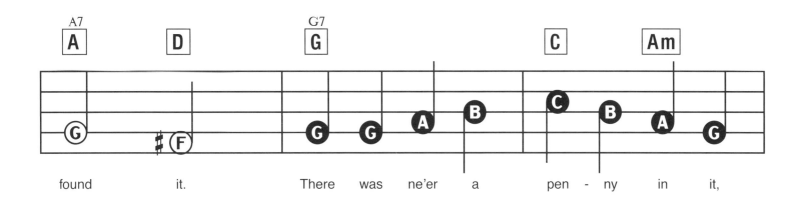

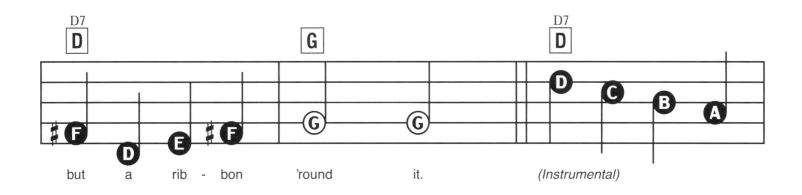

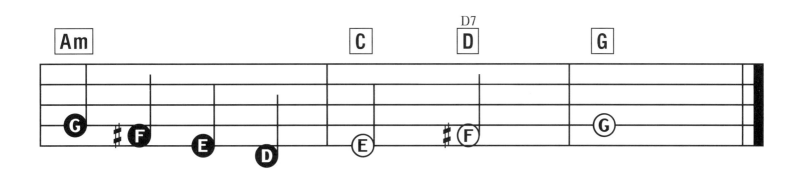

Mary Had a Little Lamb

Registration 4
Rhythm: Fox Trot or Swing

Traditional

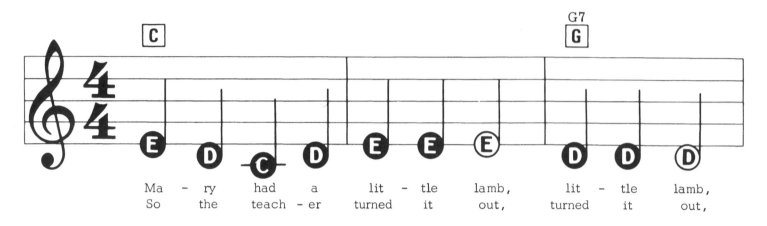

Ma - ry   had   a   lit - tle   lamb,   lit - tle   lamb,
So   the   teach - er   turned   it   out,   turned   it   out,

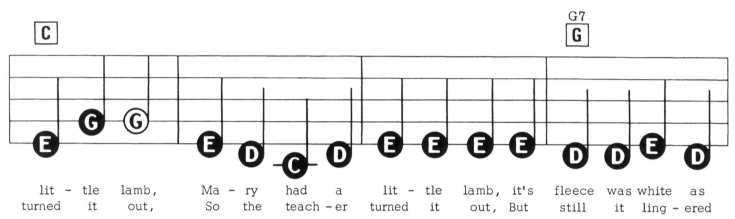

lit - tle   lamb,   Ma - ry   had   a   lit - tle   lamb, it's   fleece   was white   as
turned   it   out,   So   the   teach - er   turned   it   out, But   still   it   ling - ered

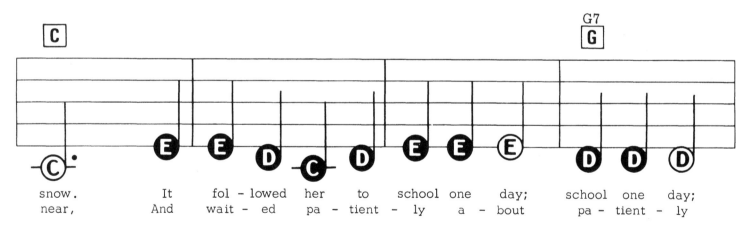

snow.   It   fol - lowed   her   to   school one   day;   school   one   day;
near,   And   wait - ed   pa - tient - ly   a - bout   pa - tient - ly

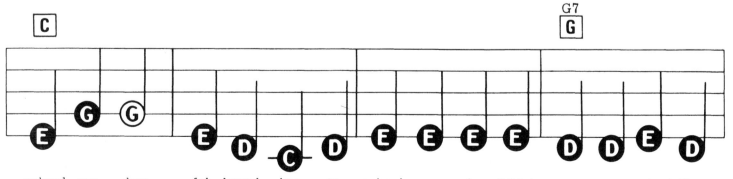

school   one   day;   fol - lowed   her   to   school   one   day; Which   was   a - gainst the
pa - tient - ly   wait - ed   pa - tient - ly   a - bout Till   Ma - ry   did   ap-

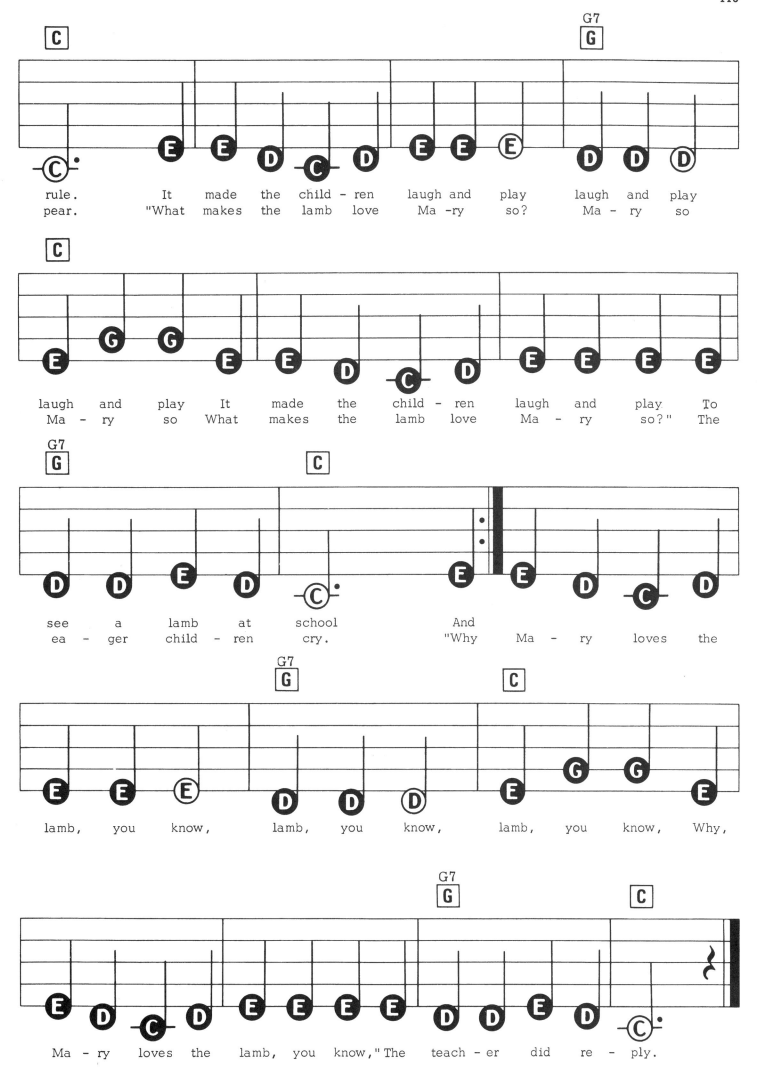

Mary, Mary Quite Contrary

Registration 5
Rhythm: Fox Trot

Traditional

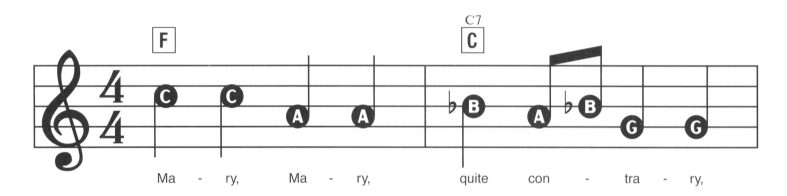

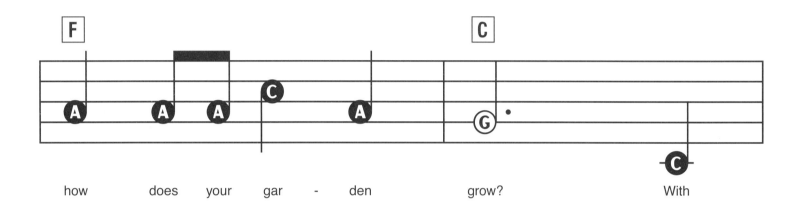

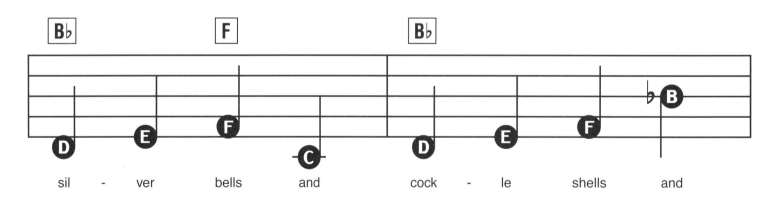

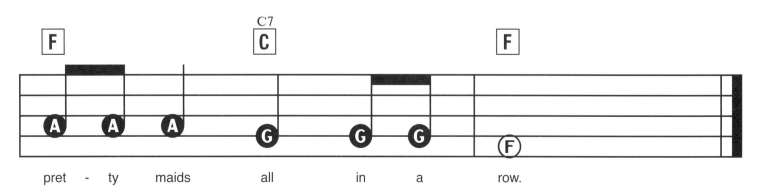

Merrily We Roll Along

Registration 2
Rhythm: Rock or 8-Beat

Traditional

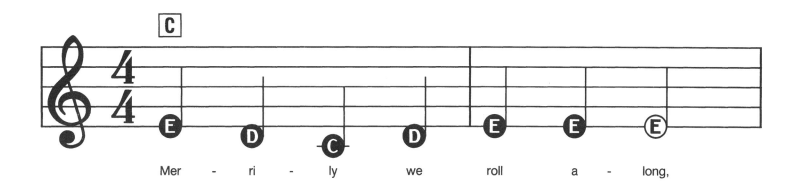

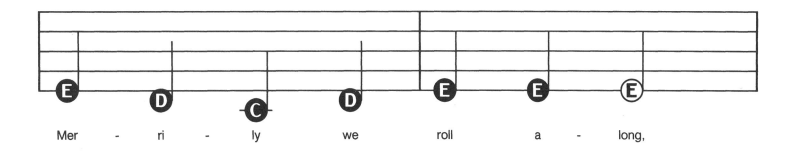

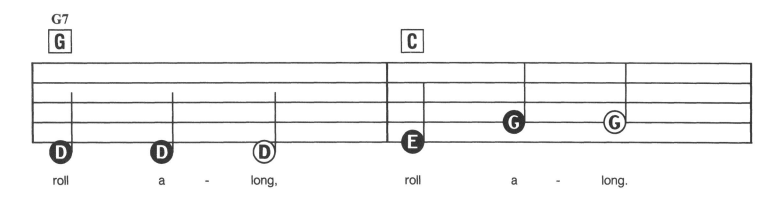

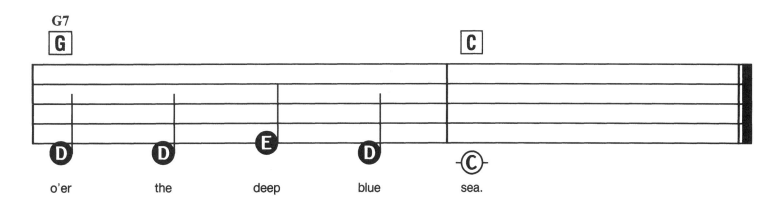

Michael Finnegan

Registration 4
Rhythm: Fox Trot or Polka

Traditional

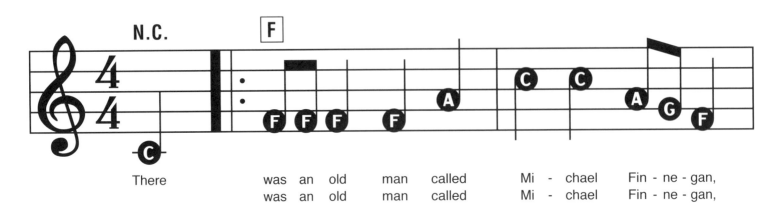

There
was an old man called Mi - chael Fin - ne - gan,
was an old man called Mi - chael Fin - ne - gan,

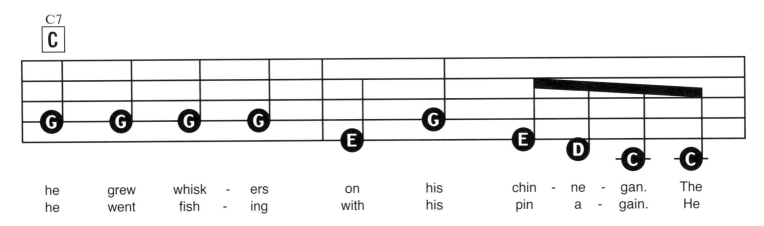

he grew whisk - ers on his chin - ne - gan. The
he went fish - ing on with his pin a - gain. He

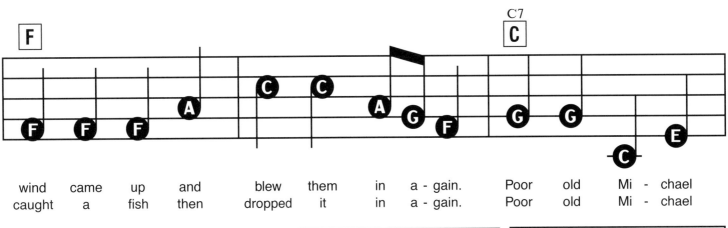

wind came up and blew them in a - gain. Poor old Mi chael
caught a fish then dropped it in a - gain. Poor old Mi chael

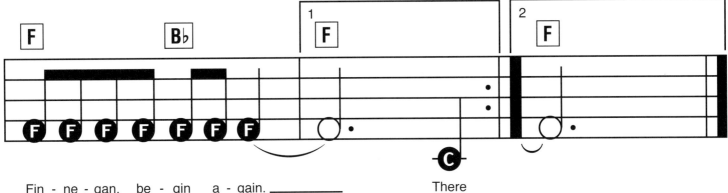

Fin - ne - gan, be - gin a - gain. _____
Fin - ne - gan, be - gin a - gain. _____

There

Michael, Row the Boat Ashore

Registration 2
Rhythm: Swing

Traditional Folksong

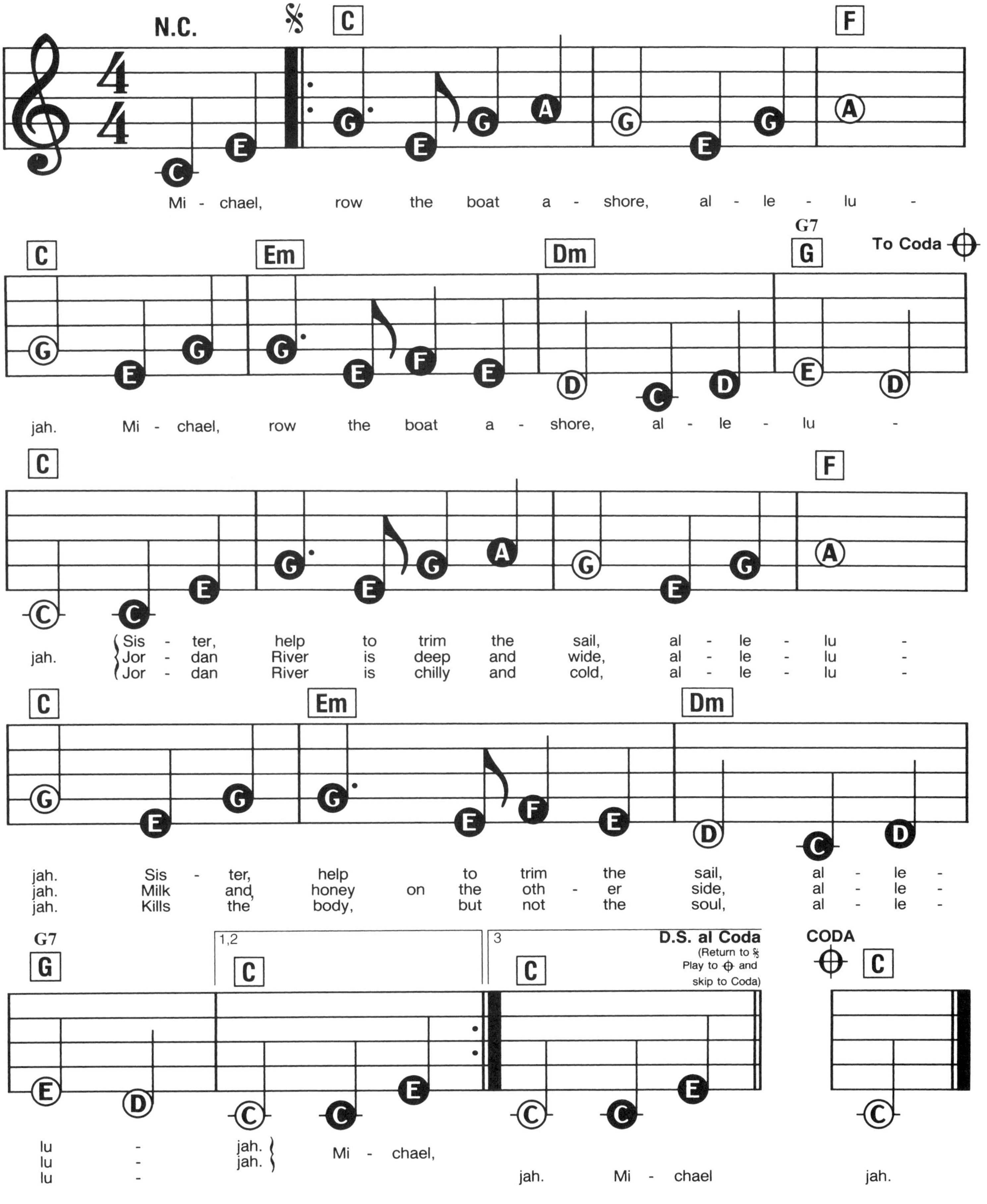

Miss Polly Had a Dolly

Registration 4
Rhythm: Fox Trot or Polka

Traditional

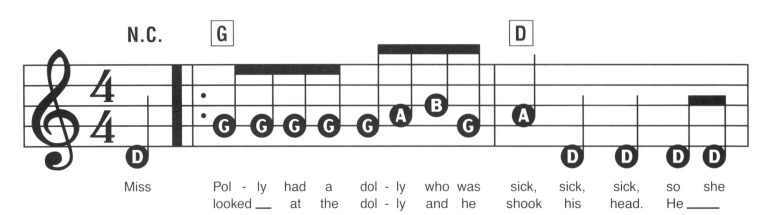

Miss Pol - ly had a dol - ly who was sick, sick, sick, so she
looked __ at the dol - ly and he shook his head. He ____

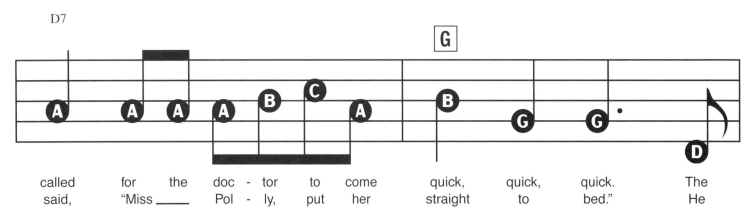

called for the doc - tor to come quick, quick, quick. The
said, "Miss ____ Pol - ly, put her straight to bed." He

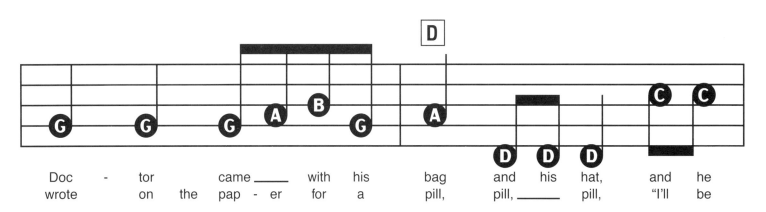

Doc - tor came ____ with his bag and his hat, and he
wrote on the pap - er for a pill, pill, ____ pill, "I'll be

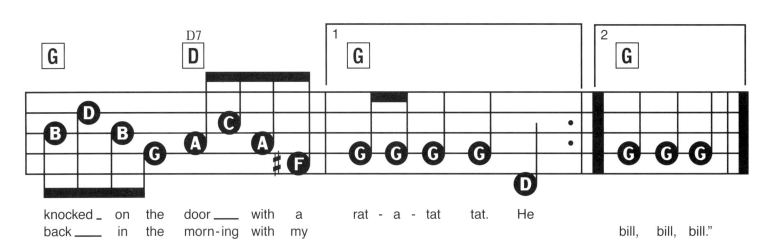

knocked _ on the door ____ with a rat - a - tat tat. He
back ____ in the morn - ing with my   bill, bill, bill."

The Muffin Man

Registration 4
Rhythm: March or Polka

Traditional

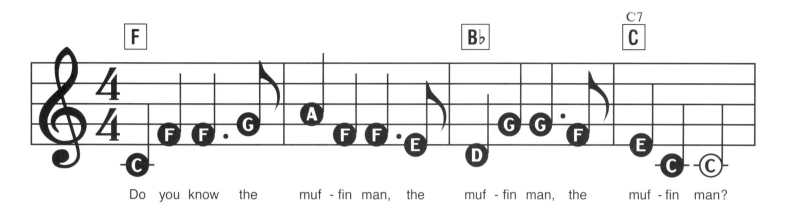

Do you know the muf-fin man, the muf-fin man, the muf-fin man?

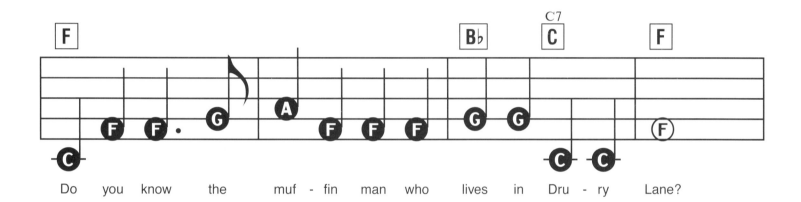

Do you know the muf-fin man who lives in Dru-ry Lane?

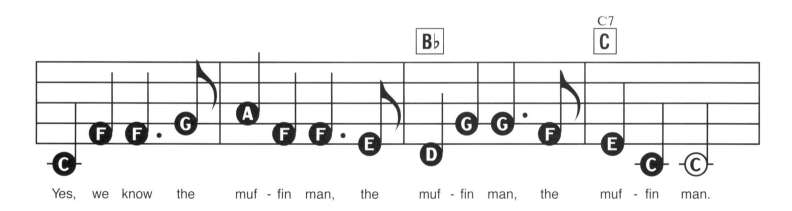

Yes, we know the muf-fin man, the muf-fin man, the muf-fin man.

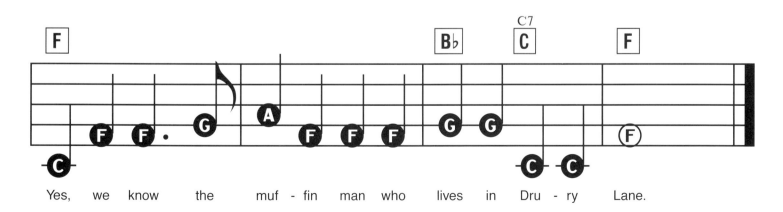

Yes, we know the muf-fin man who lives in Dru-ry Lane.

The Mulberry Bush

Registration 8
Rhythm: Waltz

Traditional

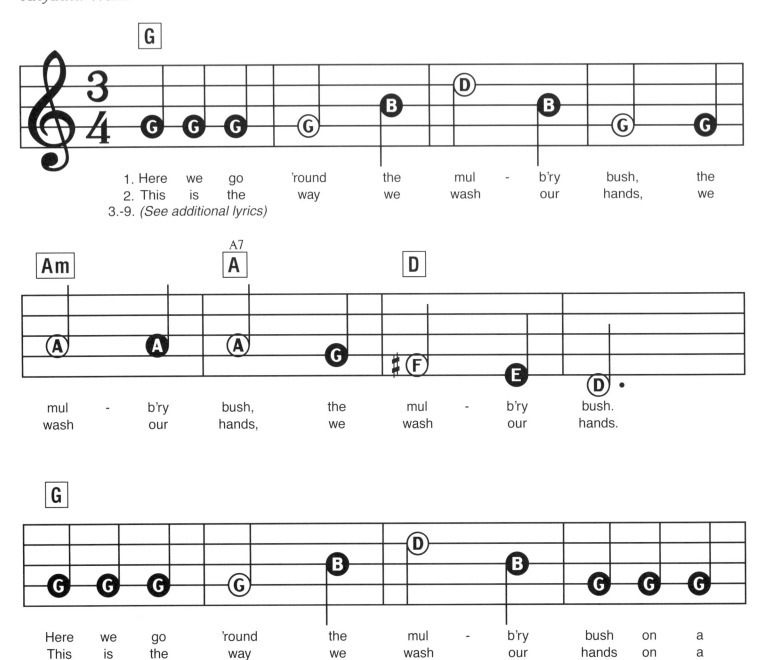

1. Here we go 'round the mul - b'ry bush, the
2. This is the way we wash our hands, the
3.-9. *(See additional lyrics)*

mul - b'ry bush, the mul - b'ry bush.
wash our hands, we wash our hands.

Here we go 'round the mul - b'ry bush on a
This is the way we wash our hands on a

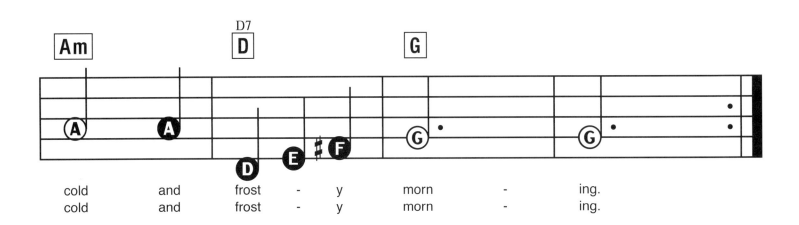

cold and frost - y morn - ing.
cold and frost - y morn - ing.

Additional Lyrics

3. This is the way we wash our clothes,
   We wash our clothes, we wash our clothes.
   This is the way we wash our clothes
   On a cold and frosty morning.

4. This is the way we dry our clothes,
   We dry our clothes, we dry our clothes.
   This is the way we dry our clothes
   On a cold and frosty morning.

5. This is the way we iron our clothes,
   We iron our clothes, we iron our clothes.
   This is the way we iron our clothes
   On a cold and frosty morning.

6. This is the way we sweep the floor,
   We sweep the floor, we sweep the floor.
   This is the way we sweep the floor
   On a cold and frosty morning.

7. This is the way we brush our hair,
   We brush our hair, we brush our hair.
   This is the way we brush our hair
   On a cold and frosty morning.

8. This is the way we go to school,
   We go to school, we go to school.
   This is the way we go to school
   On a cold and frosty morning.

9. This is the way we come back from school,
   We come back from school, we come back from school.
   This is the way we come back from school
   On a cold and frosty morning.

The Music Man

Registration 9
Rhythm: March

Traditional

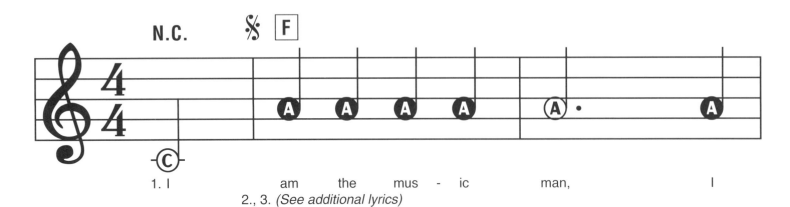

1. I   am   the   mus - ic   man,   I
2., 3. *(See additional lyrics)*

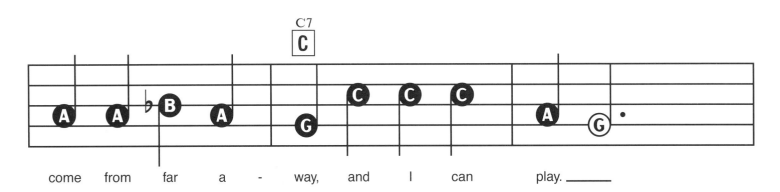

come   from   far   a -   way,   and   I   can   play. _____

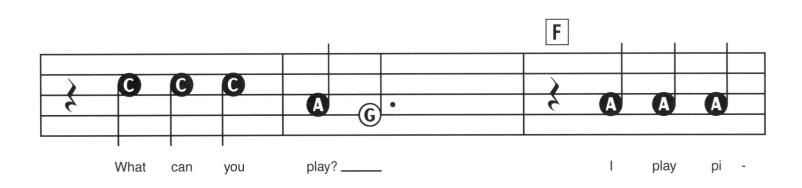

What   can   you   play? _____   I   play   pi -

Repeat for each instrument

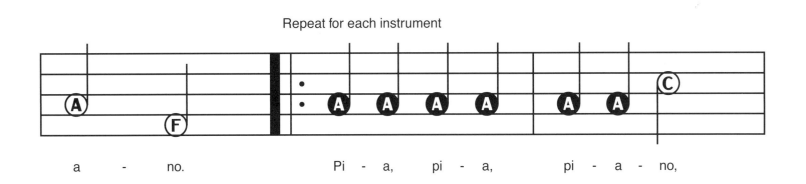

a -   no.   Pi - a,   pi - a,   pi - a - no,

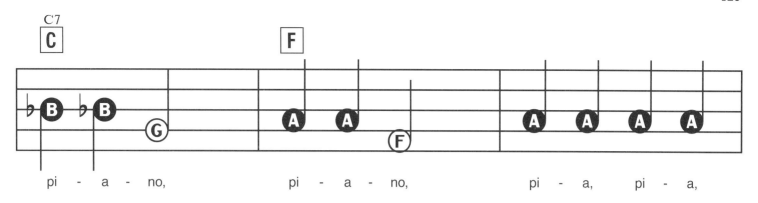

pi - a - no,   pi - a - no,   pi - a, pi - a,

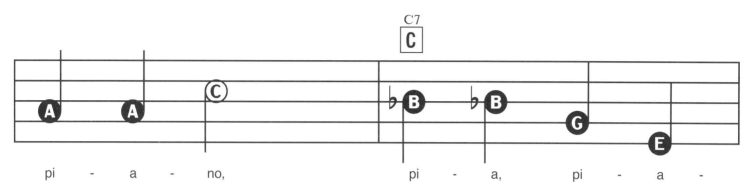

pi - a - no,   pi - a, pi - a -

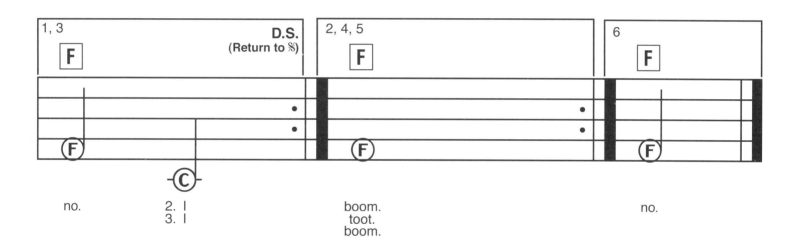

no.   2. I   boom.   no.
        3. I   toot.
                 boom.

Additional Lyrics

2. I am the music man,
   I come from far away,
   And I can play.
   What can you play?
   I play the bass drum.

   Boom-di, boom-di, boom-di-boom,
   Boom-di-boom, boom-di-boom,
   Boom-di, boom-di, boom-di-boom,
   Boom-di, boom-di-boom.
   Pi-a, pi-a, pi-a-no, *etc.*

3. I am the music man,
   I come from far away,
   And I can play.
   What can you play?
   I play the trumpet.

   Toot-ti, toot-ti, toot-ti-toot,
   Toot-ti-toot, toot-ti-toot,
   Toot-ti, toot-ti, toot-ti-toot,
   Toot-ti, toot-ti-toot.
   Boom-di-boom, boom-di-boom, *etc.*
   Pi-a, pi-a, pi-a-no, *etc.*

My Hat, It Has Three Corners

Registration 9
Rhythm: Waltz

Traditional

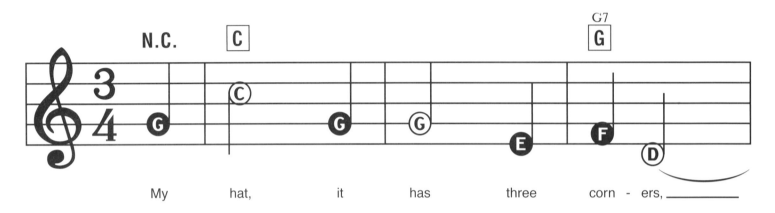

My hat, it has three corn - ers, _____

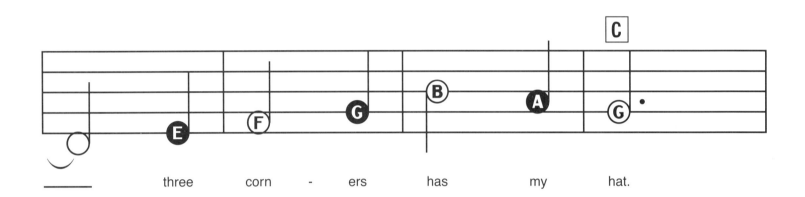

_____ three corn - ers has my hat.

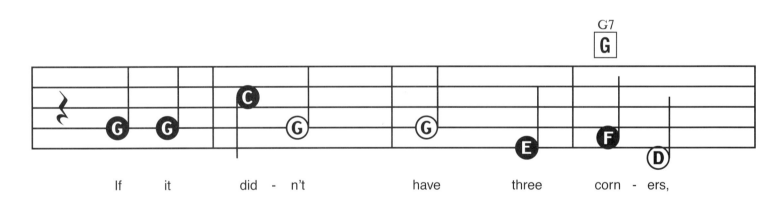

If it did - n't have three corn - ers,

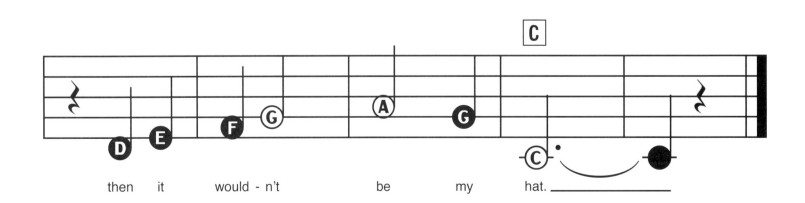

then it would - n't be my hat. _____

My Lady's Garden

Registration 3
Rhythm: 6/8 March

Traditional

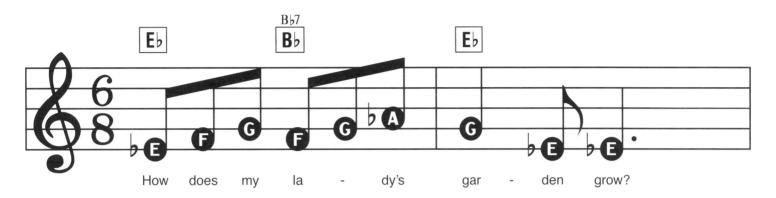

How does my la - dy's gar - den grow?

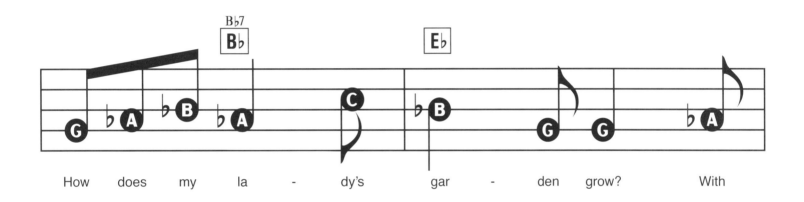

How does my la - dy's gar - den grow? With

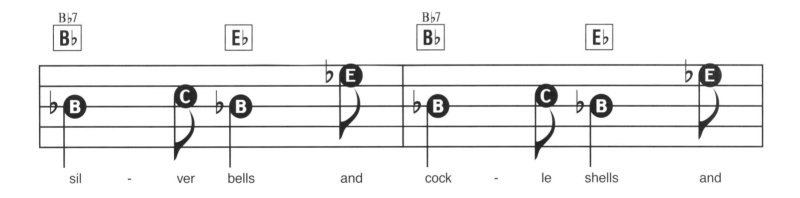

sil - ver bells and cock - le shells and

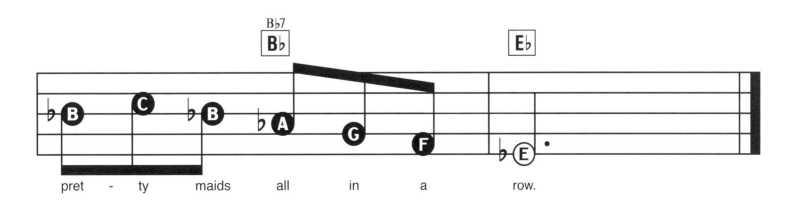

pret - ty maids all in a row.

Nobody Loves Me

Registration 8
Rhythm: Polka or Fox Trot

Traditional

The North Wind Doth Blow

Registration 2
Rhythm: Waltz

Traditional

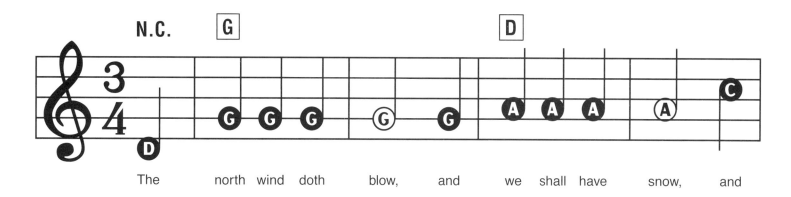

The north wind doth blow, and we shall have snow, and

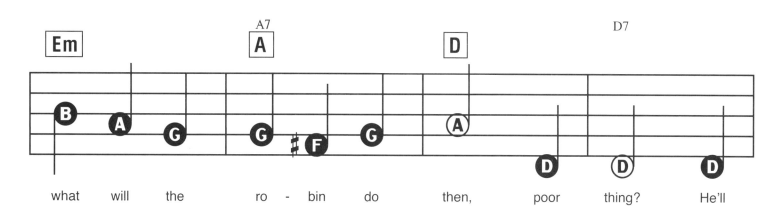

what will the ro - bin do then, poor thing? He'll

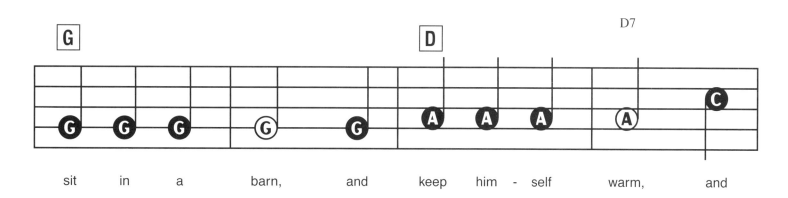

sit in a barn, and keep him - self warm, and

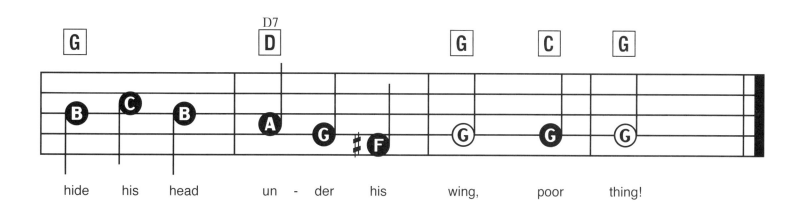

hide his head un - der his wing, poor thing!

Now I Lay Me Down to Sleep

Registration 1
Rhythm: Ballad

Traditional

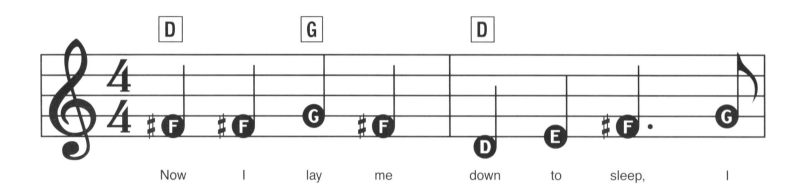

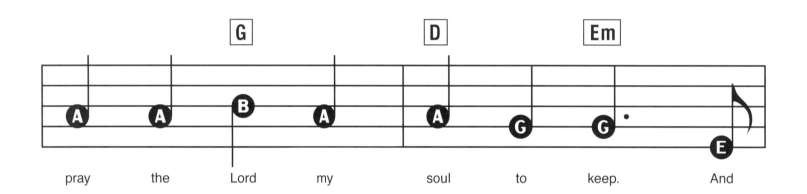

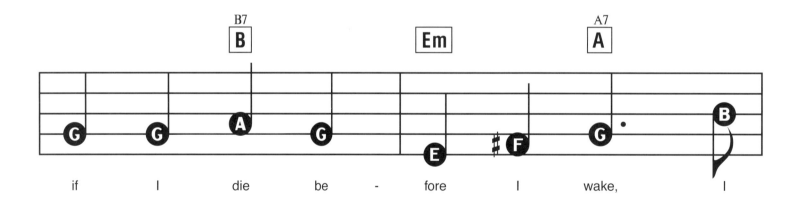

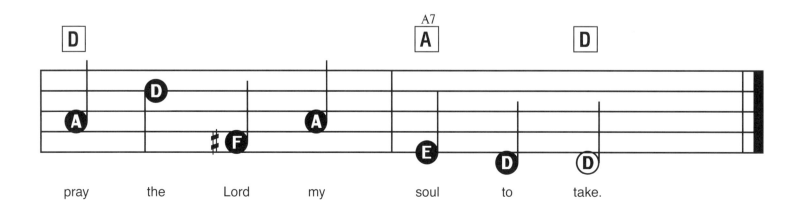

Now the Day Is Over

Registration 6
Rhythm: Ballad

Traditional

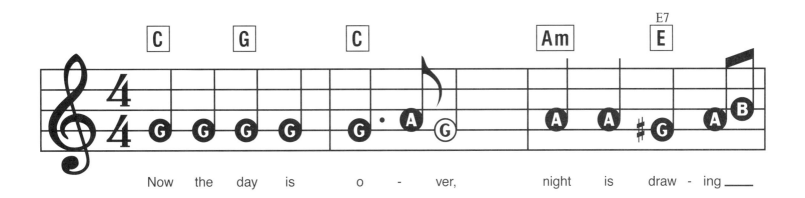

Now the day is o - ver, night is draw - ing ___

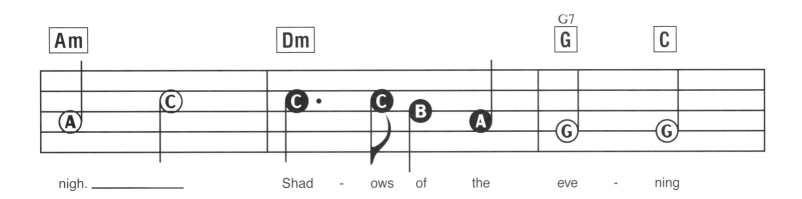

nigh. _____ Shad - ows of the eve - ning

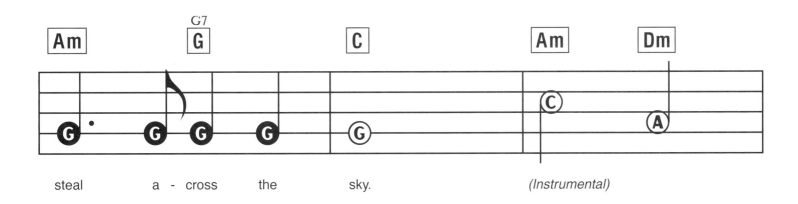

steal a - cross the sky. *(Instrumental)*

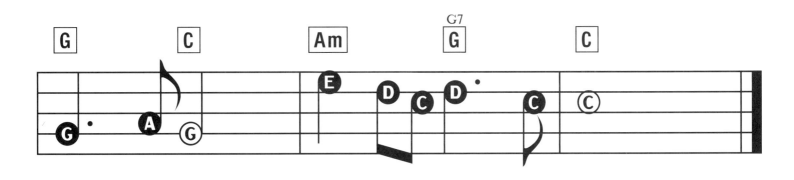

Oh, Dear! What Can the Matter Be?

Registration 2
Rhythm: Waltz

Traditional

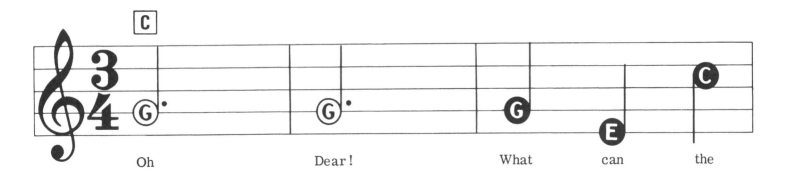

Oh   Dear!   What   can   the

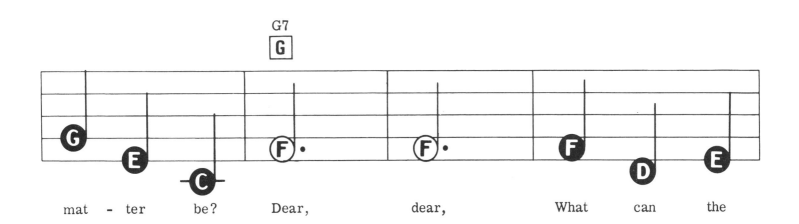

mat - ter be?   Dear,   dear,   What   can   the

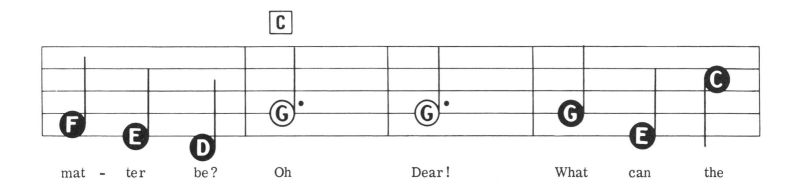

mat - ter be?   Oh   Dear!   What   can   the

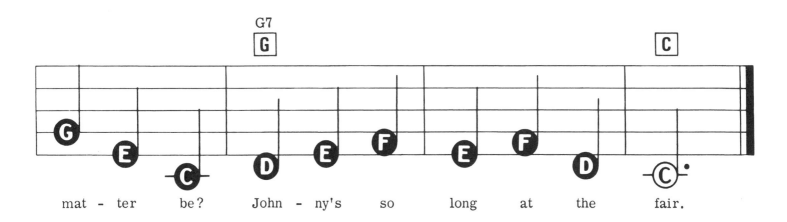

mat - ter be?   John - ny's   so   long   at   the   fair.

Oh, We Can Play
on the Big Bass Drum

Registration 2
Rhythm: March

Traditional

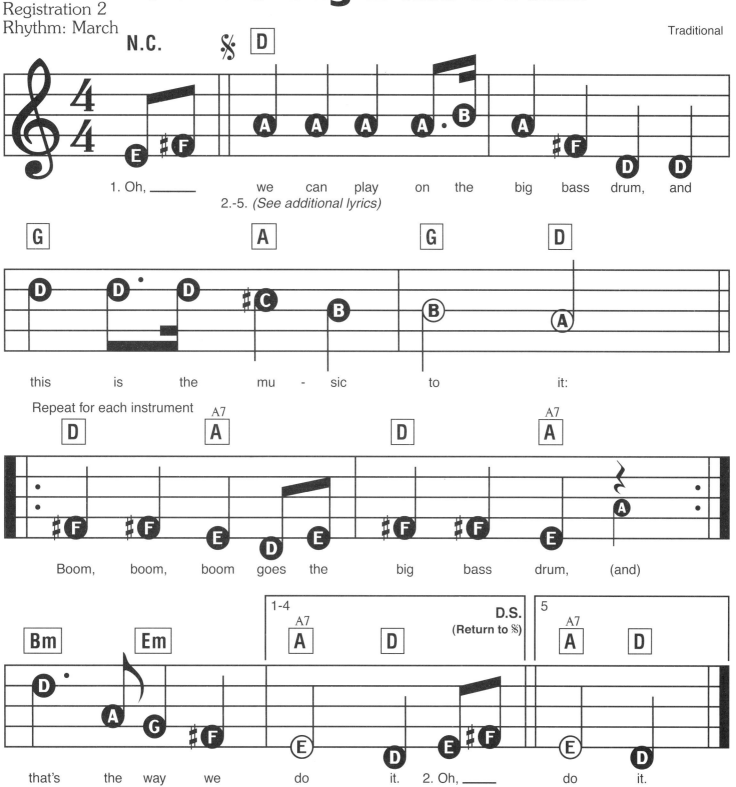

Additional Lyrics

2. Oh, we can play on the tambourine,
   And this is the music to it:
   Chink, chink, chink goes the tambourine,
   Boom, boom, boom goes the big bass drum,
   And that's the way we do it.

3. Oh, we can play on the castanets,
   And this is the music to it:
   Click, clickety-click go the castanets,
   Chink, chink, chink goes the tambourine, *etc.*

4. Oh, we can play on the triangle,
   And this is the music to it:
   Ping, ping, ping goes the triangle,
   Click, clickety-click go the castanets, *etc.*

5. Oh, we can play on the old banjo,
   And this is the music to it:
   Tum, tum, tum goes the old banjo,
   Ping, ping, ping goes the triangle, *etc.*

Oh Where, Oh Where
Has My Little Dog Gone

Registration 5
Rhythm: Waltz

Words by Sep. Winner
Traditional Melody

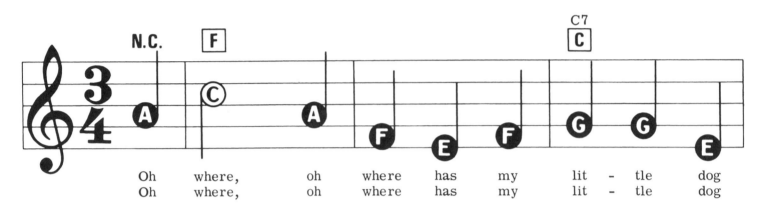

Oh   where,   oh   where   has   my   lit – tle   dog
Oh   where,   oh   where   has   my   lit – tle   dog

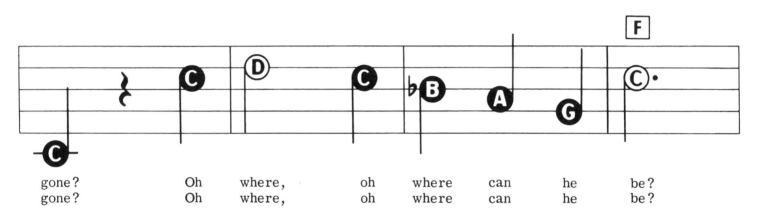

gone?   Oh   where,   oh   where   can   he   be?
gone?   Oh   where,   oh   where   can   he   be?

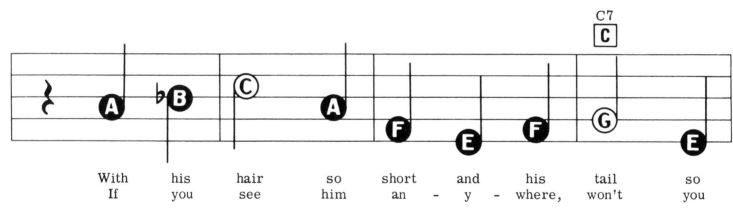

With   his   hair   so   short   and   his   tail   so
If   you   see   him   an – y – where,   won't   you

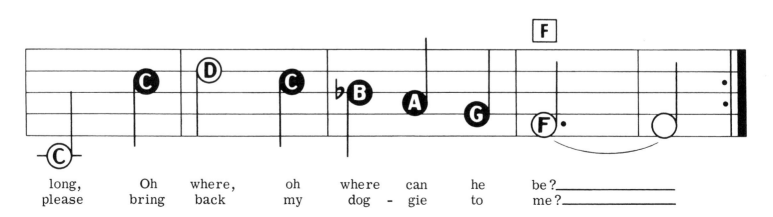

long,   Oh   where,   oh   where   can   he   be?_____
please   bring   back   my   dog – gie   to   me?_____

Old King Cole

Registration 4
Rhythm: Polka or March

Traditional

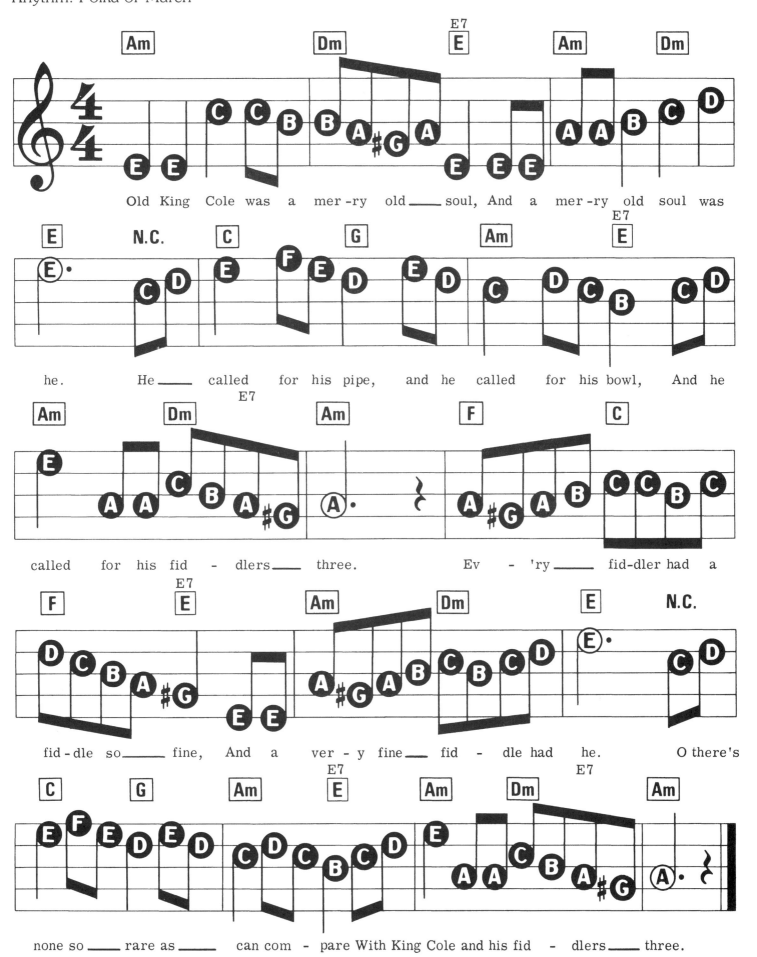

Old Blue

Registration 4
Rhythm: Fox Trot or Swing

Traditional

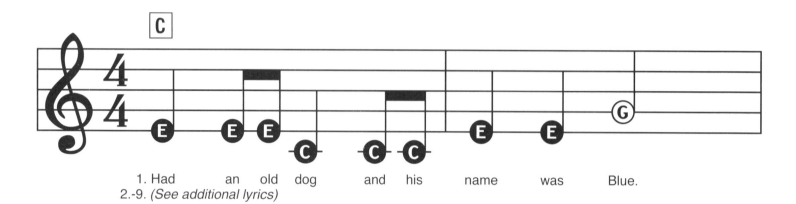

1. Had an old dog and his name was Blue.
2.-9. *(See additional lyrics)*

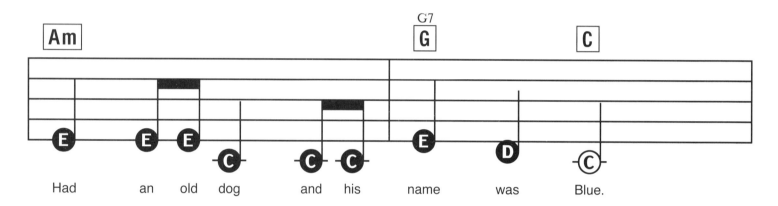

Had an old dog and his name was Blue.

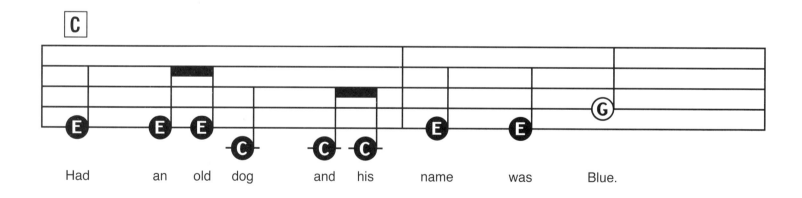

Had an old dog and his name was Blue.

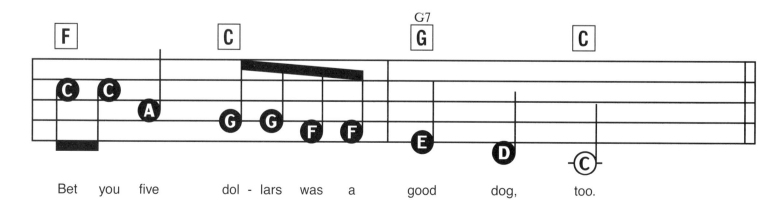

Bet you five dol - lars was a good dog, too.

Chorus

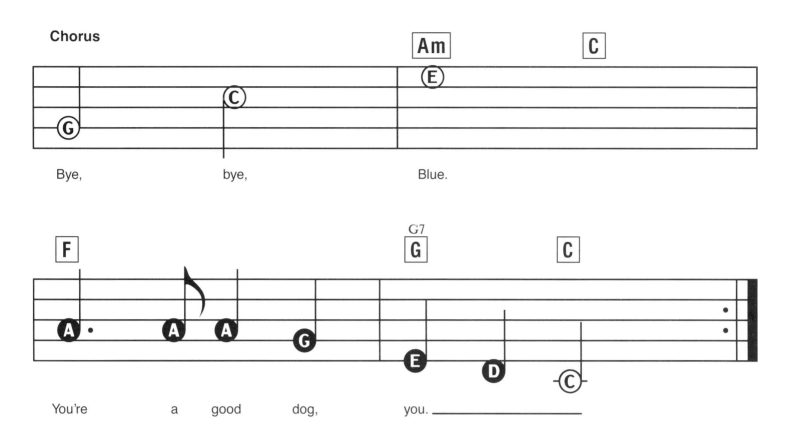

Bye,   bye,   Blue.

You're   a   good   dog,   you. _____

Additional Lyrics

2. Every night just about dark, *(3 times)*
Blue goes out and begins to bark.
Chorus

3. Everything just in a rush, *(3 times)*
He treed a possum in a white-oak bush.
Chorus

4. Possum walked out to the end of a limb, *(3 times)*
Blue set down and talked to him.
Chorus

5. Blue got sick and very sick, *(3 times)*
Sent for the doctor to come here quick.
Chorus

6. Doctor come and he come in a run, *(3 times)*
Says, "Old Blue, your hunting's done."
Chorus

7. Blue he died and died so hard, *(3 times)*
Scratched little holes all around the yard.
Chorus

8. Laid him out in a shady place, *(3 times)*
Covered him o'er with a possum's face.
Chorus

9. When I get to heaven I'll tell you what I'll do,
(3 times)
I'll take my horn and blow for Blue.
Chorus

Old Davey Jones

Registration 4
Rhythm: Swing

Traditional

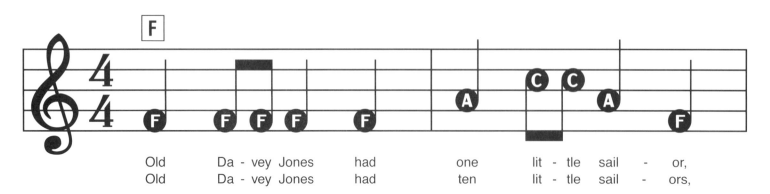

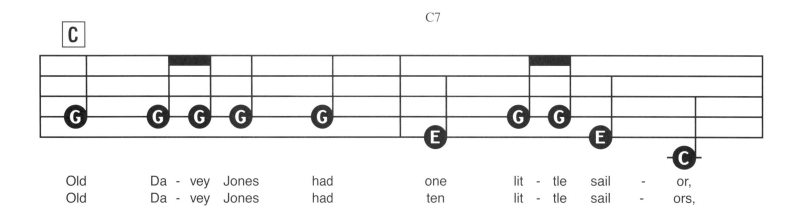

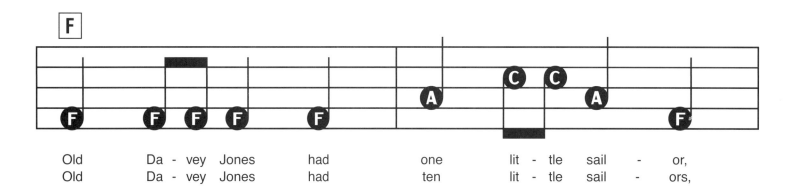

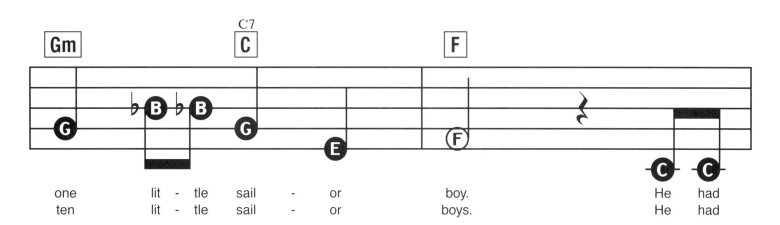

143

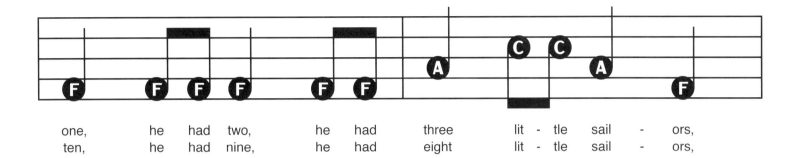

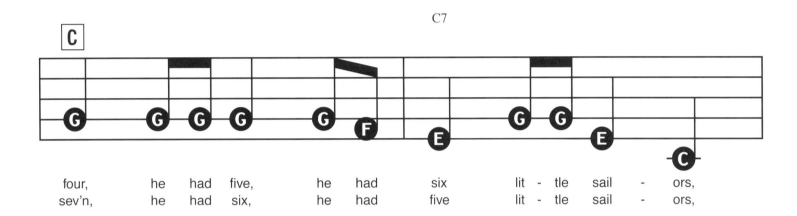

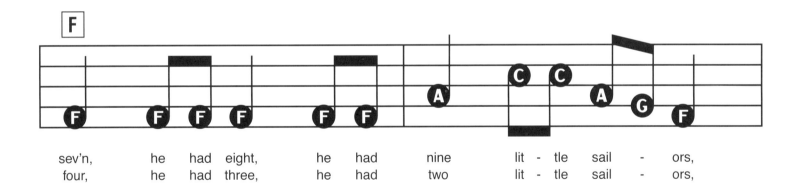

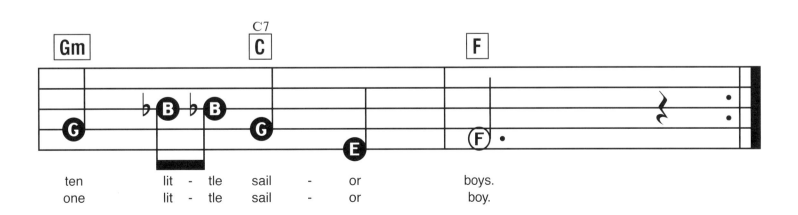

Old Hogan's Goat

Registration 9
Rhythm: Fox Trot

Traditional

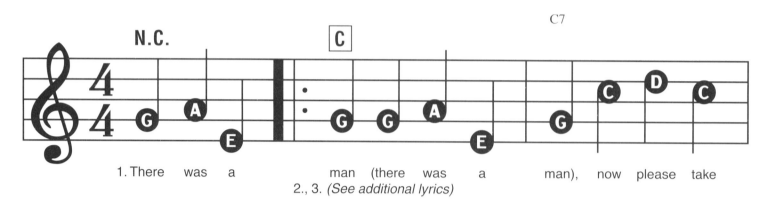

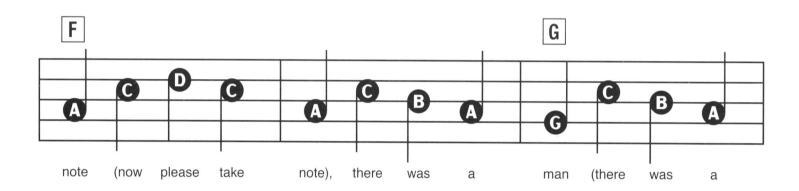

1. There was a man (there was a man), now please take
2., 3. *(See additional lyrics)*

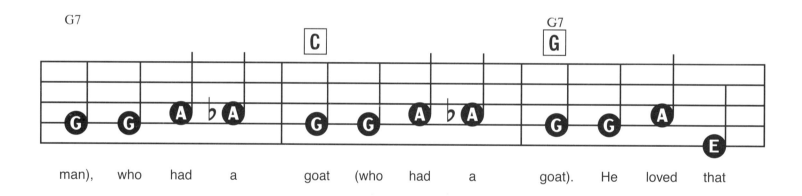

note (now please take note), there was a man (there was a

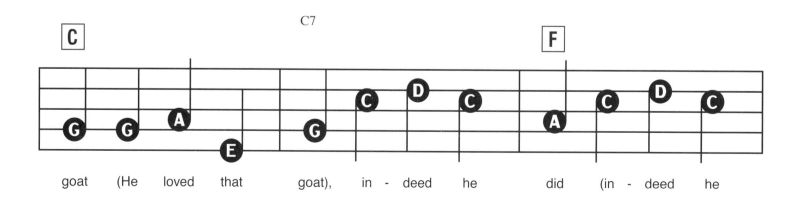

man), who had a goat (who had a goat). He loved that

goat (He loved that goat), in - deed he did (in - deed he

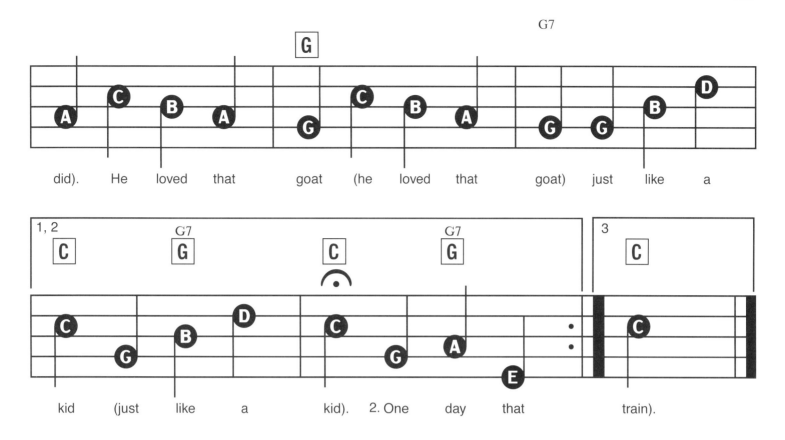

Additional Lyrics

2. One day that goat   (one day that goat)
   Was feeling fine   (was feeling fine)
   Ate three red shirts   (ate three red shirts)
   From off the line   (from off the line)
   The old man grabbed   (the old man grabbed)
   Her by the back   (her by the back)
   And tied her to   (and tied her to)
   The railway track   (the railway track)

3. Now when the train   (now when the train)
   Came into sight   (came into sight)
   The goat grew pale   (the goat grew pale)
   And grey with fright   (and grey with fright)
   She struggled hard   (she struggled hard)
   And then again   (and then again)
   Coughed up the shirts   (coughed up the shirts)
   And flagged the train   (and flagged the train)

Old MacDonald Had a Farm

Registration 4
Rhythm: Fox Trot

Traditional

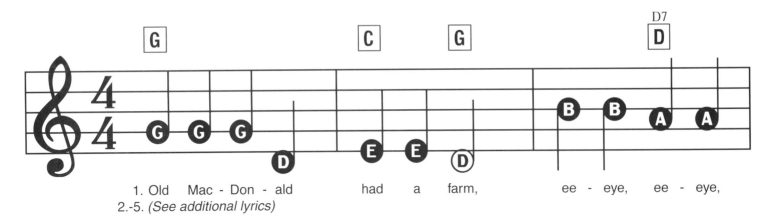

1. Old Mac - Don - ald had a farm, ee - eye, ee - eye,
2.-5. *(See additional lyrics)*

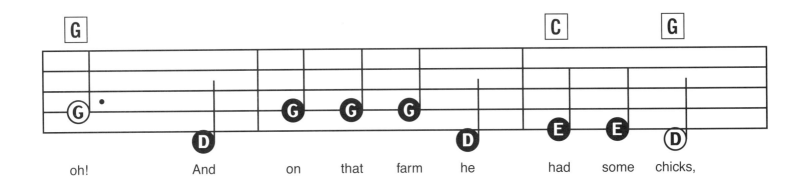

oh! And on that farm he had some chicks,

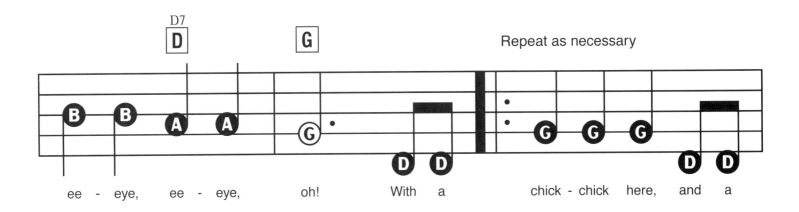

Repeat as necessary

ee - eye, ee - eye, oh! With a chick - chick here, and a

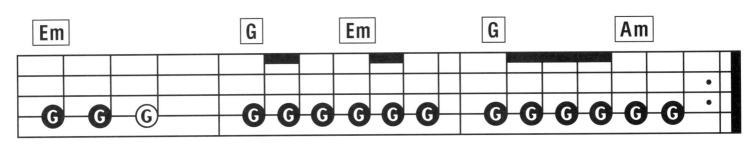

chick - chick there, here a chick, there a chick, ev - 'ry - where a chick - chick.

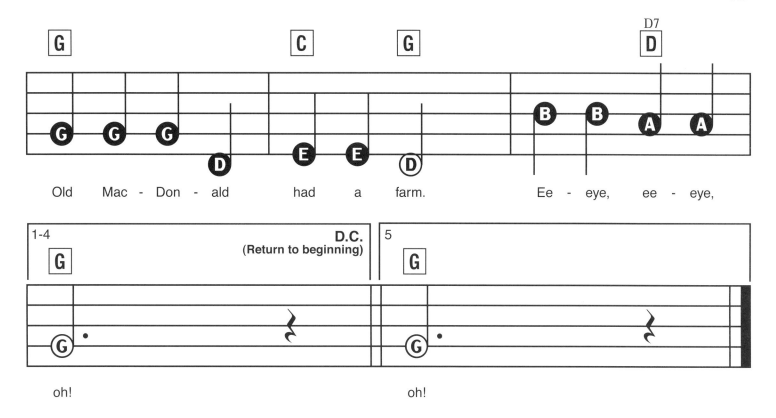

Old   Mac - Don - ald   had   a   farm.   Ee - eye,   ee - eye,

1-4
G

D.C.
(Return to beginning)

5
G

oh!   oh!

Additional Lyrics

2. Old MacDonald had a farm,
   Ee-eye, ee-eye, oh!
   And on that farm he had some ducks,
   Ee-eye, ee-eye, oh!
   With a quack-quack here and a quack-quack there,
   Here a quack, there a quack, everywhere a quack-quack.
   Chick-chick here and a chick-chick there,
   Here a chick, there a chick, everywhere a chick-chick.
   Old MacDonald had a farm,
   Ee-eye, ee-eye, oh!

3. …and on that farm he had some cows…
   With a moo-moo here and a moo-moo there,
   Here a moo, there a moo, everywhere a moo-moo,
   Quack-quack here and a quack-quack there…
   Chick-chick here and a chick-chick there…

4. …and on that farm he had some pigs…
   With an oink-oink here and an oink-oink there,
   Here an oink, there an oink, everywhere an oink-oink,
   Moo-moo here…
   Quack-quack here…
   Chick-chick here…

5. …and on that farm he had some sheep…
   With a baa-baa here and a baa-baa there…
   Oink-oink here…
   Moo-moo here…
   Quack-quack here…
   Chick-chick here…

Old Mother Hubbard

Registration 8
Rhythm: 6/8 March

Traditional

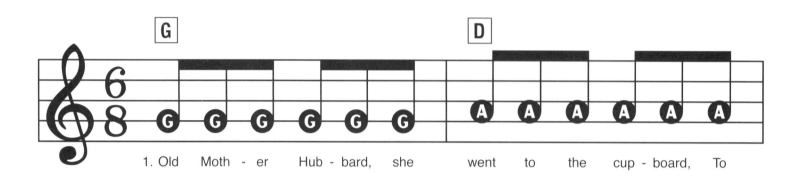

1. Old Moth - er Hub - bard, she went to the cup - board, To

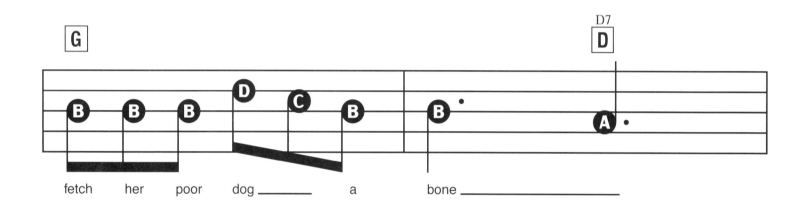

fetch her poor dog _____ a bone _____

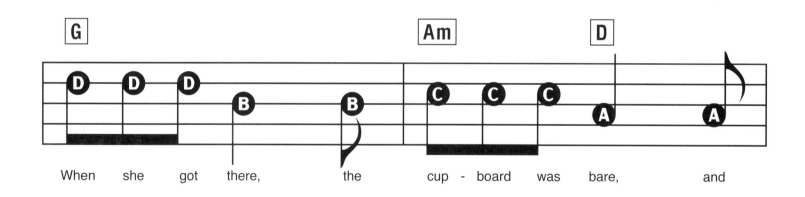

When she got there, the cup - board was bare, and

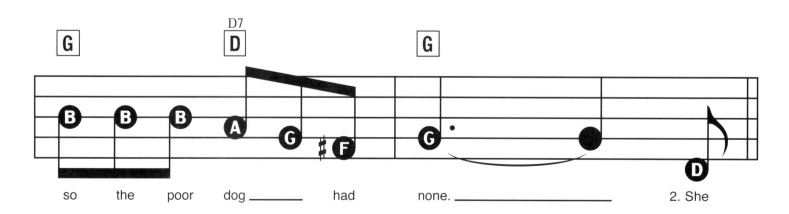

so the poor dog _____ had none. _____ 2. She

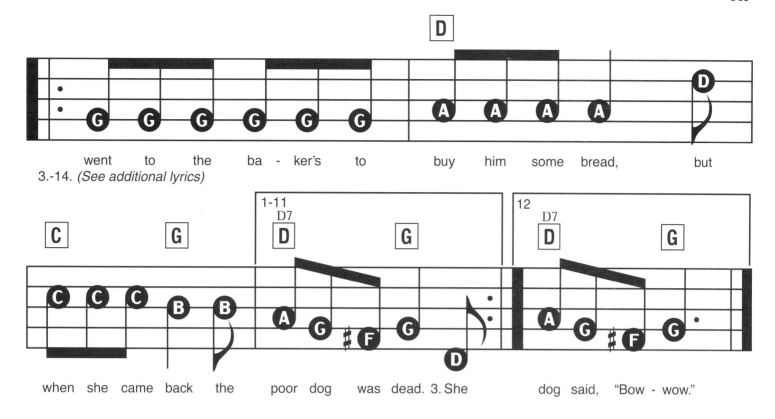

went   to   the   ba - ker's   to   buy   him   some   bread,   but

3.-14. *(See additional lyrics)*

when   she   came   back   the   poor   dog   was   dead. 3. She   dog   said,   "Bow - wow."

Additional Lyrics

3. She went to the undertaker's
   To buy him a coffin:
   But when she came back,
   The poor dog was laughing.

4. She took a clean dish
   To get him some tripe:
   But when she got back,
   He was smoking a pipe.

5. She went to the fishmonger's
   To buy him some fish:
   But when she came back,
   He was licking the dish.

6. She went to the tavern
   For white wine and red:
   But when she got back,
   The dog stood on his head.

7. She went to the fruiterer's
   To buy him some fruit:
   But when she came back,
   He was playing the flute.

8. She went to the tailor's
   To buy him a coat:
   But when she came back,
   He was riding a goat.

9. She went to the hatter's
   To buy him a hat:
   But when she came back,
   He was feeding the cat.

10. She went to the barber's
    To buy him a wig:
    But when she came back,
    He was dancing a jig.

11. She went to the cobbler's
    To buy him some shoes:
    But when she came back,
    He was reading the news.

12. She went to the seamstress
    To buy him some linen:
    But when she came back,
    The dog was a-spinning.

13. She went to the hosier's
    To buy him some hose:
    But when she came back,
    He was dressed in his clothes.

14. The Dame made a curtsey,
    The dog made a bow;
    The Dame said, "Your servant,"
    The dog said, "Bow-wow."

On Top of Old Smoky

Registration 1
Rhythm: Waltz

Kentucky Mountain Folksong

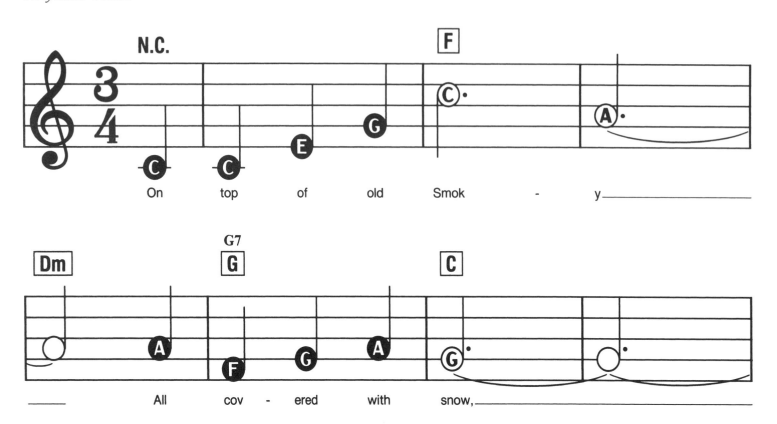

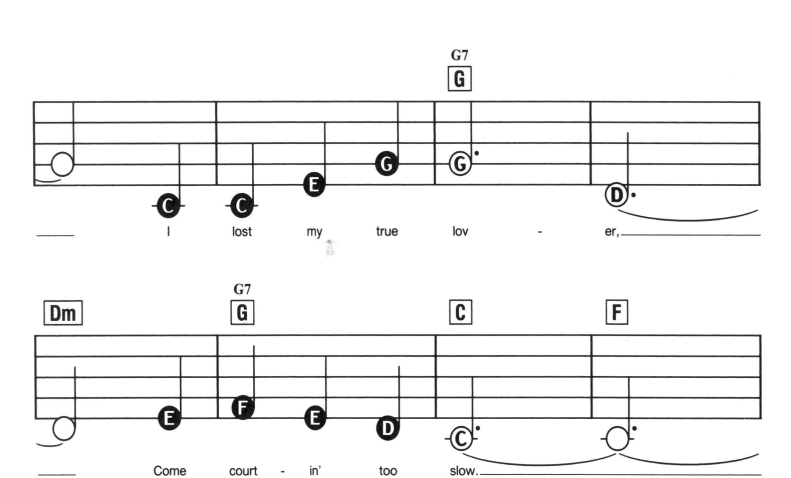

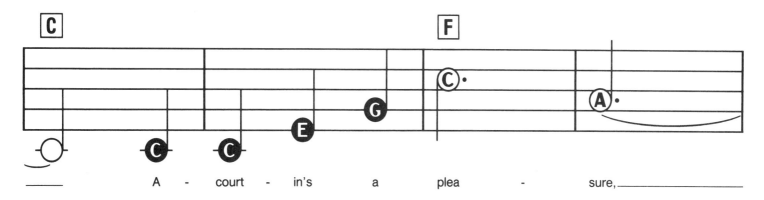

A - court - in's a plea - sure,

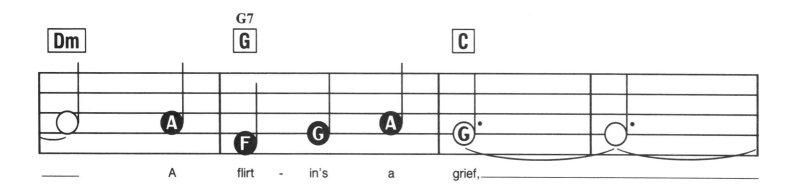

A flirt - in's a grief,

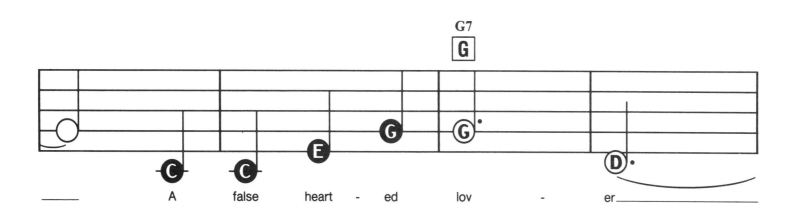

A false heart - ed lov - er

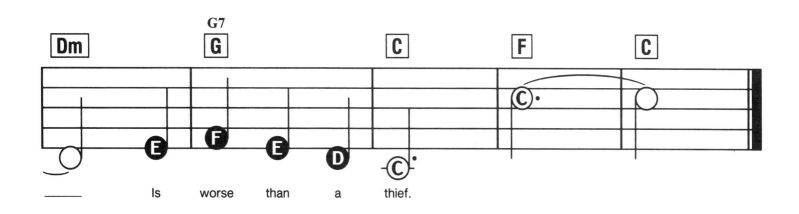

Is worse than a thief.

One Elephant

Registration 9
Rhythm: Fox Trot or March

Traditional

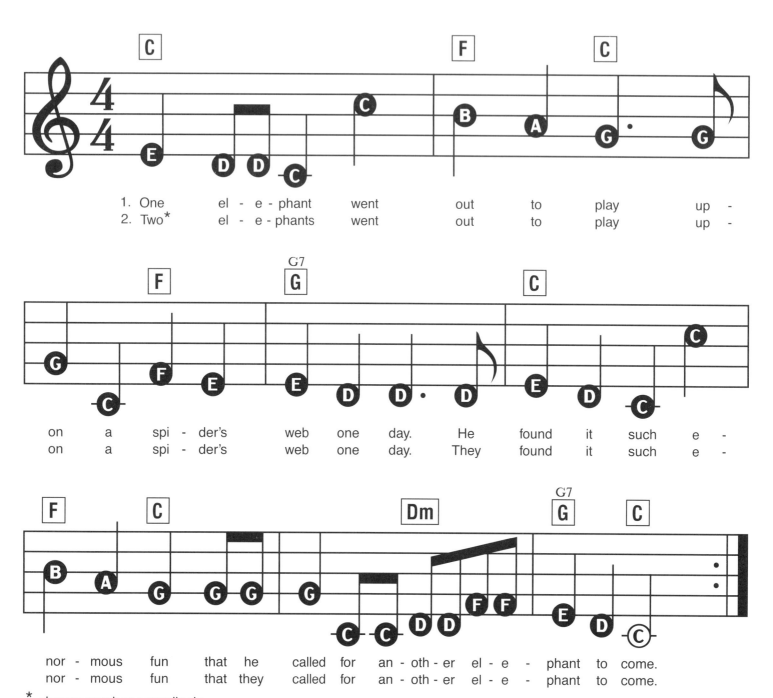

* change number accordingly

Activity

Get everyone into a circle. Pick one person to be the elephant and ask them to stand in the middle. While singing, the elephant in the middle skips around having fun. Those on the outside can mime appropriate actions to match the song. On the line "that he called for another elephant to come," everyone wiggles their bottom and the elephant in the middle points at someone to come and join him/her. Keep going until everyone is an elephant!

One Finger, One Thumb

Registration 9
Rhythm: 6/8 March

Traditional

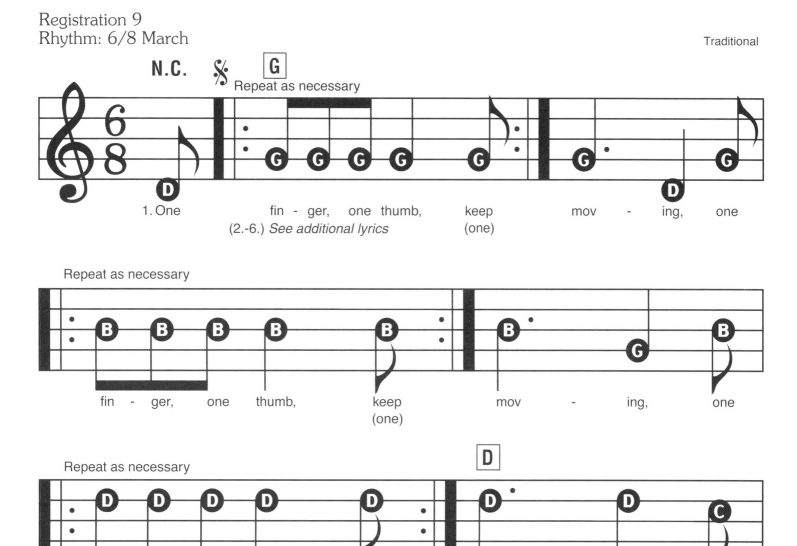

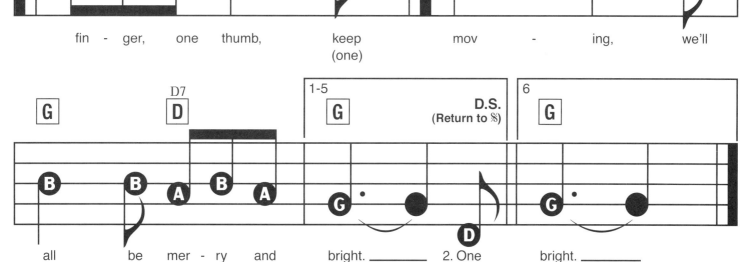

Additional Lyrics

2. One finger, one thumb, one arm,
   keep moving, *etc.*

3. One finger, one thumb, one arm, one leg,
   keep moving, *etc.*

4. One finger, one thumb, one arm, one leg,
   One nod of the head, keep moving, *etc.*

5. One finger, one thumb, one arm, one leg,
   One nod of the head, stand up, sit down,
   keep moving, *etc.*

6. One finger, one thumb, one arm, one leg,
   One nod of the head, stand up, sit down,
   Turn around, keep moving, *etc.*

One Man Went to Mow

Registration 9
Rhythm: Polka or March

Traditional

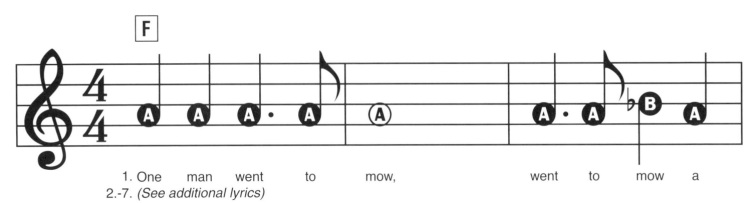

1. One man went to mow,
2.-7. *(See additional lyrics)*

went to mow a

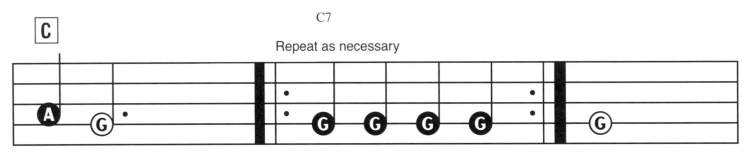

mea - dow.   One   man   and   his   dog

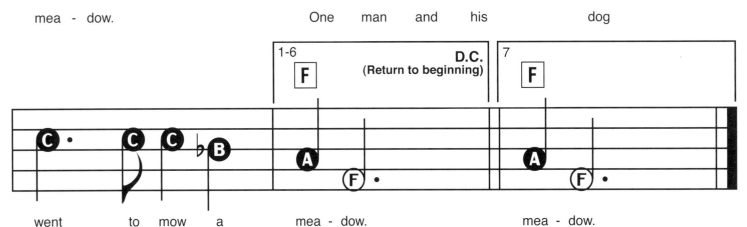

went   to   mow   a   mea - dow.   mea - dow.

Additional Lyrics

2. Two men went to mow,
   Went to mow a meadow.
   Two men, one man and his dog
   Went to mow a meadow.

3. Three men went to mow,
   Went to mow a meadow,
   Three men, two men, one man and his dog
   Went to mow a meadow.

4. Four men went to mow, *etc.*

5. Five men went to mow, *etc.*

6. Six men went to mow, *etc.*

7. Seven men went to mow, *etc.*

One, Two, Three, Four, Five

Registration 4
Rhythm: Fox Trot

Traditional

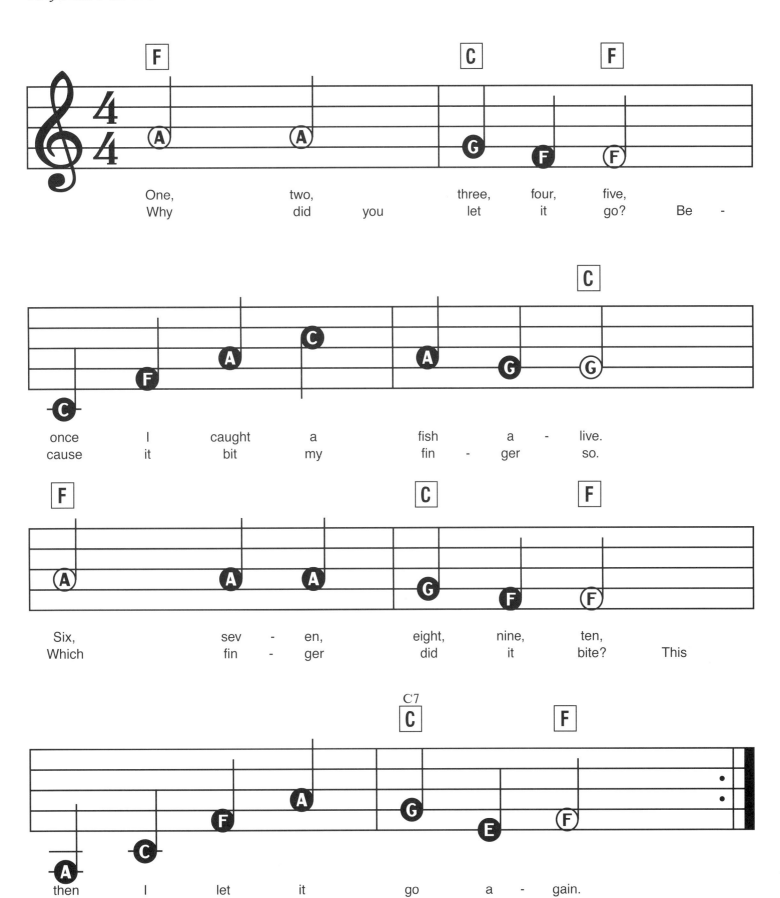

One, Two, Buckle My Shoe

Registration 5
Rhythm: 6/8 March

Traditional

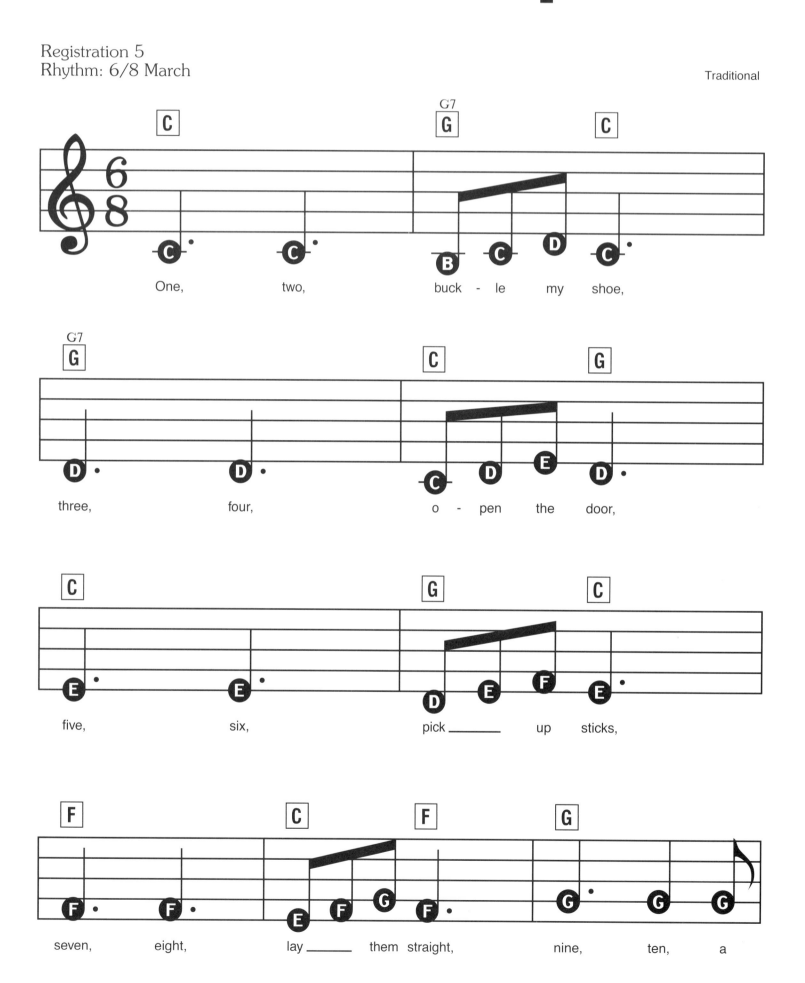

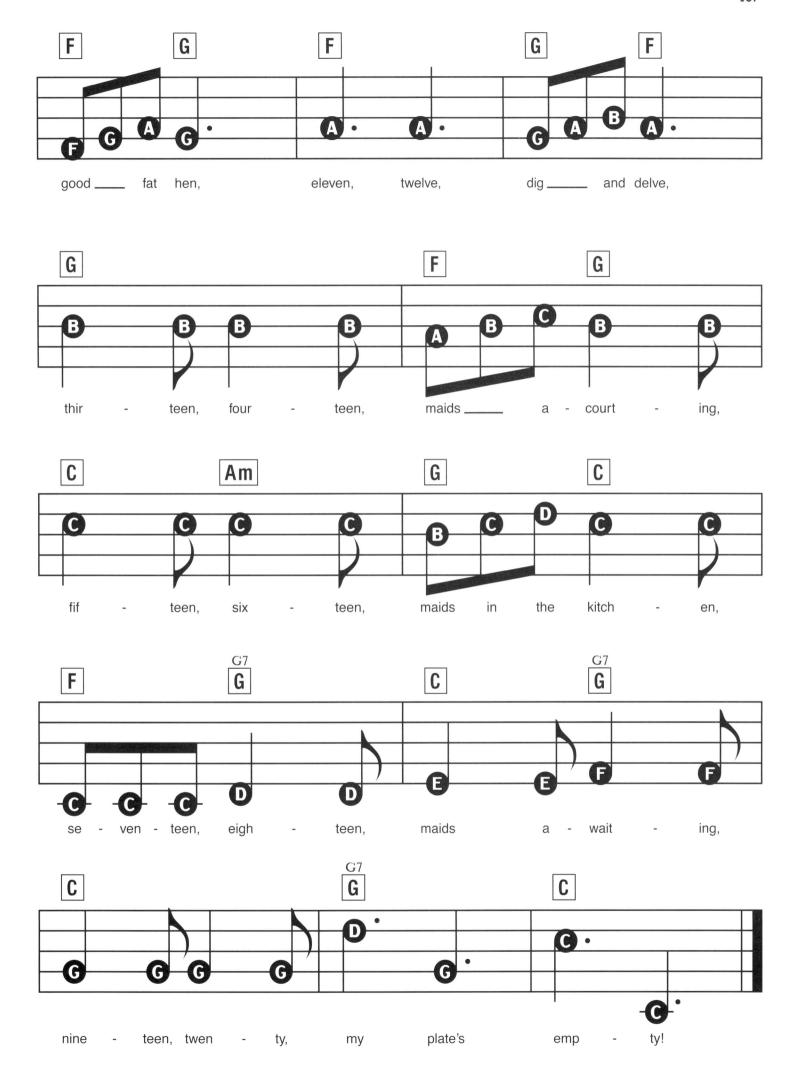

Oranges and Lemons

Registration 6
Rhythm: Waltz

Traditional

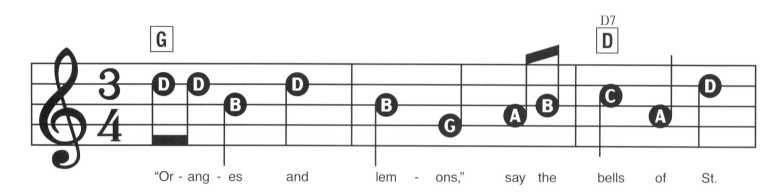

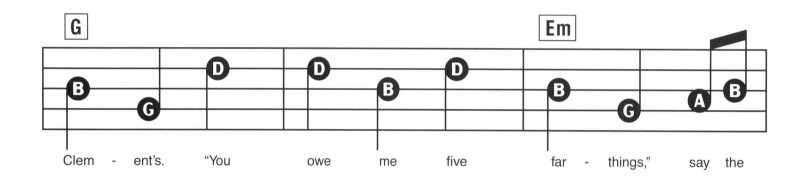

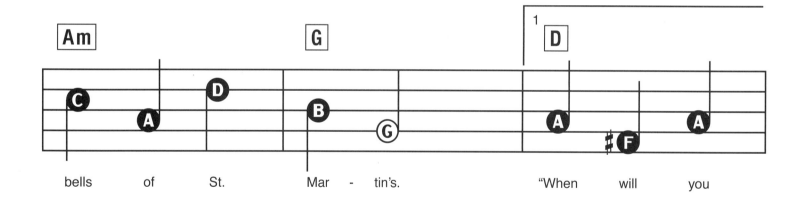

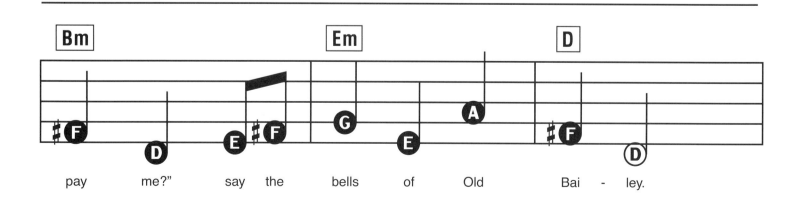

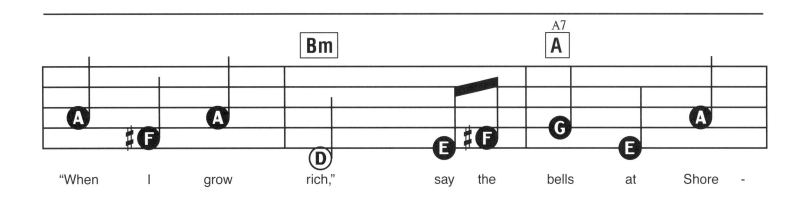

"When I grow rich," say the bells at Shore -

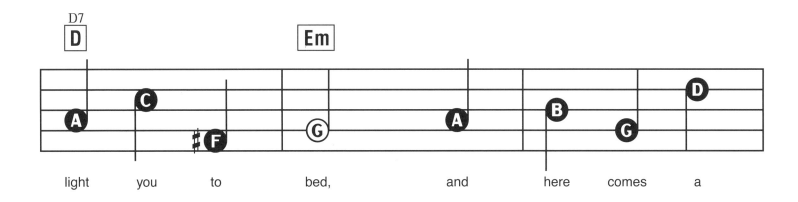

ditch. Here comes a can - dle to _____

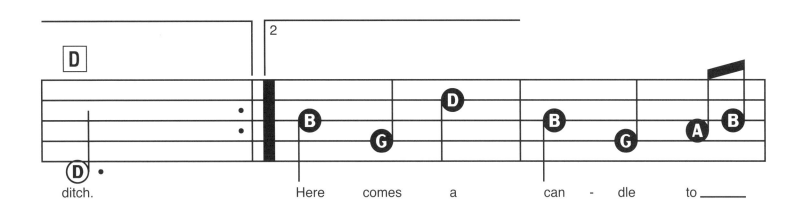

light you to bed, and here comes a

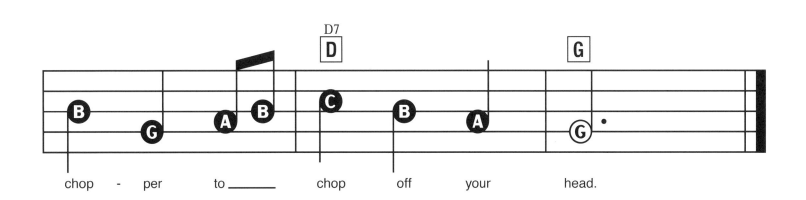

chop - per to _____ chop off your head.

The Owl and the Pussycat

Registration 1
Rhythm: 6/8 March

Traditional

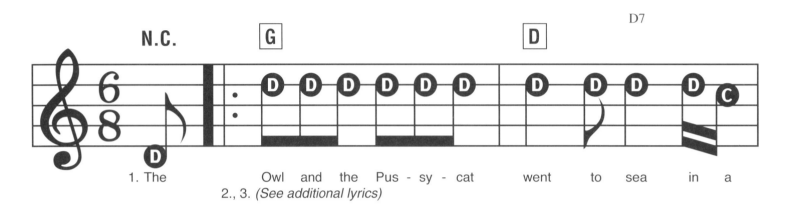

1. The Owl and the Pus - sy - cat went to sea in a
2., 3. *(See additional lyrics)*

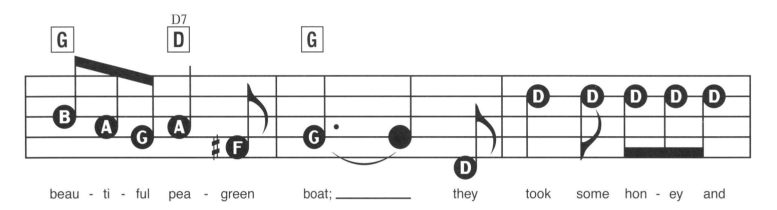

beau - ti - ful pea - green boat; _____ they took some hon - ey and

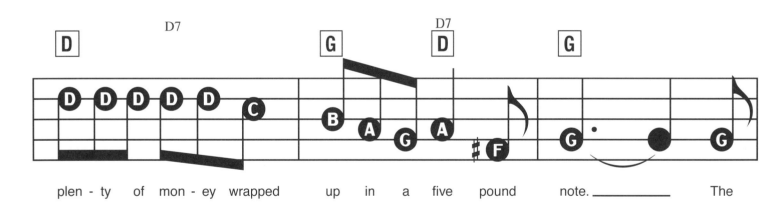

plen - ty of mon - ey wrapped up in a five pound note. _____ The

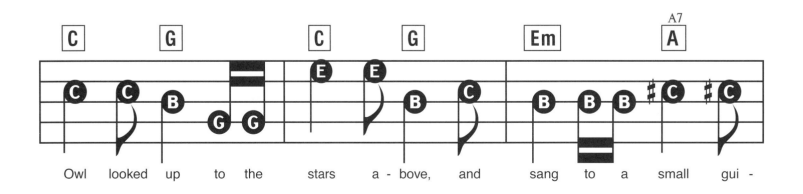

Owl looked up to the stars a - bove, and sang to a small gui -

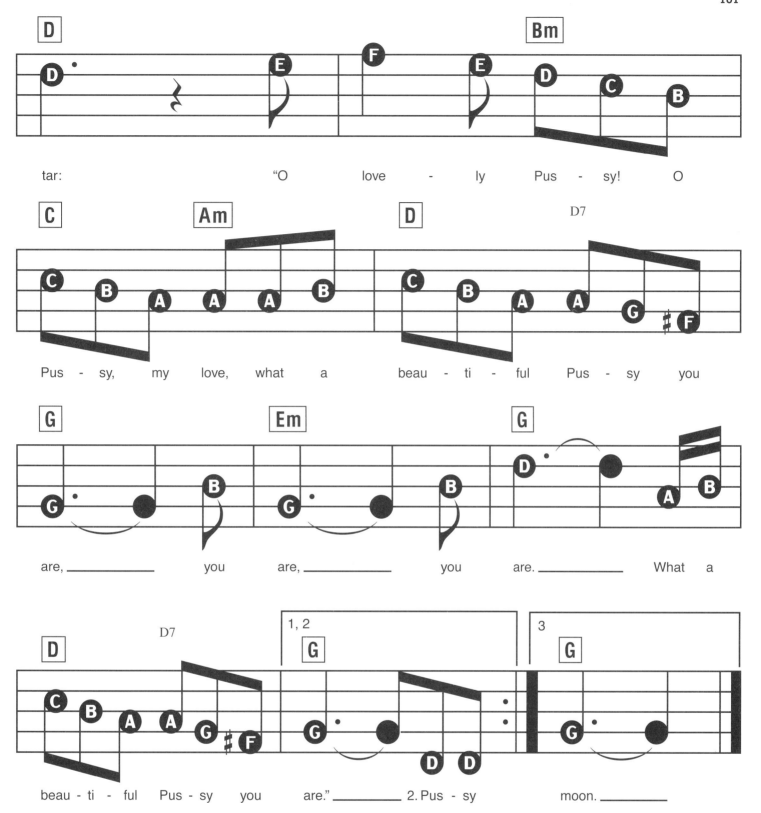

Additional Lyrics

2. Pussy said to the Owl: "You elegant fowl,
   How charmingly sweet you sing!
   Oh, let us be married; too long we have tarried;
   But what shall we do for a ring?"
   They sailed away for a year and a day
   To the land where the bong tree grows;
   And there in the woods, a piggy-wig stood
   With a ring at the end of his nose,
   His nose, his nose,
   With a ring at the end of his nose..

3. "Dear Pig, are you willing to sell for one shilling
   Your ring?" Said the piggy, "I will."
   So they took it away, and were married next day
   By the turkey who lives on the hill.
   They dined on mince and slices of quince,
   Which they ate with a runcible spoon.
   And hand in hand on the edge of the sand,
   They danced by the light of the moon,
   The moon, the moon.
   They danced by the light of the moon.

Pat-a-Cake

Registration 4
Rhythm: Waltz

Traditional

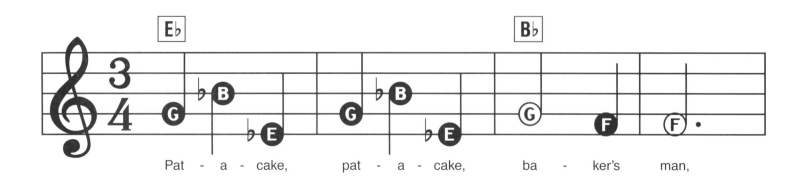

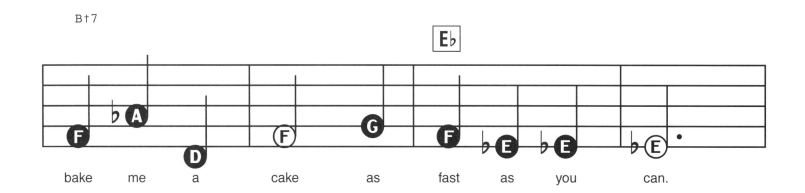

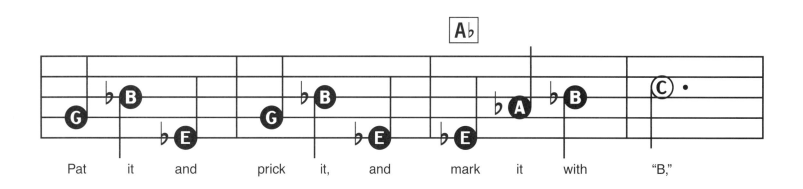

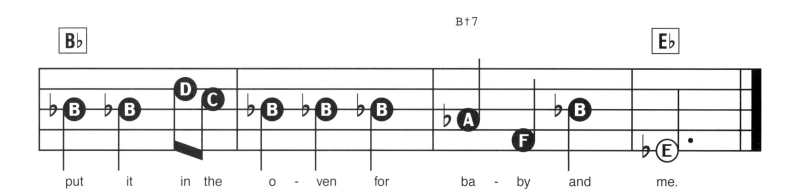

Peanut Sat on a Railroad Track

Registration 8
Rhythm: Polka or March

Traditional

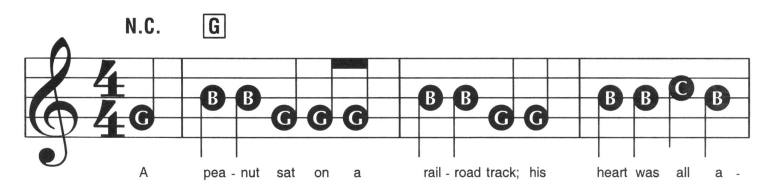

A pea - nut sat on a rail - road track; his heart was all a -

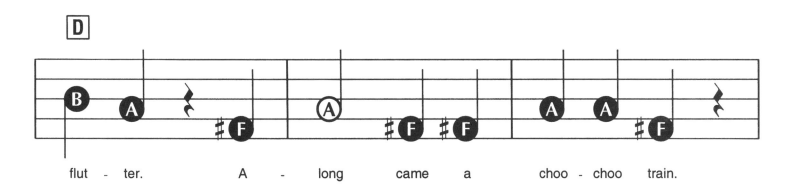

flut - ter. A - long came a choo - choo train.

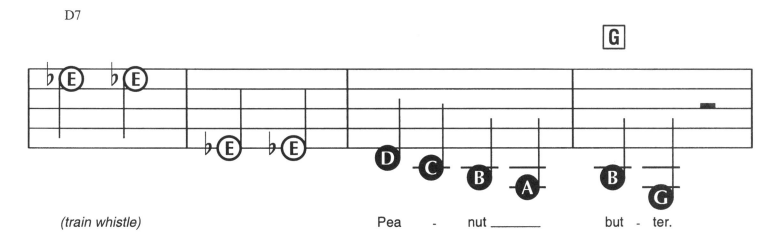

(train whistle)

Pea - nut _____ but - ter.

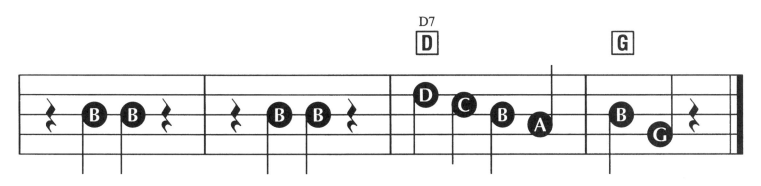

Pease Porridge Hot

Registration 8
Rhythm: Fox Trot

Traditional

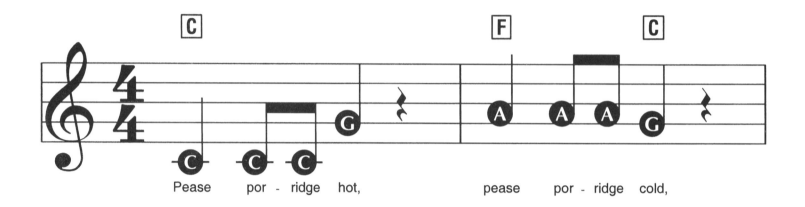

Pease por - ridge hot, pease por - ridge cold,

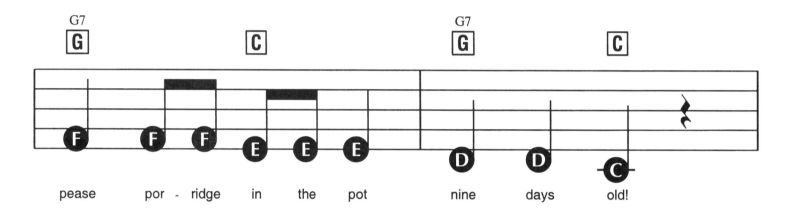

pease por - ridge in the pot nine days old!

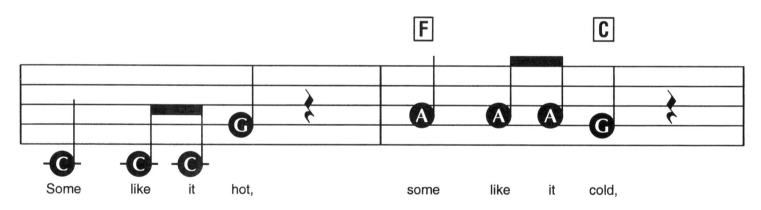

Some like it hot, some like it cold,

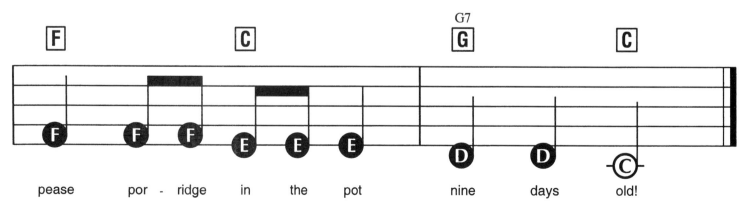

pease por - ridge in the pot nine days old!

Peter Piper

Registration 9
Rhythm: Fox Trot

Traditional

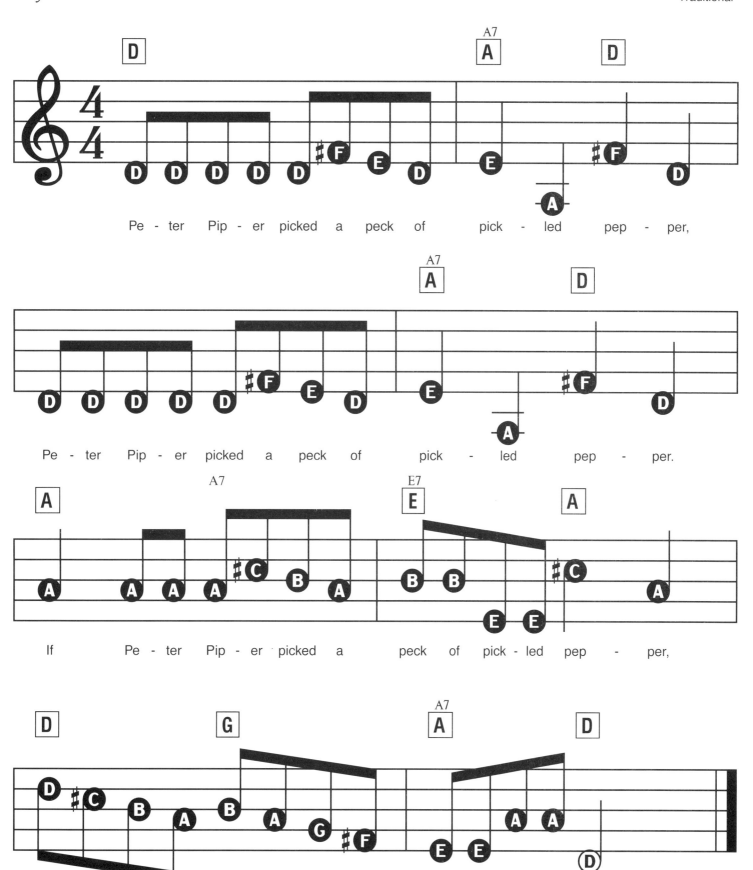

Peter, Peter, Pumpkin Eater

Registration 7
Rhythm: Polka or March

Traditional

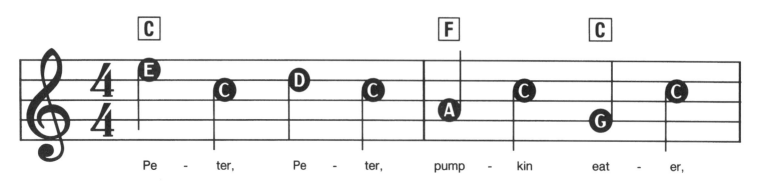

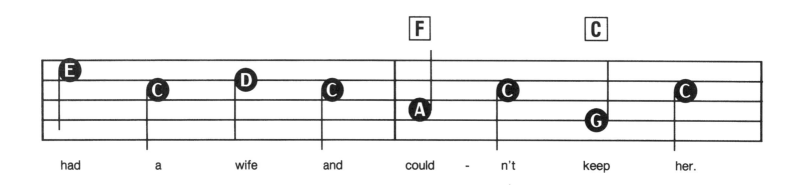

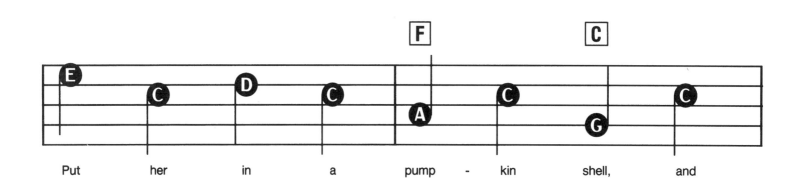

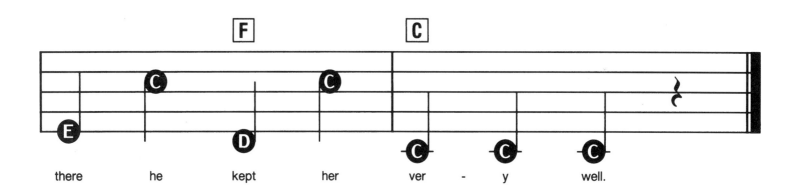

Polly Put the Kettle On

Registration 4
Rhythm: Fox Trot or Swing

Traditional

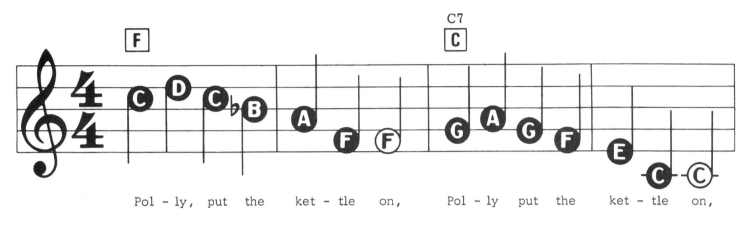

Pol - ly, put the ket - tle on, Pol - ly put the ket - tle on,

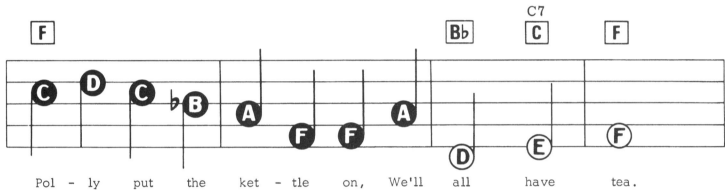

Pol - ly put the ket - tle on, We'll all have tea.

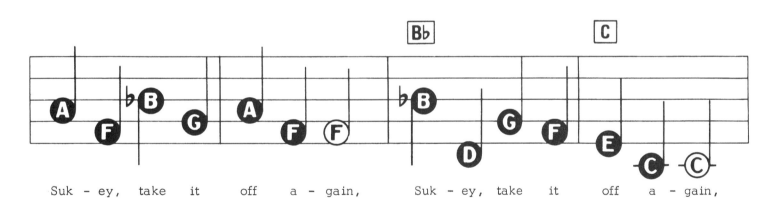

Suk - ey, take it off a - gain, Suk - ey, take it off a - gain,

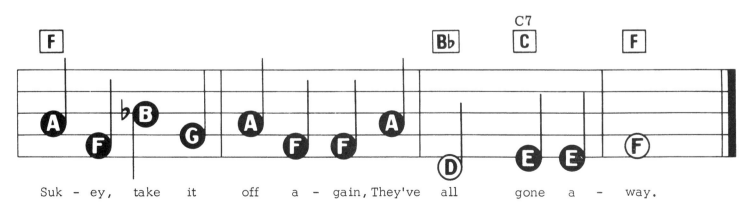

Suk - ey, take it off a - gain, They've all gone a - way.

Polly Wolly Doodle

Registration 4
Rhythm: Fox Trot

Traditional American Minstrel Song

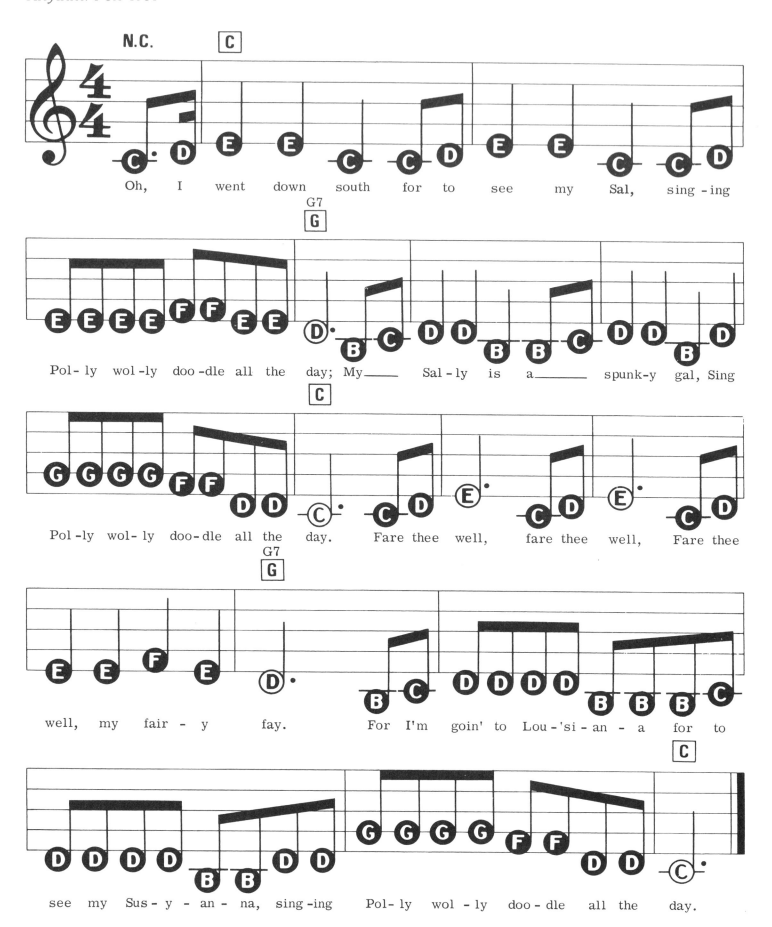

Pop Goes the Weasel

Registration 5
Rhythm: Waltz

Traditional

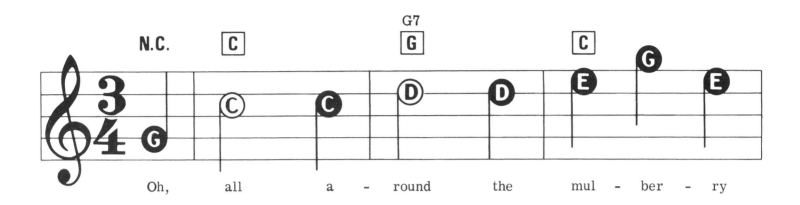

Oh, all a - round the mul - ber - ry

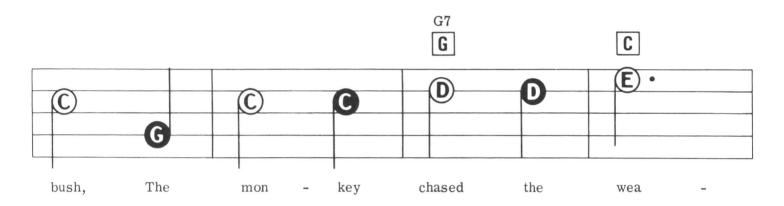

bush, The mon - key chased the wea -

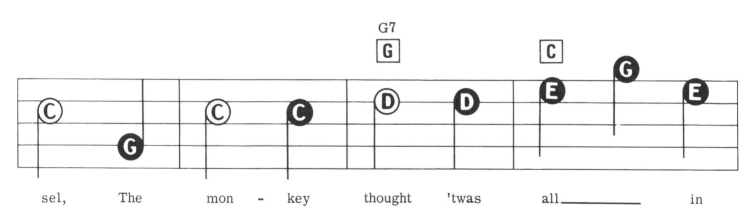

sel, The mon - key thought 'twas all_____ in

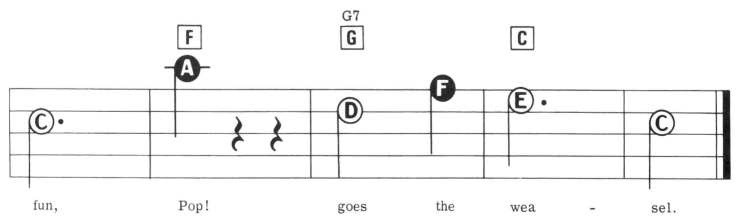

fun, Pop! goes the wea - sel.

Pussy Cat

Registration 1
Rhythm: 6/8 March

Traditional

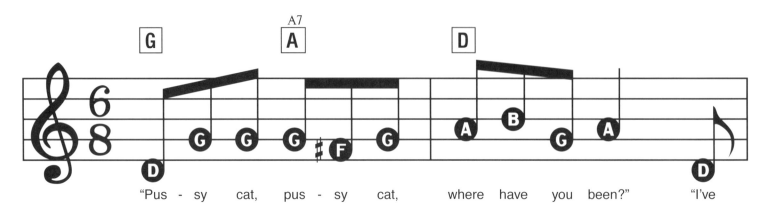

"Pus - sy cat, pus - sy cat, where have you been?" "I've

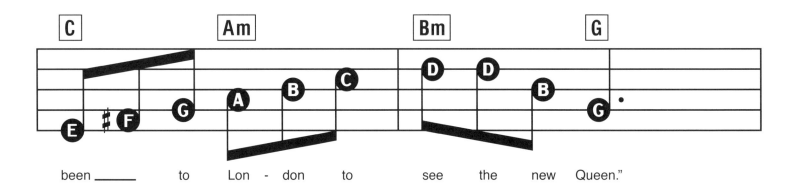

been _____ to Lon - don to see the new Queen."

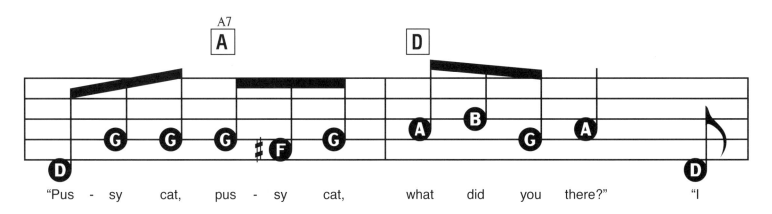

"Pus - sy cat, pus - sy cat, what did you there?" "I

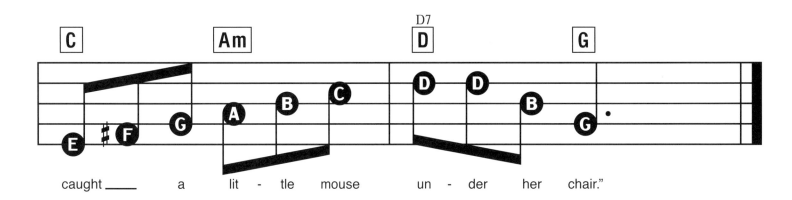

caught _____ a lit - tle mouse un - der her chair."

Ride a Cock Horse

Registration 7
Rhythm: Waltz

Traditional

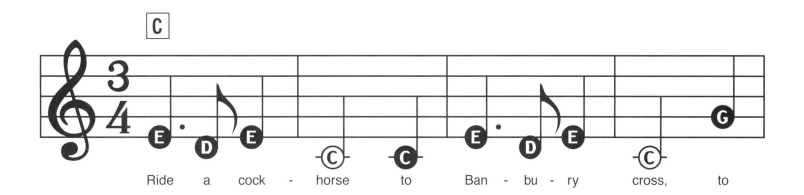

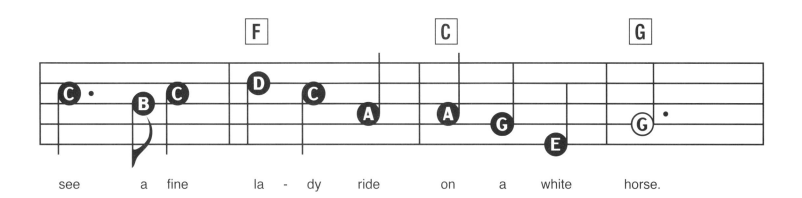

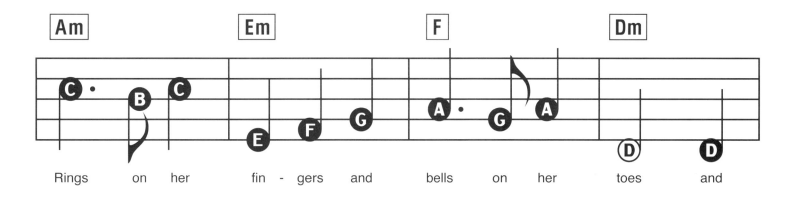

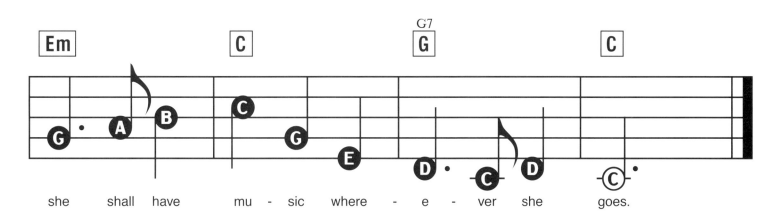

The Quartermaster's Store

Registration 2
Rhythm: March

Traditional

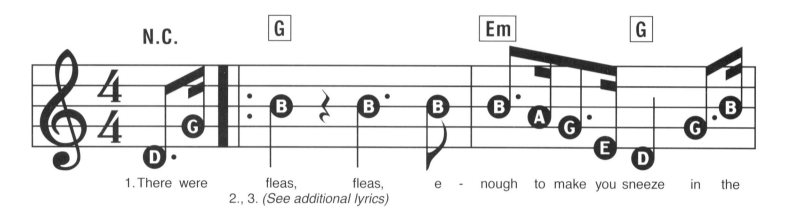

1. There were fleas, fleas, e - nough to make you sneeze in the
2., 3. *(See additional lyrics)*

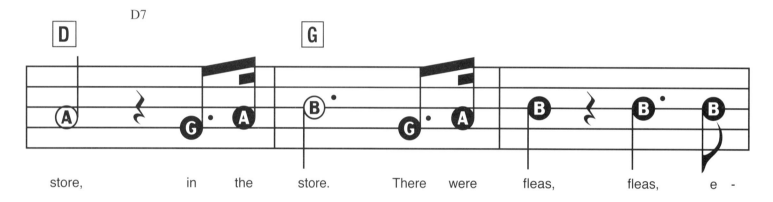

store, in the store. There were fleas, fleas, e -

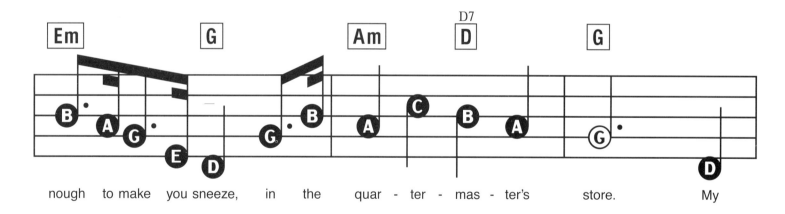

nough to make you sneeze, in the quar - ter - mas - ter's store. My

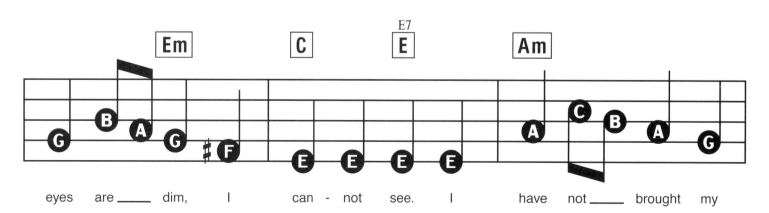

eyes are ___ dim, I can - not see. I have not ___ brought my

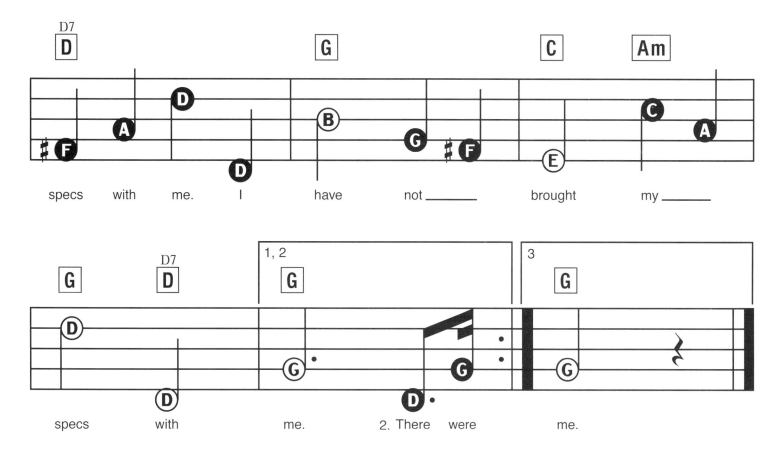

specs with me. I have not _____ brought my _____
specs with me. me. 2. There were me.

Additional Lyrics

2. There were rats, rats,
   As big as bloomin' cats,
   In the store, in the store.
   There were rats, rats,
   As big as bloomin' cats,
   In the quartermaster's store.
   My eyes are dim, I cannot see.
   I have not brought my specs with me.
   I have not brought my specs with me.

3. There was bread, bread,
   Harder than your head,
   In the store, in the store.
   There was bread, bread,
   Harder than your head,
   In the quartermaster's store.
   My eyes are dim, I cannot see.
   I have not brought my specs with me.
   I have not brought my specs with me.

The Rainbow Song

Registration 4
Rhythm: Fox Trot or March

Traditional

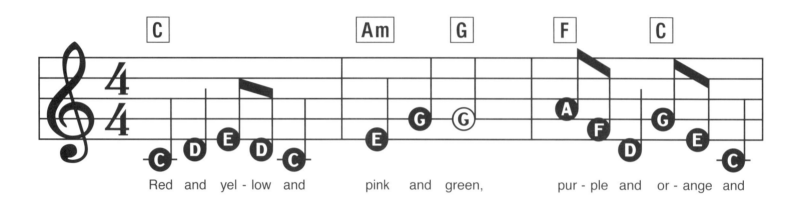

Red and yel - low and   pink and green,   pur - ple and or - ange and

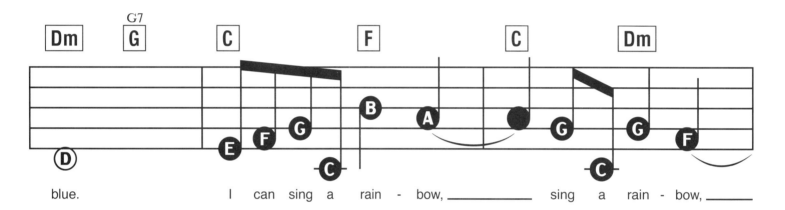

blue.   I can sing a rain - bow, _____ sing a rain - bow, _____

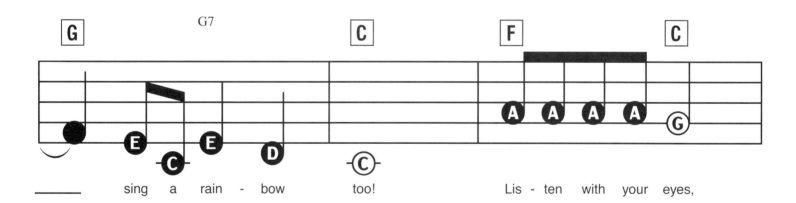

_____ sing a rain - bow too!   Lis - ten with your eyes,

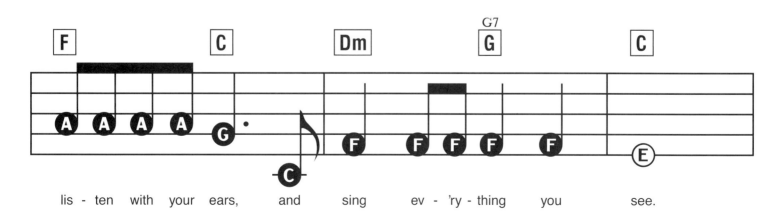

lis - ten with your ears, and sing ev - 'ry - thing you see.

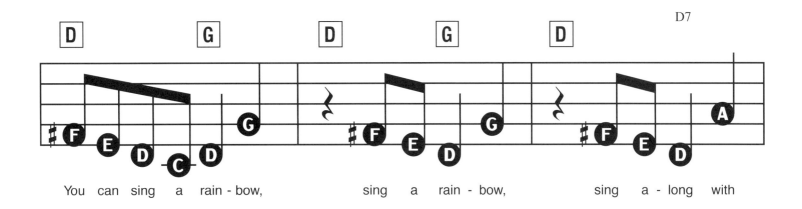

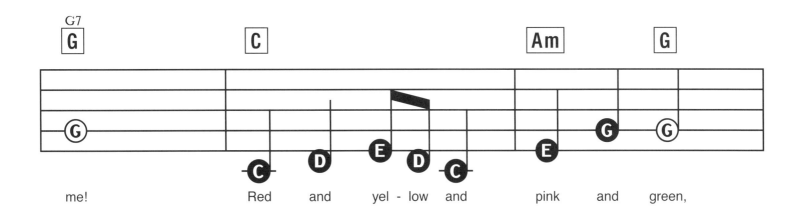

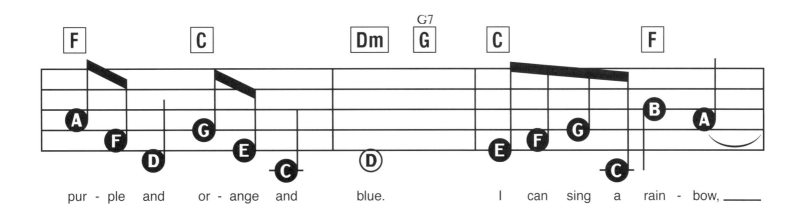

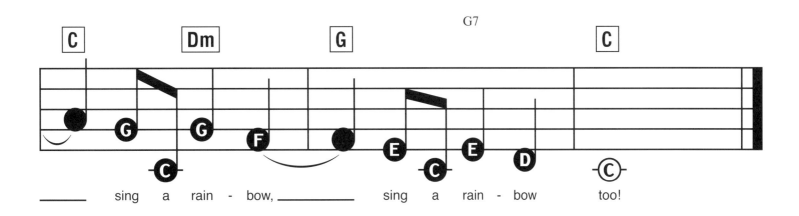

Rock-a-Bye Baby

Registration 3
Rhythm: Waltz

Traditional

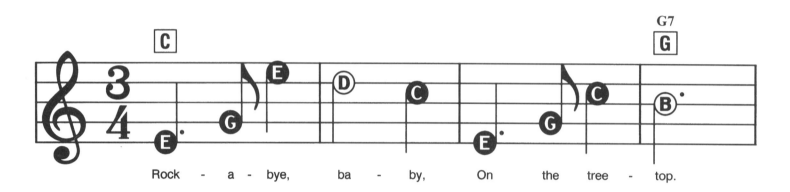

Rock - a - bye, ba - by, On the tree - top.

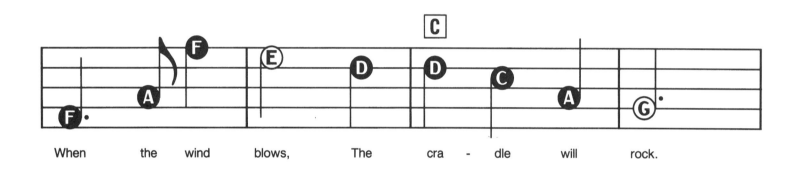

When the wind blows, The cra - dle will rock.

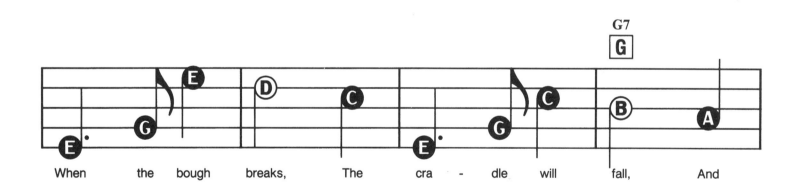

When the bough breaks, The cra - dle will fall, And

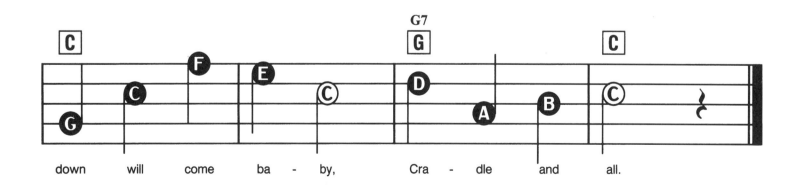

down will come ba - by, Cra - dle and all.

Round and Round the Garden

Registration 9
Rhythm: 6/8 March

Traditional

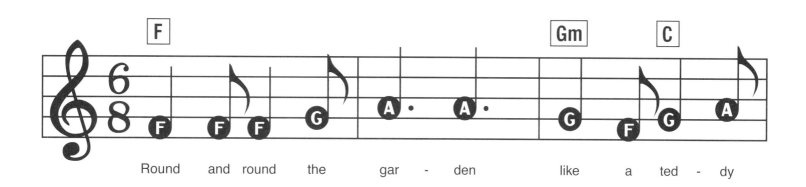

Round and round the gar - den like a ted - dy

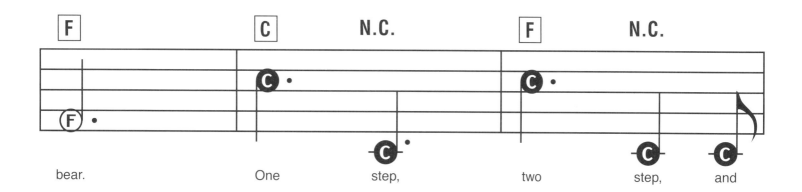

bear. One step, two step, and

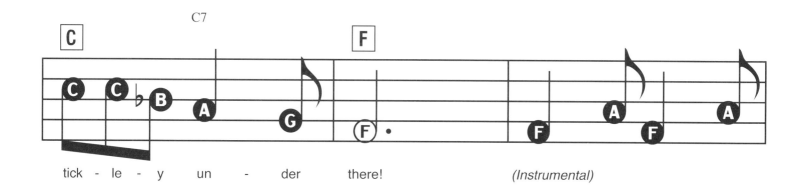

tick - le - y un - der there! *(Instrumental)*

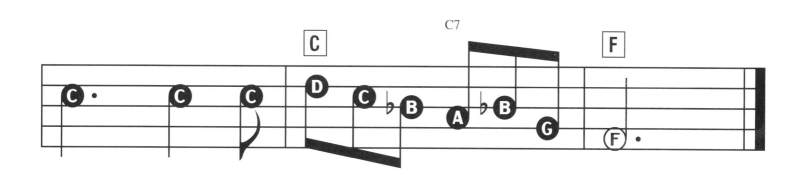

Round the Village

Registration 4
Rhythm: Polka or Fox Trot

Traditional

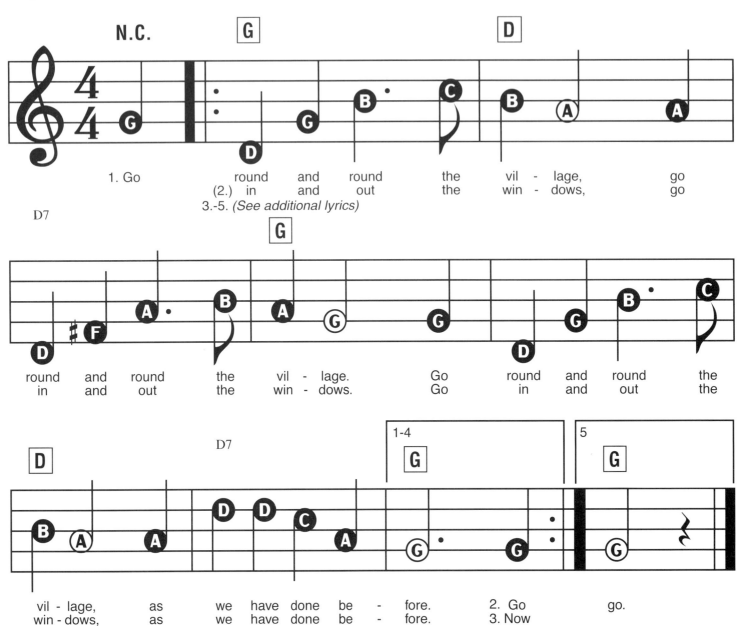

Additional Lyrics

3. Now stand and face your partner,
   Now stand and face your partner,
   Now stand and face your partner,
   And bow before you go.

4. Now follow me to London,
   Now follow me to London,
   Now follow me to London,
   As we have done before.

5. Now shake his hand and leave him,
   Now shake his hand and leave him,
   Now shake his hand and leave him,
   And bow before you go.

Row, Row, Row Your Boat

Registration 5
Rhythm: Waltz

Traditional

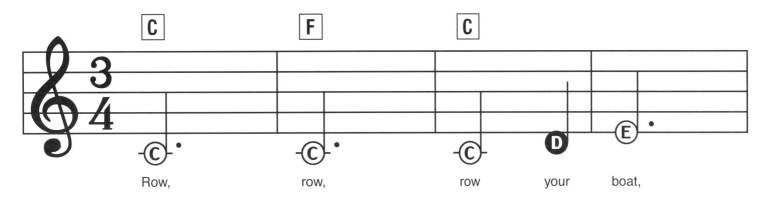

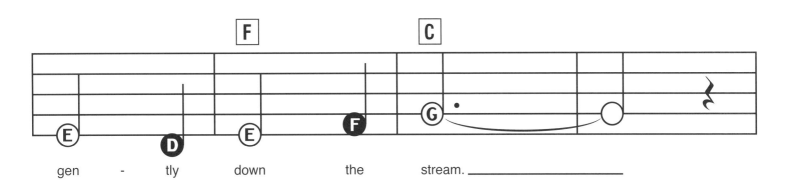

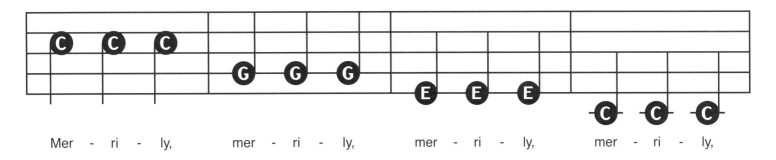

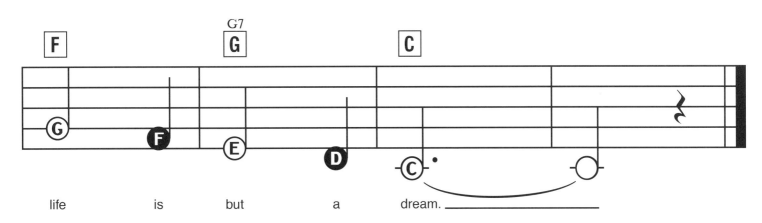

Rub-a-Dub-Dub, Three Men in a Tub

Registration 9
Rhythm: 6/8 March

Traditional

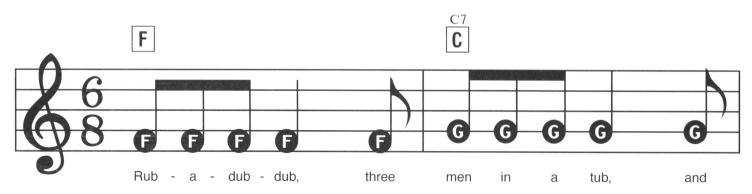

Rub - a - dub - dub,   three   men   in   a   tub,   and

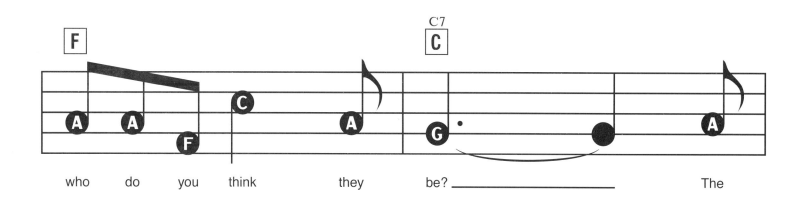

who   do   you   think   they   be? _____   The

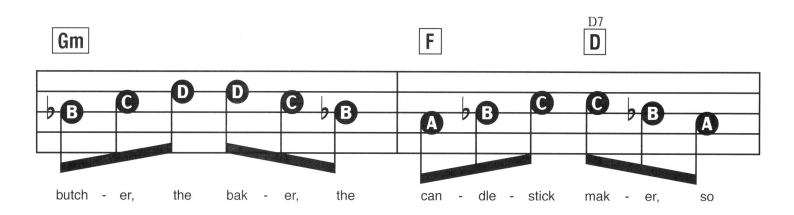

butch - er,   the   bak - er,   the   can - dle - stick   mak - er,   so

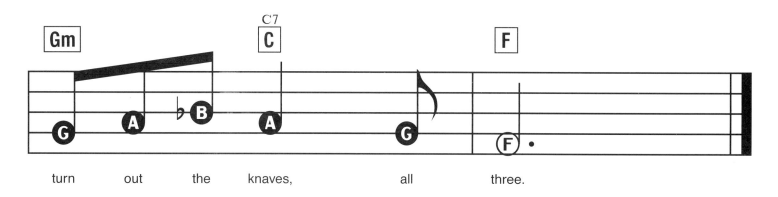

turn   out   the   knaves,   all   three.

Short'nin' Bread

Registration 8
Rhythm: Country or Shuffle

Plantation Song

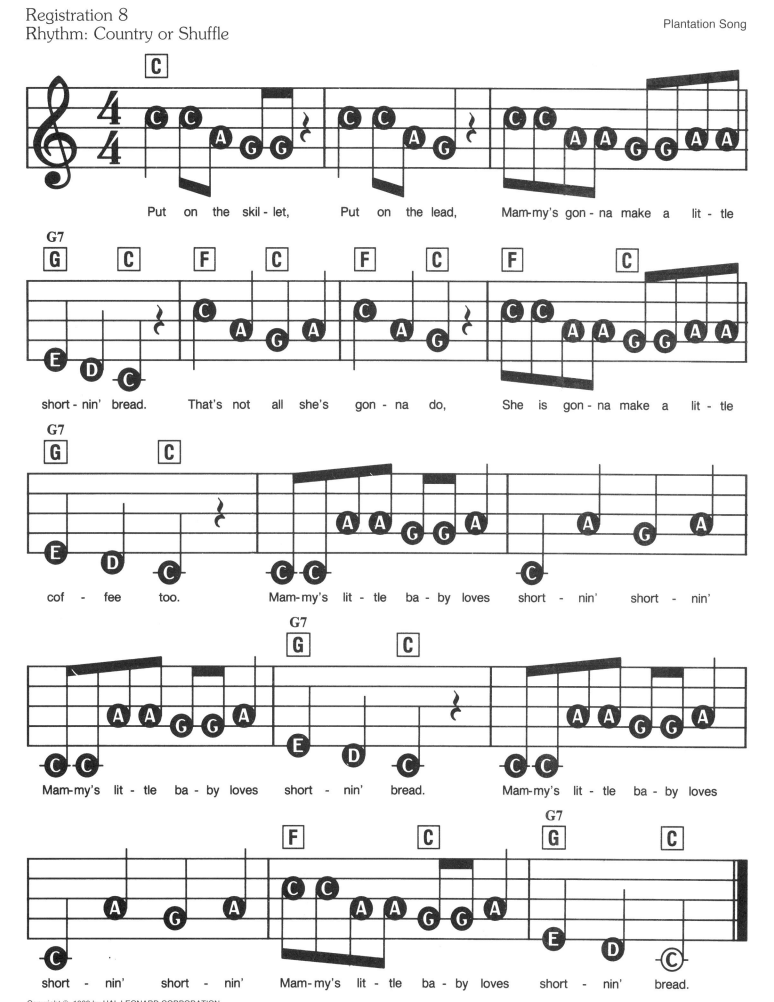

See Saw, Margery Daw

Registration 10
Rhythm: Waltz

Traditional

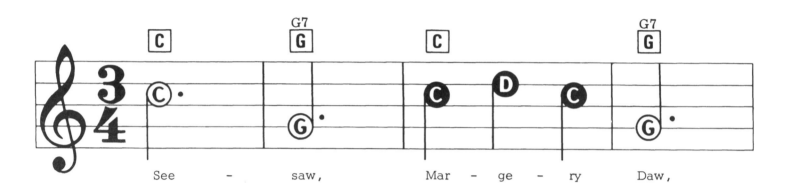

See - saw, Mar - ge - ry Daw,

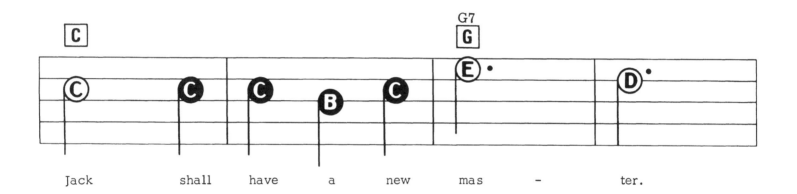

Jack shall have a new mas - ter.

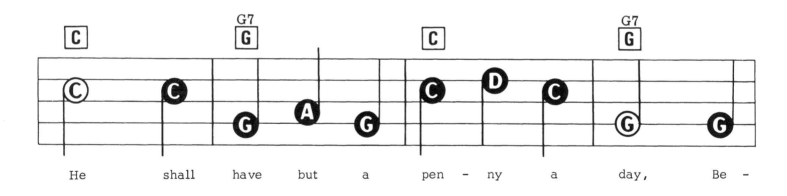

He shall have but a pen - ny a day, Be -

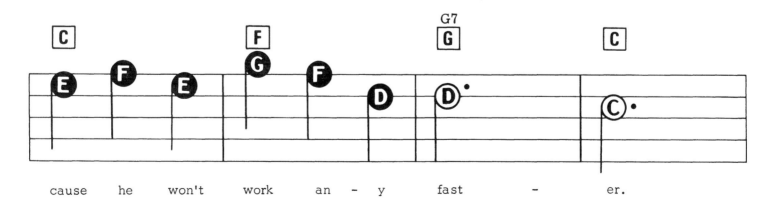

cause he won't work an - y fast - er.

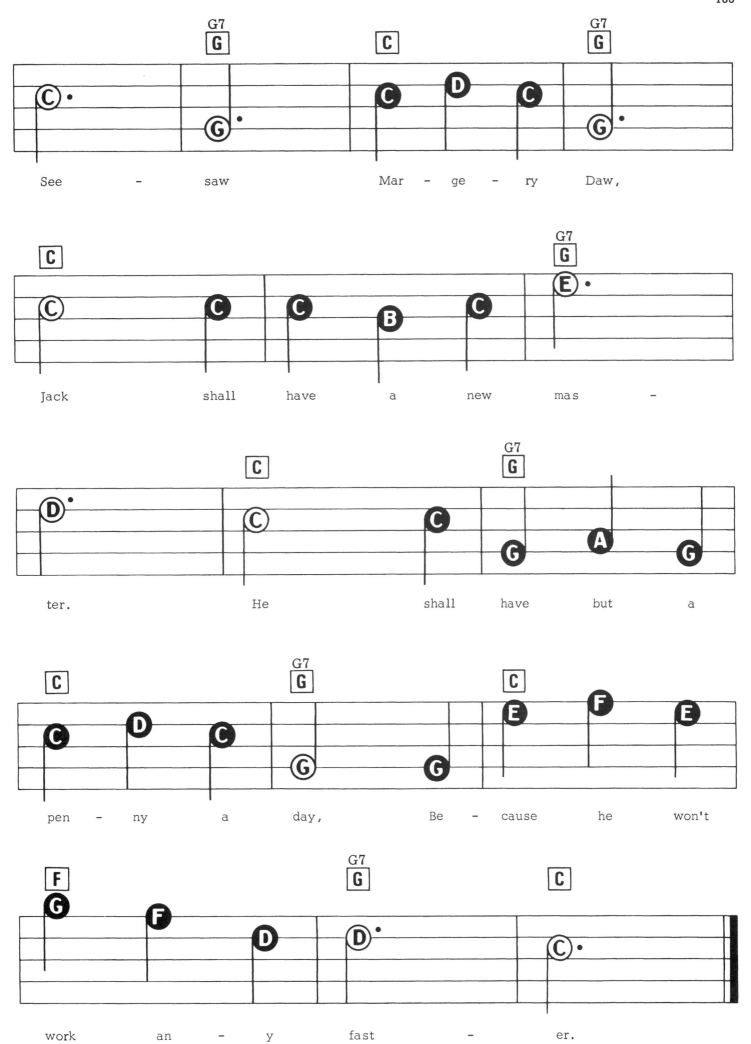

She'll Be Comin' 'Round the Mountain

Registration 4
Rhythm: Bluegrass or Fox Trot

Traditional

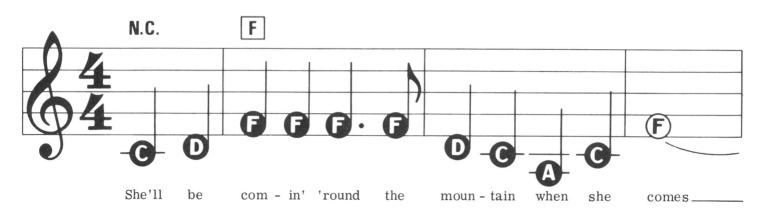

She'll be com - in' 'round the moun - tain when she comes

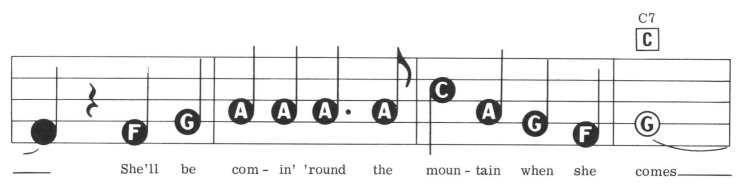

She'll be com - in' 'round the moun - tain when she comes

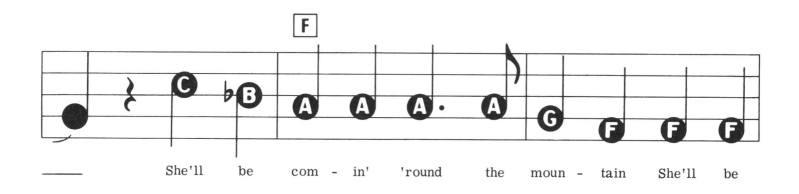

She'll be com - in' 'round the moun - tain She'll be

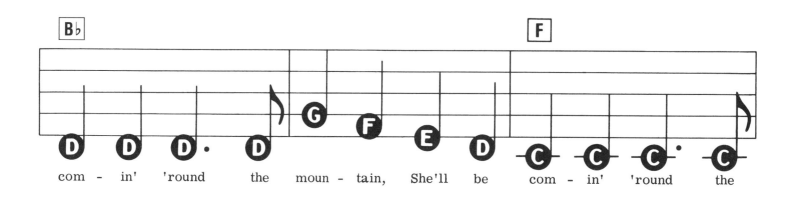

com - in' 'round the moun - tain, She'll be com - in' 'round the

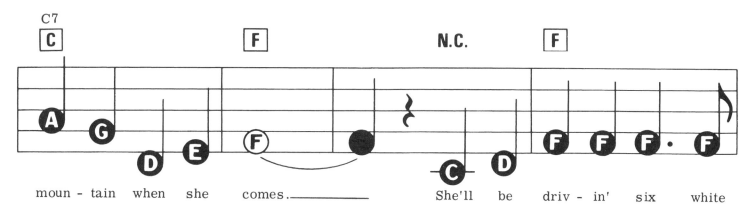

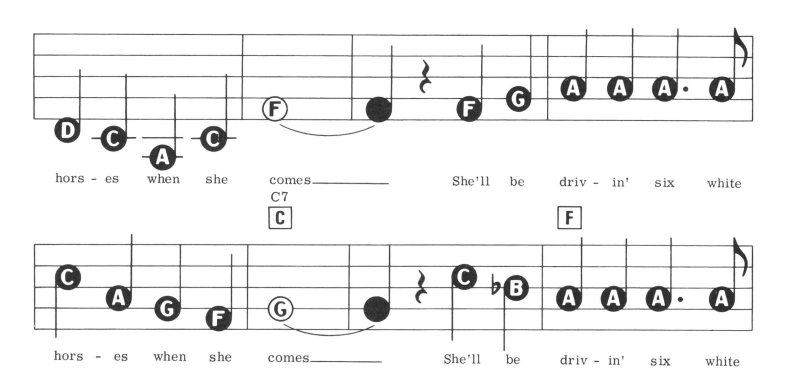

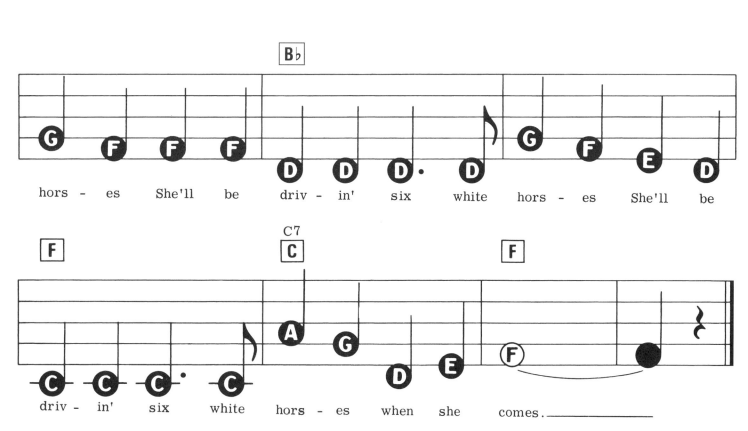

Simple Simon

Registration 9
Rhythm: Fox Trot

Traditional

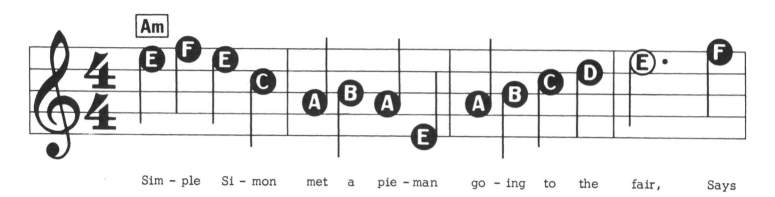

Sim - ple Si - mon met a pie - man go - ing to the fair, Says

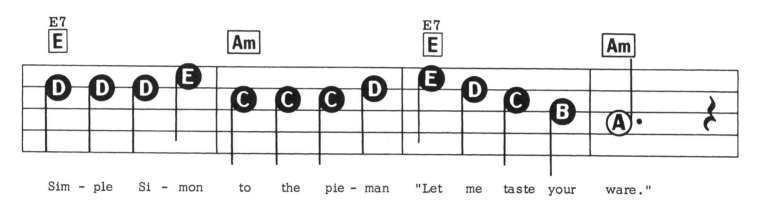

Sim - ple Si - mon to the pie - man "Let me taste your ware."

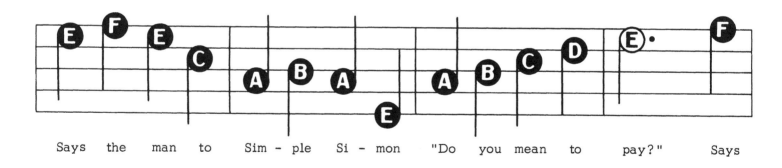

Says the man to Sim - ple Si - mon "Do you mean to pay?" Says

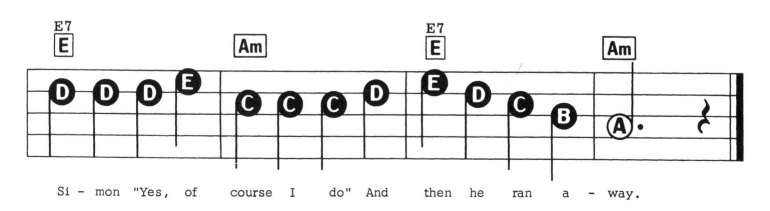

Si - mon "Yes, of course I do" And then he ran a - way.

Skip to My Lou

Registration 10
Rhythm: Fox Trot

Traditional

Choose your part - ners, skip to my Lou, Choose your part - ners,

skip to my Lou, Choose your part - ners, skip to my Lou,

Skip to my Lou, my dar - ling. Fly's in the but - ter-milk,

shoo fly, shoo, Fly's in the but - ter-milk, shoo fly, shoo,

Fly's in the but - ter-milk, shoo fly, shoo, Skip to my Lou, my dar - ling.

Sing a Song of Sixpence

Registration 4
Rhythm: Fox Trot or Swing

Traditional

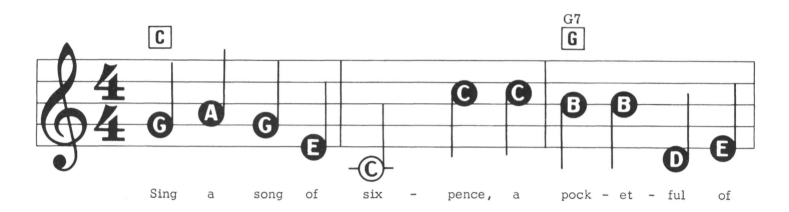

Sing a song of six - pence, a pock - et - ful of

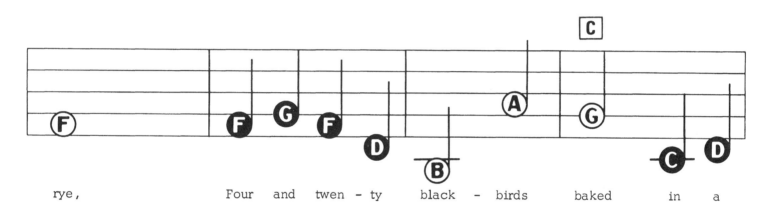

rye, Four and twen - ty black - birds baked in a

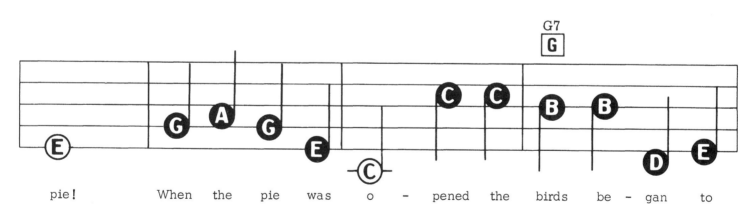

pie! When the pie was o - pened the birds be - gan to

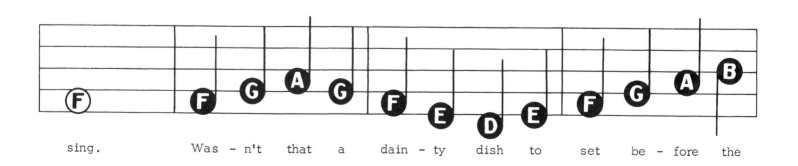

sing. Was - n't that a dain - ty dish to set be - fore the

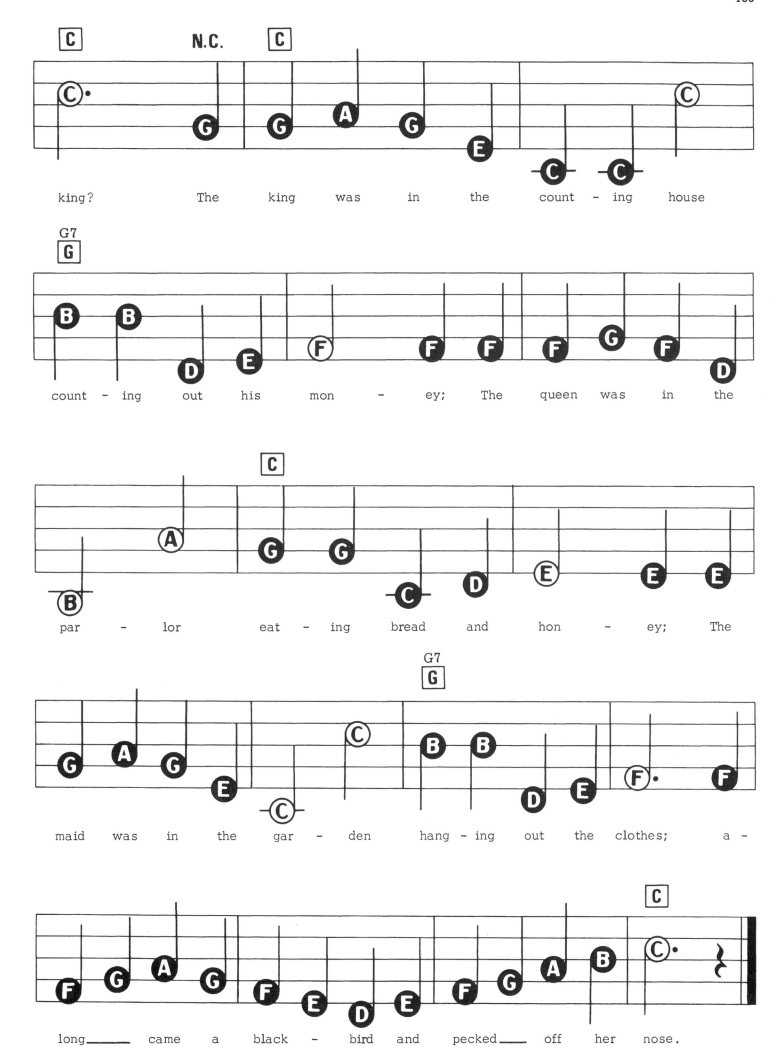

Sleep, Baby, Sleep

Registration 3
Rhythm: 6/8 March

Pennsylvania Dutch Lullaby

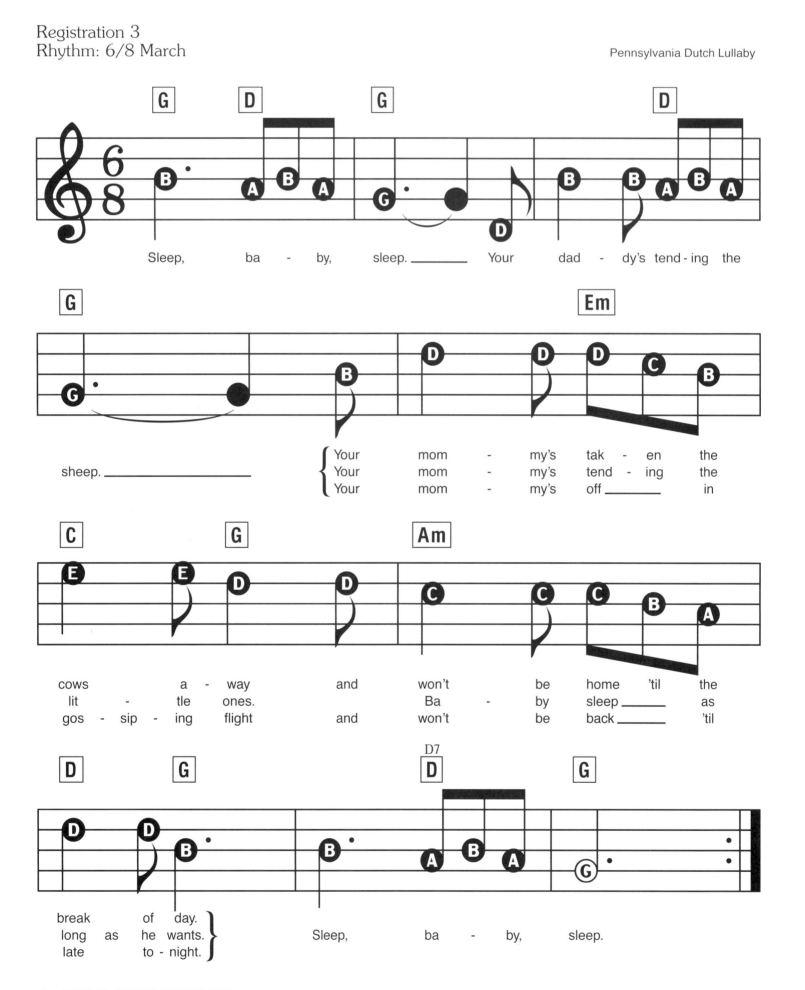

Soldier, Soldier, Will You Marry Me?

Registration 4
Rhythm: Fox Trot

Traditional

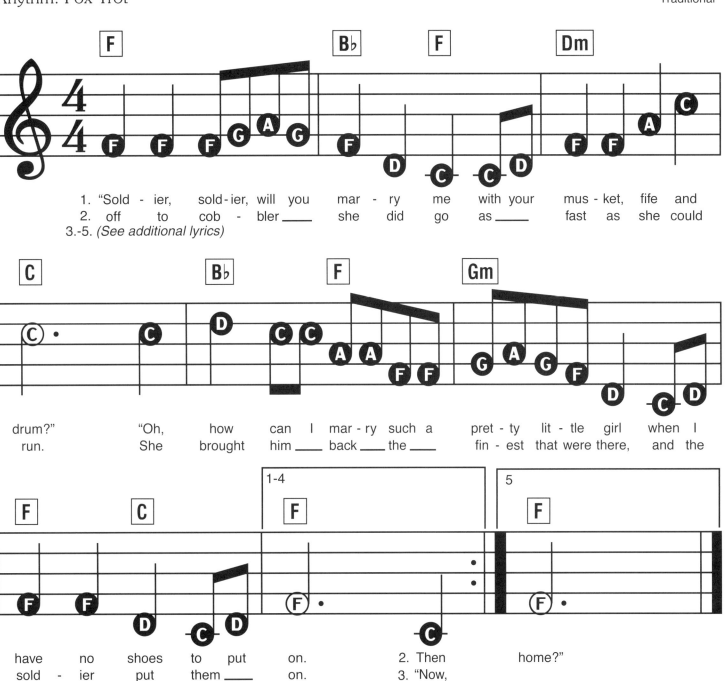

1. "Sold - ier, sold - ier, will you mar - ry me with your mus - ket, fife and
2. off to cob - bler ____ she did go as ____ fast as she could

3.-5. *(See additional lyrics)*

drum?" "Oh, how can I mar - ry such a pret - ty lit - tle girl when I
run. She brought him ____ back ____ the ____ fin - est that were there, and the

have no shoes to put on.
sold - ier put them ____ on.

2. Then home?"
3. "Now,

Additional Lyrics

3. "Now, soldier, soldier, will you marry me with your musket, fife and drum?"
   "Oh, how can I marry such a pretty little girl when I have no coat to put on?"

4. Then off to the tailor she did go as fast as she could run.
   She brought him back the finest that was there, and the soldier put it on.

5. "Now, soldier, soldier, will you marry me with your musket, fife and drum?"
   "Oh, how can I marry such a pretty little girl with a wife and baby at home?"

Sur le pont d'Avignon

Registration 2
Rhythm: Fox Trot

Traditional

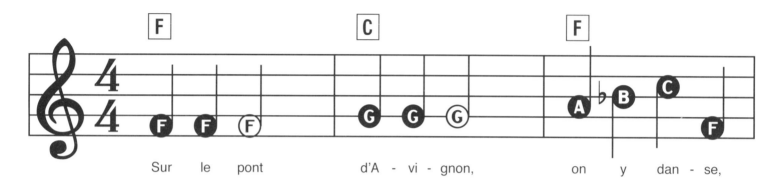

Sur le pont d'A - vi - gnon, on y dan - se,

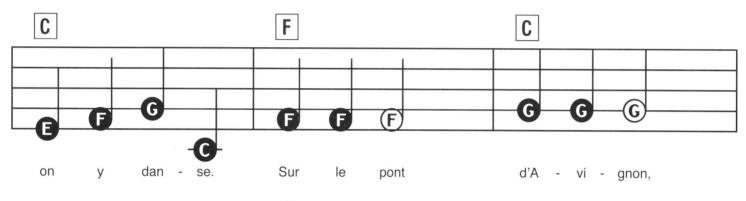

on y dan - se. Sur le pont d'A - vi - gnon,

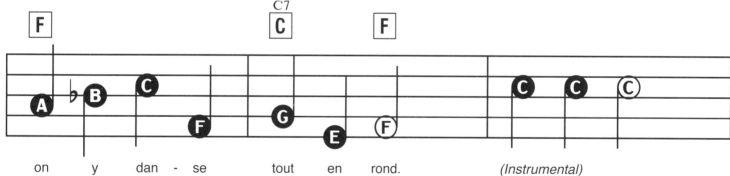

on y dan - se tout en rond. *(Instrumental)*

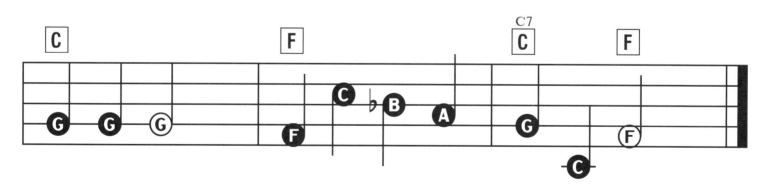

Translation

On the bridge of Avignon, they are dancing, they are dancing.
On the bridge of Avignon, they are dancing all around.

Teddy Bear

Registration 1
Rhythm: Swing

Rope-Jumping Chant

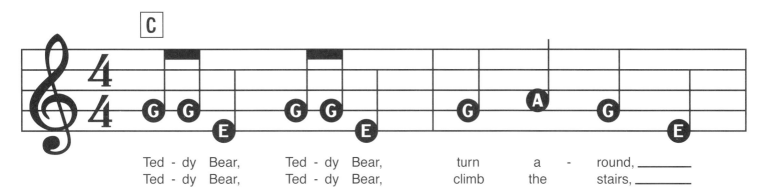

Ted - dy Bear, Ted - dy Bear, turn a - round, _____
Ted - dy Bear, Ted - dy Bear, climb the stairs, _____

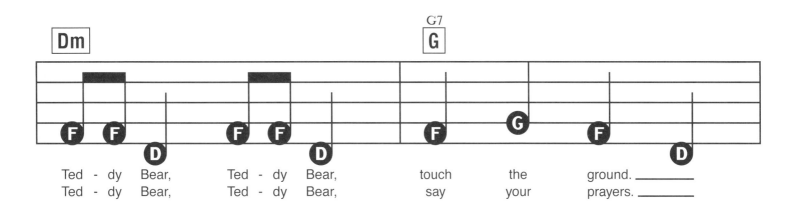

Ted - dy Bear, Ted - dy Bear, touch the ground. _____
Ted - dy Bear, Ted - dy Bear, say your prayers. _____

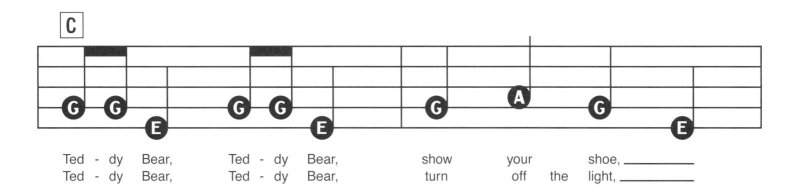

Ted - dy Bear, Ted - dy Bear, show your shoe, _____
Ted - dy Bear, Ted - dy Bear, turn off the light, _____

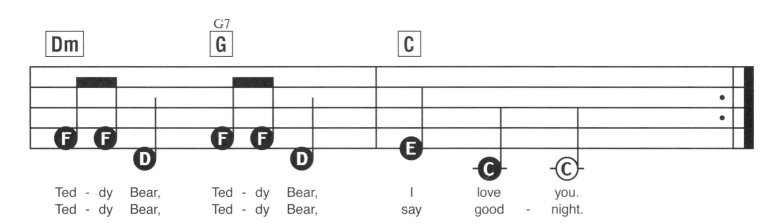

Ted - dy Bear, Ted - dy Bear, I love you.
Ted - dy Bear, Ted - dy Bear, say good - night.

Ten Green Bottles

Registration 9
Rhythm: Swing

Traditional

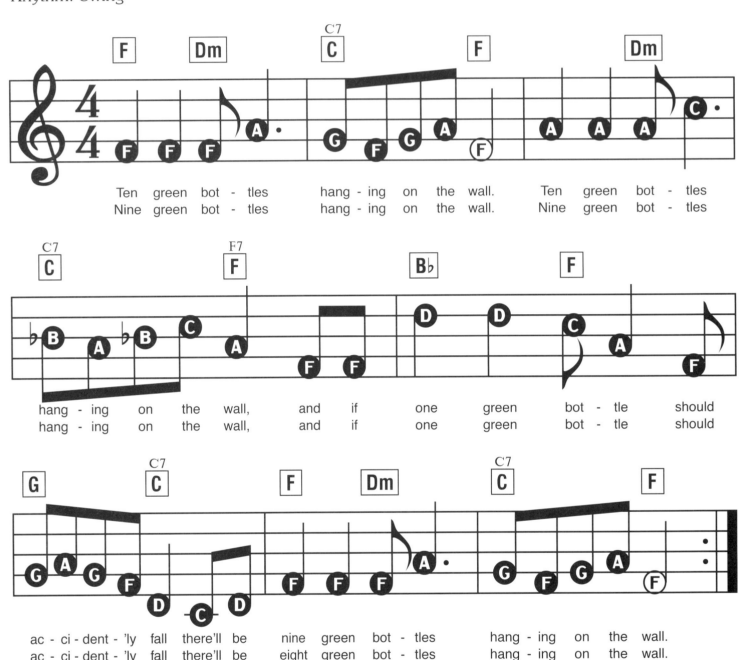

Additional Lyrics

3. Eight green bottles hanging on the wall, *etc.*

4. Seven green bottles hanging on the wall, *etc.*

5. Six green bottles hanging on the wall, *etc.*

6. Five green bottles hanging on the wall, *etc.*

7. Four green bottles hanging on the wall, *etc.*

8. Three green bottles hanging on the wall, *etc.*

9. Two green bottles hanging on the wall, *etc.*

10. One green bottle hanging on the wall.
    One green bottle hanging on the wall.
    And if that green bottle should accidenta'ly fall
    There'll be no green bottles hanging on the wall.

Ten Little Indians

Registration 9
Rhythm: Swing

Traditional

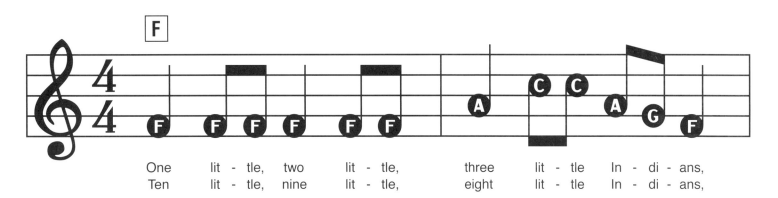

One   lit - tle, two   lit - tle,   three   lit - tle   In - di - ans,
Ten   lit - tle, nine   lit - tle,   eight   lit - tle   In - di - ans,

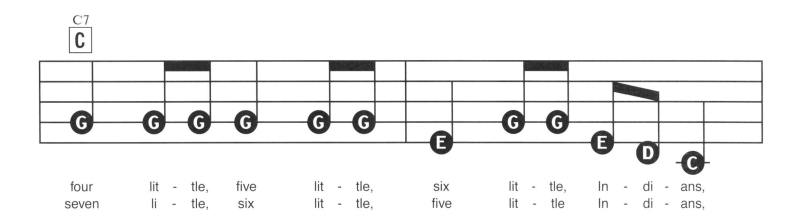

four   lit - tle, five   lit - tle,   six   lit - tle,   In - di - ans,
seven   li - tle, six   lit - tle,   five   lit - tle   In - di - ans,

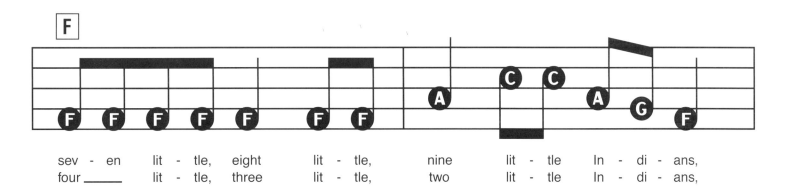

sev - en   lit - tle, eight   lit - tle,   nine   lit - tle   In - di - ans,
four ____   lit - tle, three   lit - tle,   two   lit - tle   In - di - ans,

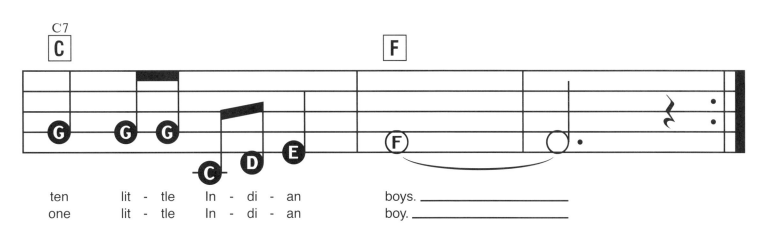

ten   lit - tle   In - di - an   boys. ____
one   lit - tle   In - di - an   boy. ____

Ten Little Pigs

Registration 2
Rhythm: March

Traditional

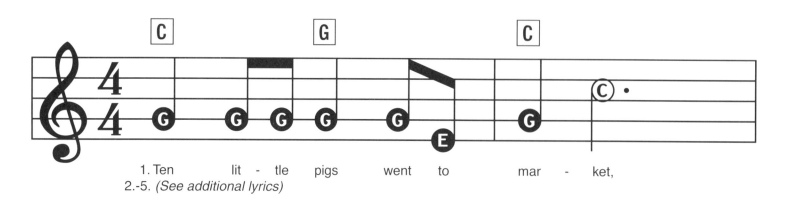

1. Ten   lit - tle   pigs   went   to   mar - ket,
2.-5. *(See additional lyrics)*

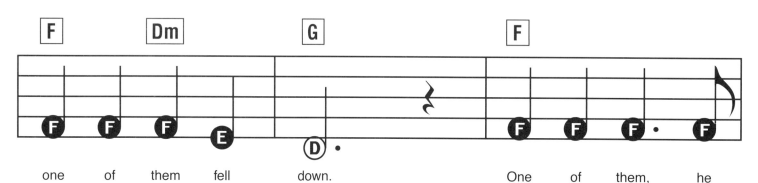

one   of   them   fell   down.   One   of   them,   he

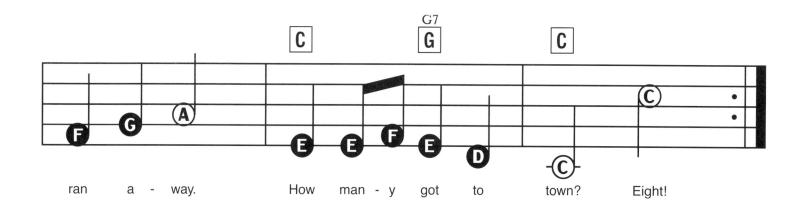

ran   a - way.   How   man - y   got   to   town?   Eight!

Additional Lyrics

2. Eight little pigs went to market,
   One of them fell down.
   One of them, he ran away.
   How many got to town?
   Six!

3. Six little pigs went to market,
   One of them fell down.
   One of them, he ran away.
   How many got to town?
   Four!

4. Four little pigs went to market,
   One of them fell down.
   One of them, he ran away.
   How many got to town?
   Two!

5. Two little pigs went to market,
   One of them fell down.
   One of them, he ran away.
   How many got to town?
   None!

There Was a Crooked Man

Registration 9
Rhythm: Fox Trot

Traditional

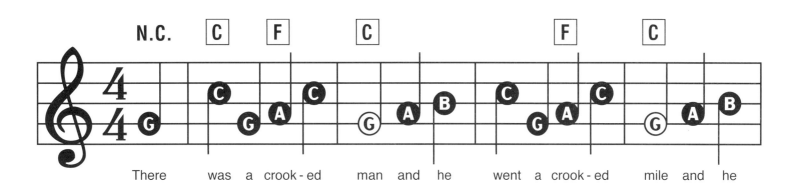

There was a crook-ed man and he went a crook-ed mile and he

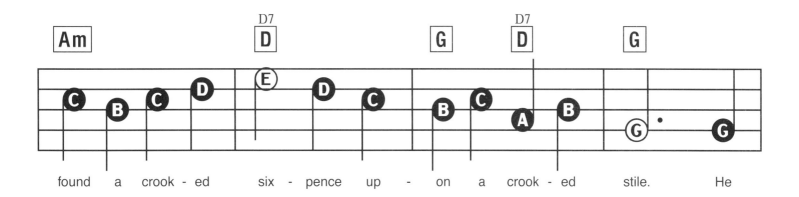

found a crook-ed six-pence up - on a crook-ed stile. He

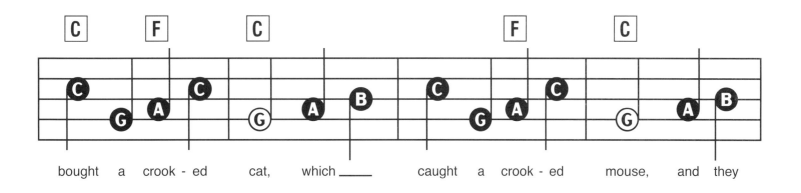

bought a crook-ed cat, which ____ caught a crook-ed mouse, and they

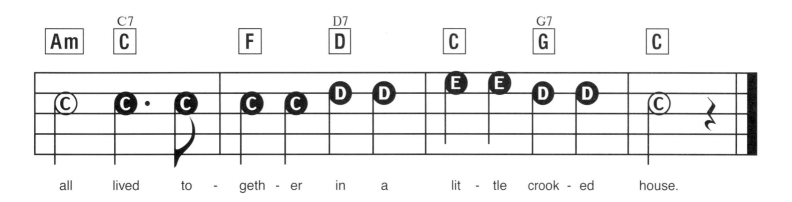

all lived to-geth-er in a lit-tle crook-ed house.

There Was a Princess

Registration 2
Rhythm: March

Traditional

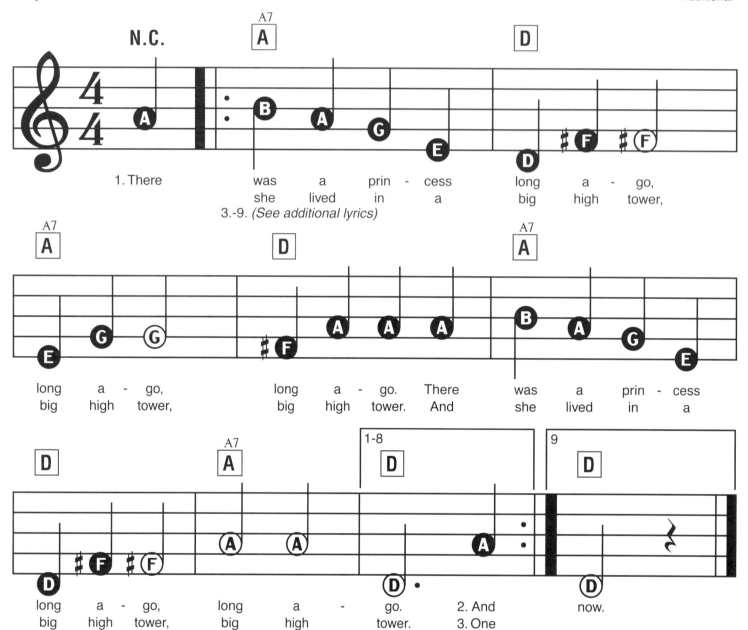

Additional Lyrics

3. One day a bad queen cast a spell,
   Cast a spell, cast a spell,
   One day a bad queen cast a spell,
   Cast a spell.

4. The princess slept a hundred years, *etc.*

5. A great big forest grew around, *etc.*

6. A gallant prince came riding by, *etc.*

7. He cut the trees down with his sword, *etc.*

8. He woke the princess with a kiss, *etc.*

9. So everybody's happy now, *etc.*

Activity

Pick three children to play the princess, prince, and queen. All other children form a circle and join hands. The prince is on the outside of the circle, the princess and the queen on the inside. While singing verse 1, the children forming the circle walk around clockwise. Mime the actions for subsequent verses. In verse 6, the prince skips around the outside of the circle, and in verse 7 he breaks through the circle to join the princess. For the final verse, everyone skips around clockwise.

There Was an Old Man

Registration 4
Rhythm: Fox Trot

Traditional

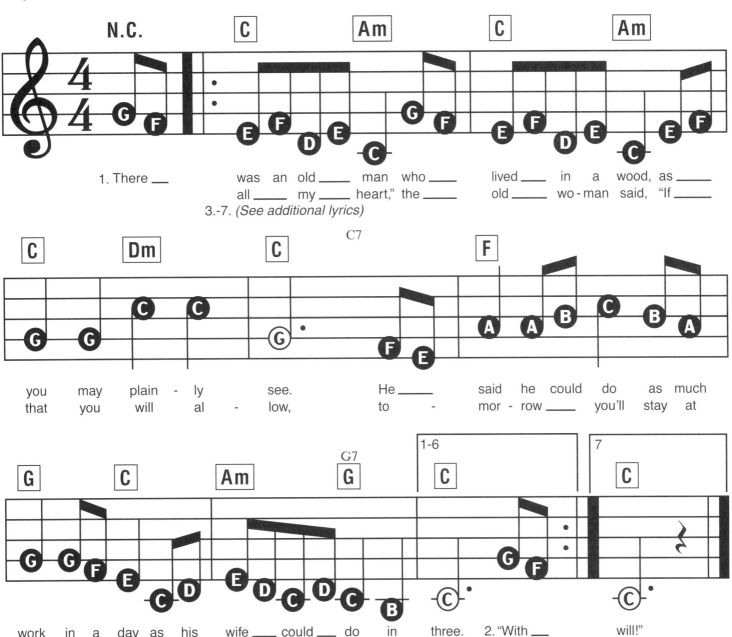

1. There ___ was an old ___ man who ___ lived ___ in a wood, as ___
all ___ my ___ heart," the ___ old ___ wo-man said, "If ___
3.-7. *(See additional lyrics)*

you may plain-ly see. He ___ said he could do as much
that you will al-low, to-mor-row ___ you'll stay at

work in a day as his wife ___ could ___ do in three. 2. "With ___ will!"
home in my stead, and ___ I'll ___ go ___ drive the plough." 3. "But ___

Additional Lyrics

3. "But you must milk the Tidy cow,
   For fear that she go dry;
   And you must feed the little pigs
   That are within the sty.

4. And you must mind the speckled hen,
   For fear she lay away;
   And you must reel a spool of yarn
   That I spun yesterday."

5. The old woman took a staff in her hand
   And went to drive the plough;
   The old man took a pail in his hand,
   And went to milk the cow.

6. But Tidy hinched and Tidy flinched,
   And Tidy broke his nose;
   And Tidy gave him such a blow
   That blood ran down to his toes.

7. "Hi, Tidy! Ho, Tidy! High!
   Tidy, do stand still!
   If ever I milk you, Tidy, again,
   'Twill be sore against my will!"

There Was an Old Frog

Registration 7
Rhythm: Fox Trot or Polka

Traditional

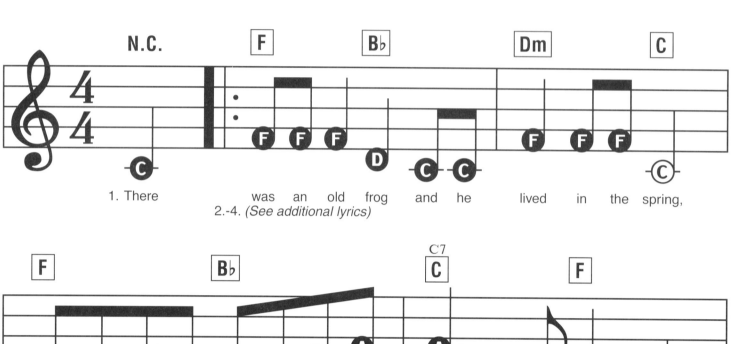

1. There   was an old frog and he   lived in the spring,
2.-4. *(See additional lyrics)*

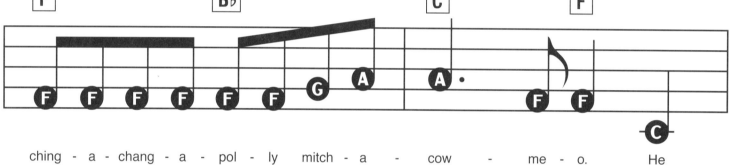

ching - a - chang - a - pol - ly mitch - a - cow - me - o. He

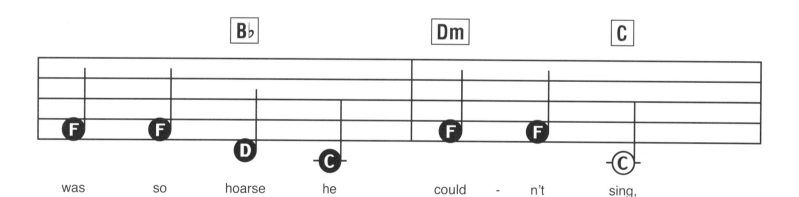

was   so   hoarse   he   could - n't   sing,

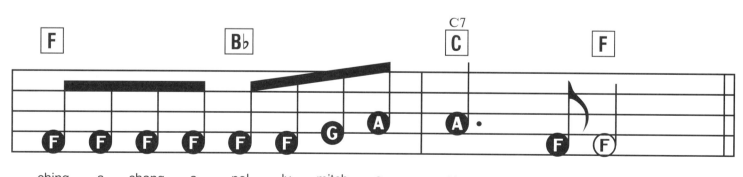

ching - a - chang - a - pol - ly mitch - a - cow - me - o.

Chorus

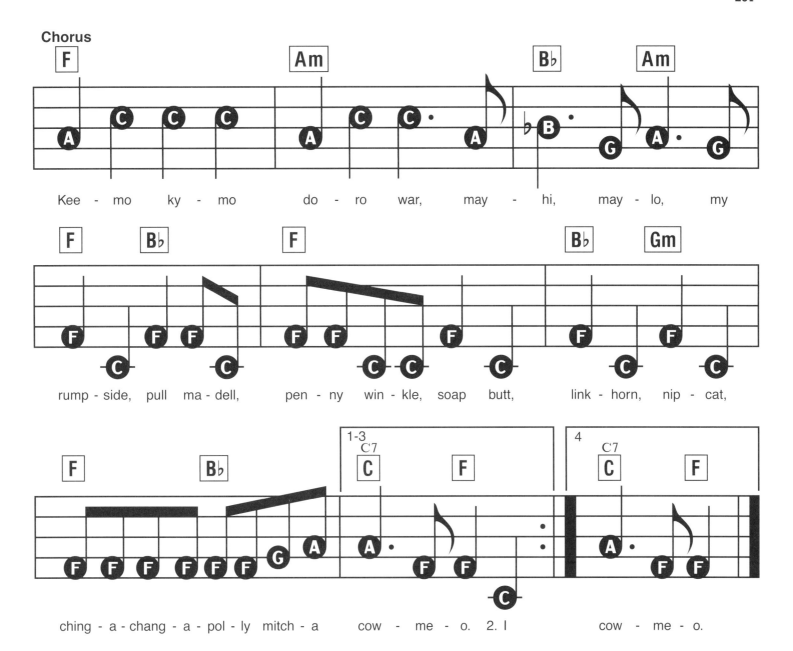

Kee - mo ky - mo do - ro war, may - hi, may - lo, my

rump - side, pull ma - dell, pen - ny win - kle, soap butt, link - horn, nip - cat,

ching - a - chang - a - pol - ly mitch - a cow - me - o. 2. I cow - me - o.

Additional Lyrics

2. I grabbed him by the leg and pulled him out,
   Ching-a-chang-a-polly mitch-a-cow-me-o.
   He hopped and he skipped and he bounced all about,
   Ching-a-chang-a-polly mitch-a-cow-me-o.
   Chorus

3. Cheese in the spring house nine days old,
   Ching-a-chang-a-polly mitch-a-cow-me-o.
   Rats and skippers is a-getting mighty bold,
   Ching-a-chang-a-polly mitch-a-cow-me-o.
   Chorus

4. Big fat rat and a bucket of souse,
   Ching-a-chang-a-polly mitch-a-cow-me-o.
   Take it back to the big white house,
   Ching-a-chang-a-polly mitch-a-cow-me-o.
   Chorus

There Was an Old Woman Who Lived in a Shoe

Registration 4
Rhythm: Rock or 8-Beat

Traditional

There was an old wom - an who lived_____ in a

shoe; she had so man - y chil - dren, she

didn't know what to do. She gave them some

broth with - out an - y bread, then she

whipped them all sound - ly and put_____ them to bed.

There Were Ten in a Bed

Registration 4
Rhythm: Swing

Traditional

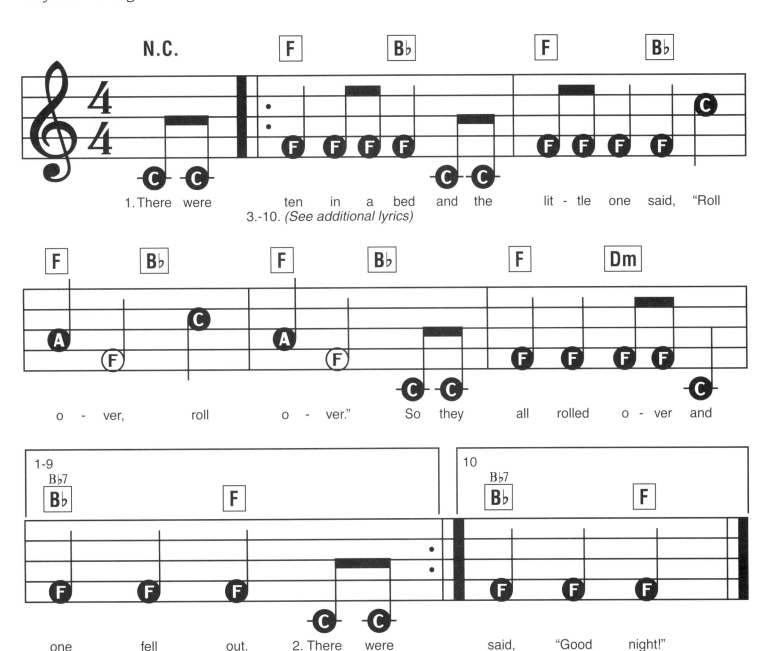

Additional Lyrics

2. There were nine in the bed, *etc.*

3. There were eight in the bed, *etc.*

4. There were seven in the bed, *etc.*

5. There were six in the bed, *etc.*

6. There were five in the bed, *etc.*

7. There were four in the bed, *etc.*

8. There were three in the bed, *etc.*

9. There were two in the bed, *etc.*

10. There was one in the bed, *etc.*
    And the little one said, "Good night!"

There's a Hole in the Bucket

Registration 10
Rhythm: Waltz

Traditional

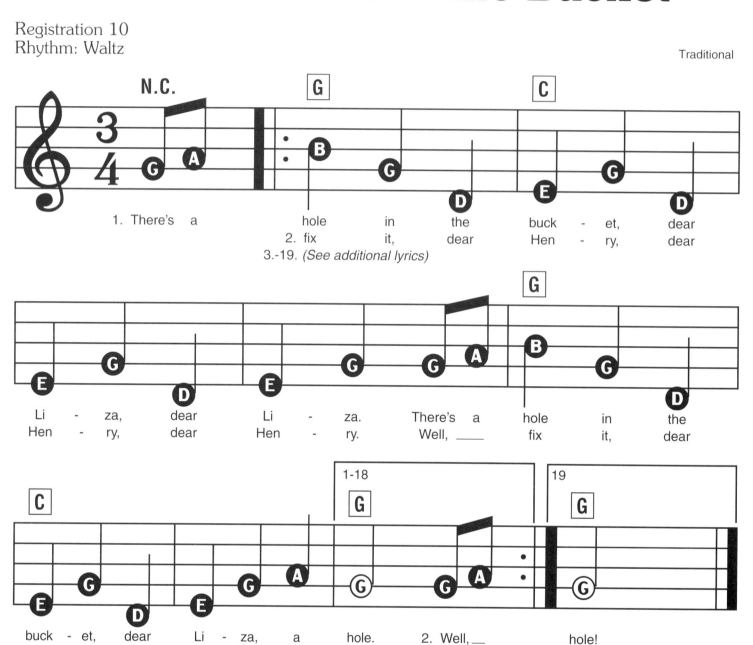

Additional Lyrics

3. With what shall I fix it, dear Liza, *etc.*
4. With a straw, dear Henry, *etc.*
5. But the straw is too long, dear Liza, *etc.*
6. Then cut it, dear Henry, *etc.*
7. With what shall I cut it, dear Liza, *etc.*
8. With a knife, dear Henry, *etc.*
9. But the knife is too dull, dear Liza, *etc.*
10. Then sharpen it, dear Henry, *etc.*
11. With what shall I sharpen it, dear Liza, *etc.*
12. With a stone, dear Henry, *etc.*
13. But the stone is too dry, dear Liza, *etc.*
14. Then wet it, dear Henry, *etc.*
15. With what shall I wet it, dear Liza, *etc.*
16. With water, dear Henry, *etc.*
17. In what shall I carry it, dear Liza, *etc.*
18. In a bucket, dear Henry, *etc.*
19. There's a hole in the bucket, dear Liza, *etc.*

This Little Pig Went to Market

Registration 9
Rhythm: 6/8 March

Traditional

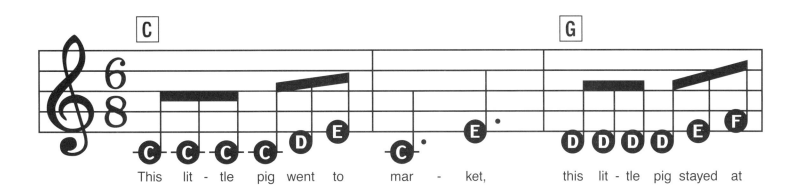

This lit - tle pig went to mar - ket, this lit - tle pig stayed at

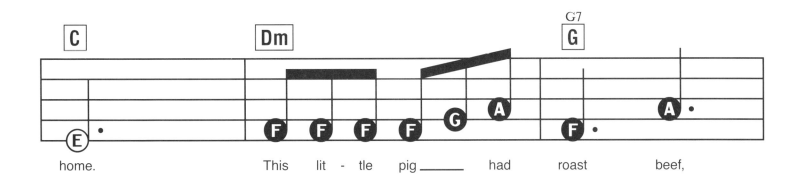

home. This lit - tle pig ___ had roast beef,

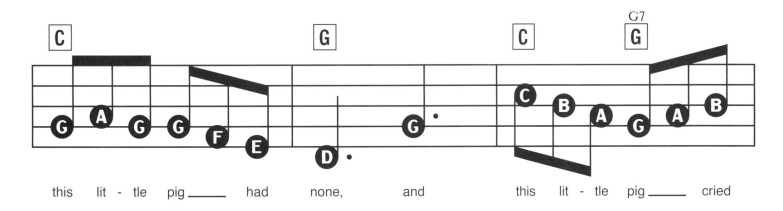

this lit - tle pig ___ had none, and this lit - tle pig ___ cried

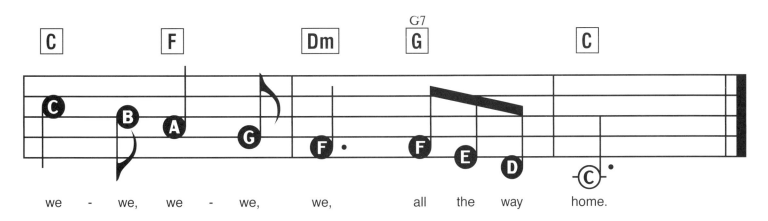

we - we, we - we, we, all the way home.

This Old Man

Registration 5
Rhythm: Fox Trot

Traditional

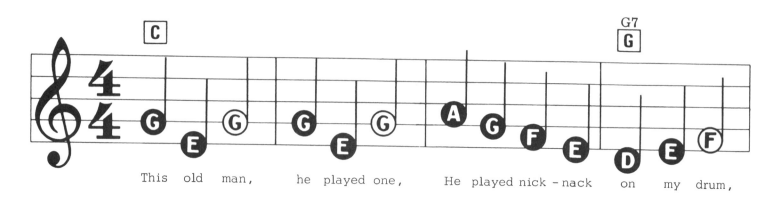

This old man, he played one, He played nick - nack on my drum,

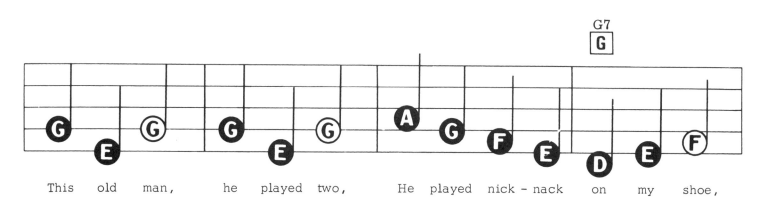

Nick-nack pad - dy whack, give a dog a bone, This old man came roll - ing home.

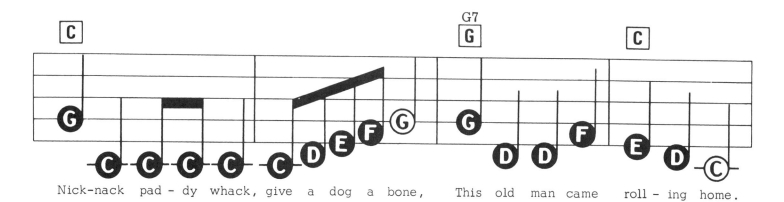

This old man, he played two, He played nick - nack on my shoe,

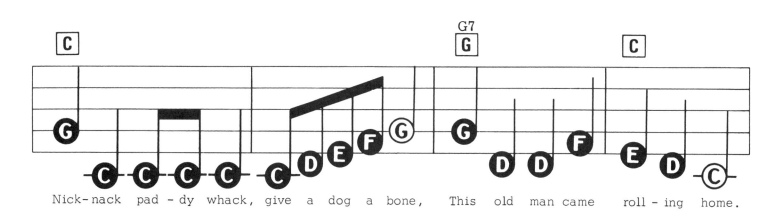

Nick-nack pad - dy whack, give a dog a bone, This old man came roll - ing home.

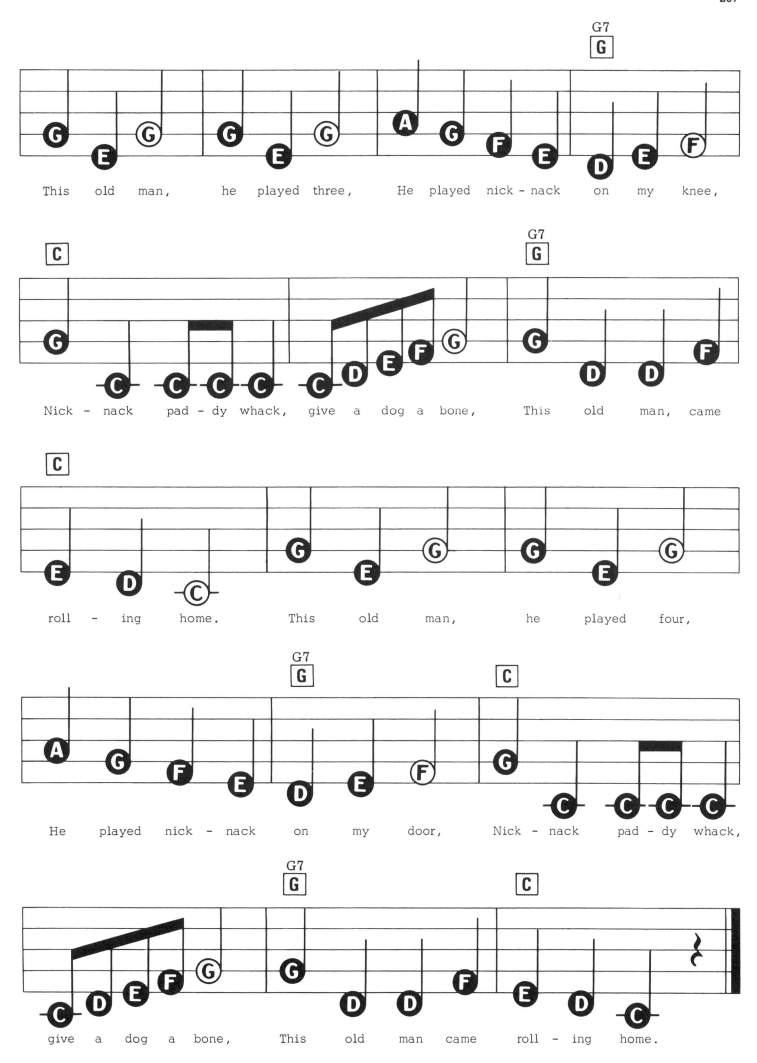

Three Blind Mice

Registration 1
Rhythm: Waltz

Traditional

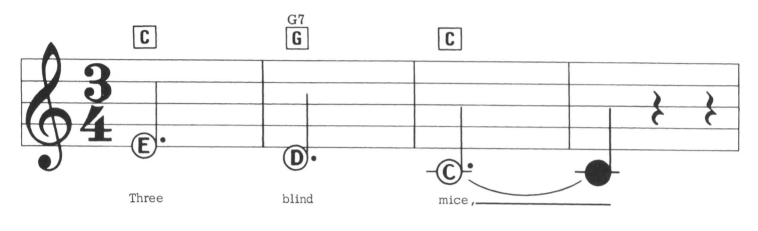

Three   blind   mice,

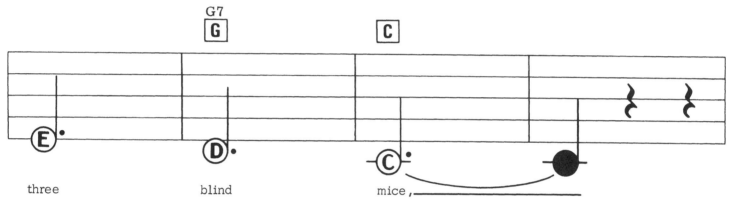

three   blind   mice,

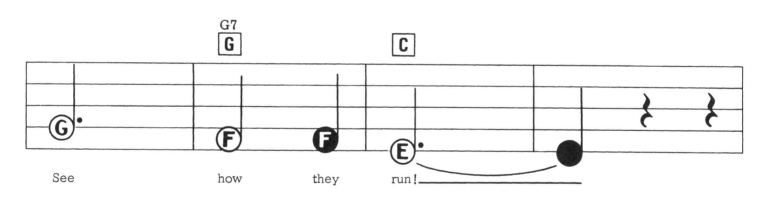

See   how   they   run!

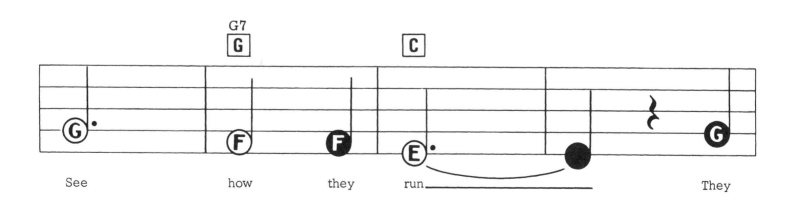

See   how   they   run   They

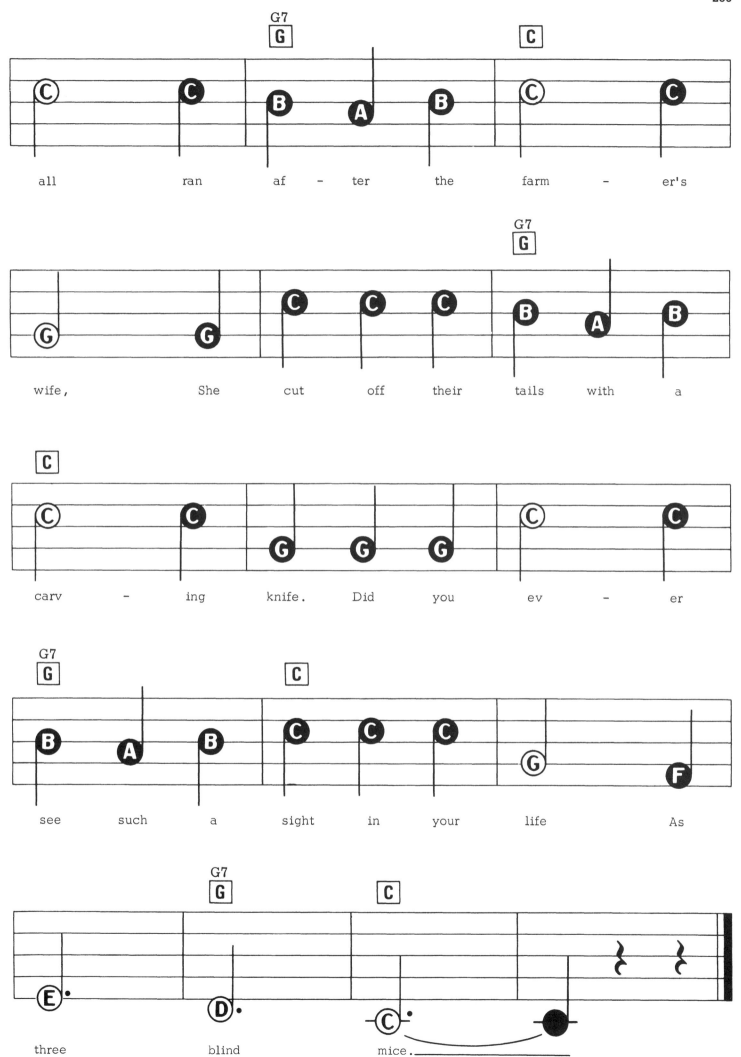

209

Three Little Kittens

Registration 7
Rhythm: Waltz

Traditional

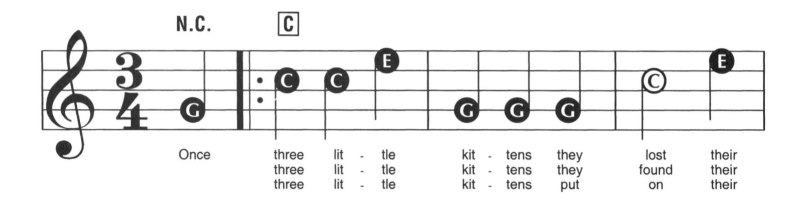

Once three lit - tle kit - tens they lost their
three lit - tle kit - tens they found their
three lit - tle kit - tens put on their

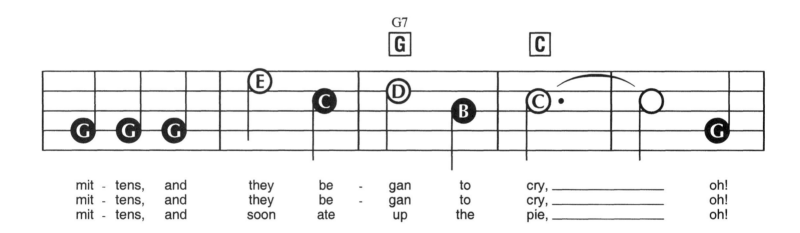

mit - tens, and they be - gan to cry, _____ oh!
mit - tens, and they be - gan to cry, _____ oh!
mit - tens, and soon ate up the pie, _____ oh!

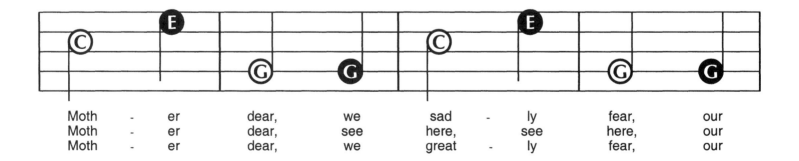

Moth - er dear, we sad - ly fear, our
Moth - er dear, we see here, see here, our
Moth - er dear, we great - ly fear, our

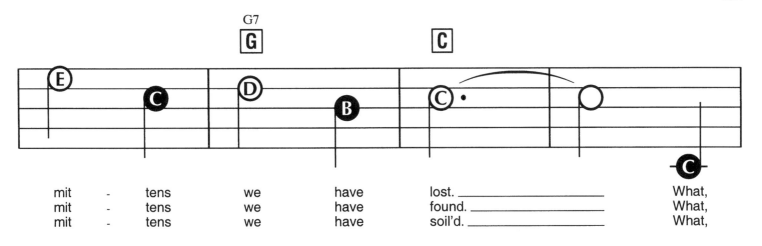

mit - tens we have lost. _____ What,
mit - tens we have found. _____ What,
mit - tens we have soil'd. _____ What,

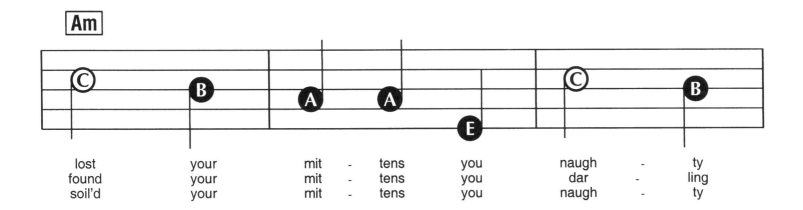

lost your mit - tens you naugh - ty
found your mit - tens you dar - ling
soil'd your mit - tens you naugh - ty

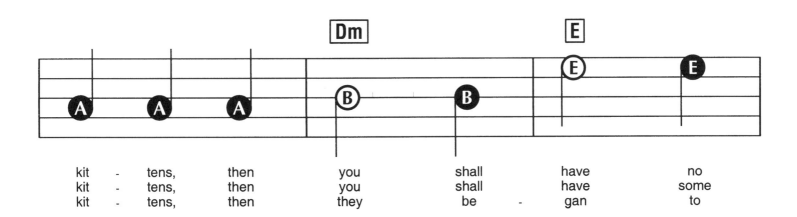

kit - tens, then you shall have no
kit - tens, then you shall have some
kit - tens, then they be - gan to

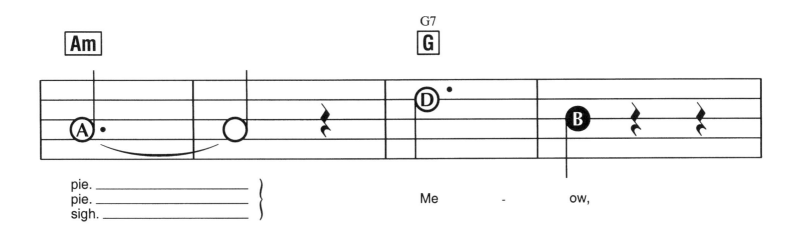

pie. _____
pie. _____
sigh. _____

Me - ow,

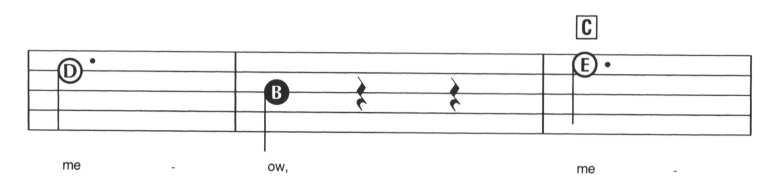

me - ow, me -

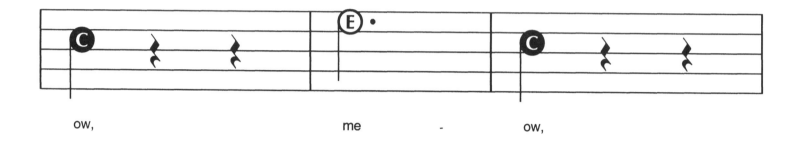

ow, me - ow,

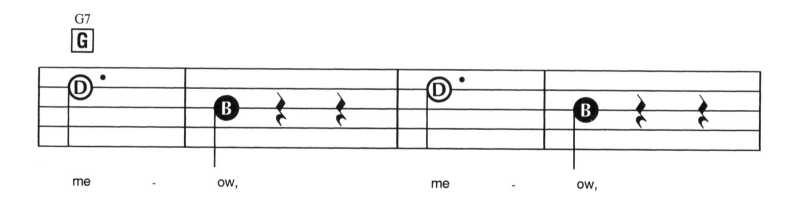

me - ow, me - ow,

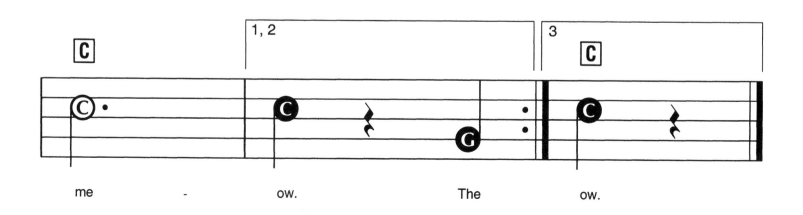

me - ow. The ow.

Tom, Tom, the Piper's Son

Registration 4
Rhythm: Fox Trot

Traditional

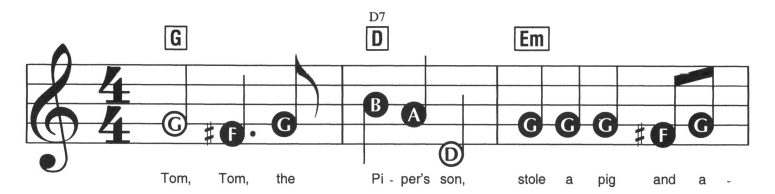

Tom, Tom, the Pi - per's son, stole a pig and a -

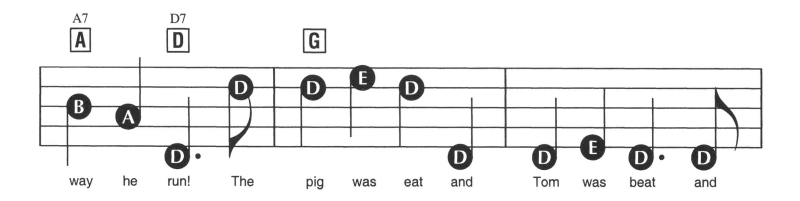

way he run! The pig was eat and Tom was beat and

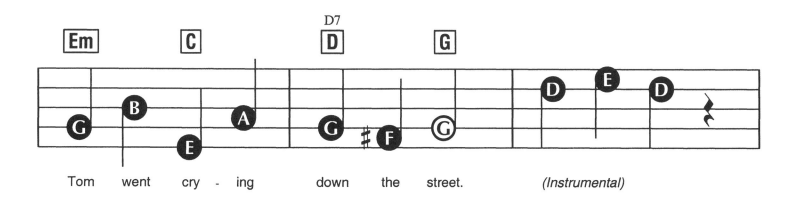

Tom went cry - ing down the street. *(Instrumental)*

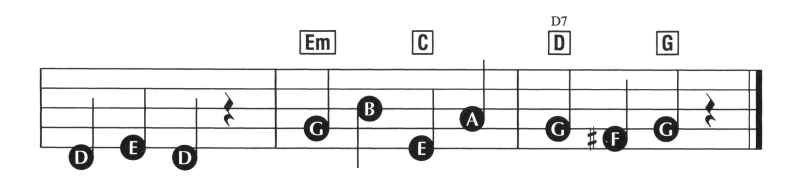

Tommy Thumb

Registration 8
Rhythm: Fox Trot

Traditional

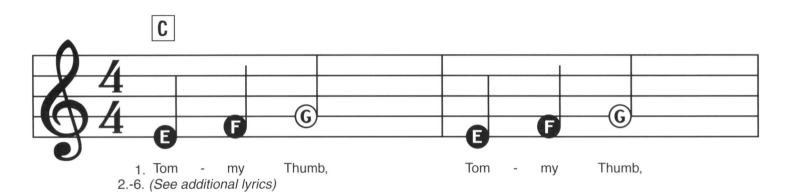

1. Tom - my Thumb, Tom - my Thumb,
2.-6. *(See additional lyrics)*

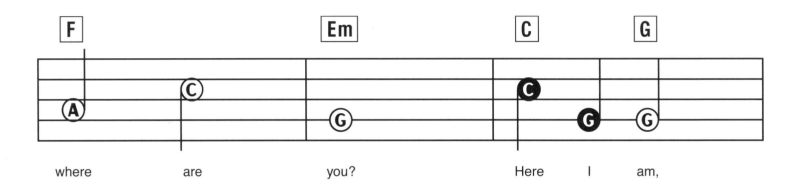

where are you? Here I am,

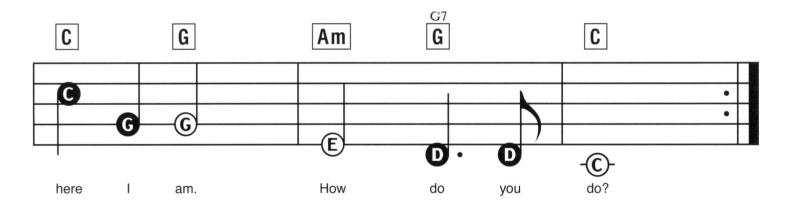

here I am. How do you do?

Additional Lyrics

2. Peter Pointer, Peter Pointer,
   Where are you?
   Here I am, here I am.
   How do you do?

3. Middle Man, Middle Man,
   Where are you?
   Here I am, here I am.
   How do you do?

4. Ruby Ring, Ruby Ring,
   Where are you?
   Here I am, here I am.
   How do you do?

5. Baby Small, Baby Small,
   Where are you?
   Here I am, here I am.
   How do you do?

6. Fingers all, fingers all,
   Where are you?
   Here we are, here we are.
   How do you do?

Turn Again, Whittington

Registration 2
Rhythm: Waltz

Traditional

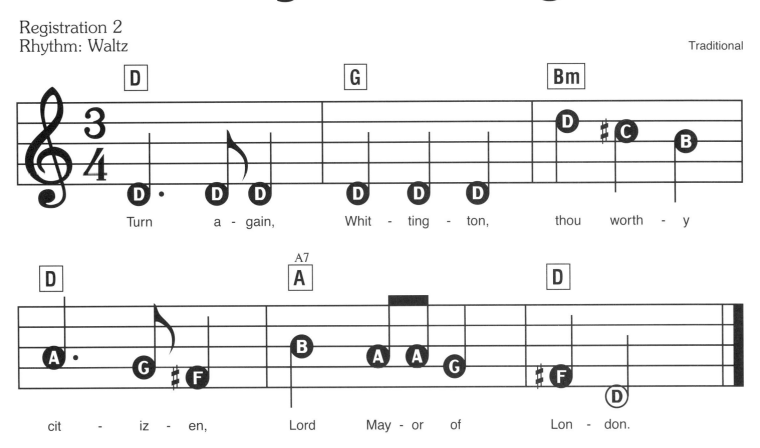

Turn a - gain, Whit - ting - ton, thou worth - y

cit - iz - en, Lord May - or of Lon - don.

Why Doesn't My Goose?

Registration 7
Rhythm: Swing

Traditional

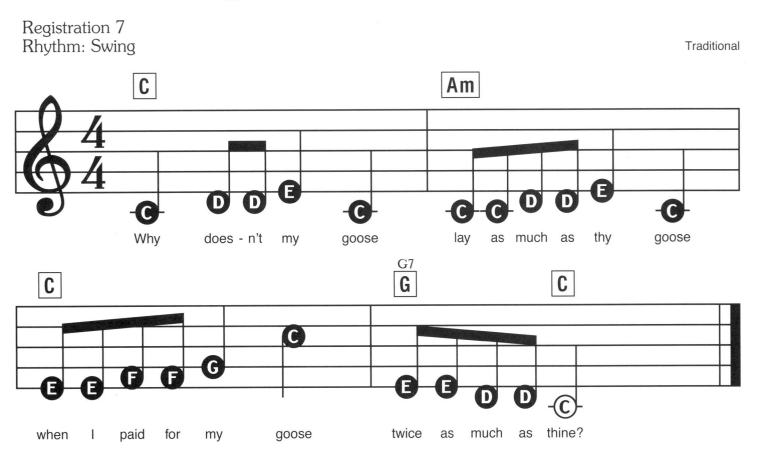

Why does - n't my goose lay as much as thy goose

when I paid for my goose twice as much as thine?

Twinkle, Twinkle Little Star

Registration 1
Rhythm: Fox Trot

Traditional

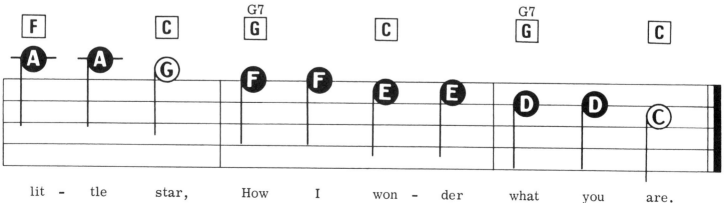

Two Little Chickens

Registration 4
Rhythm: Fox Trot or Polka

Traditional

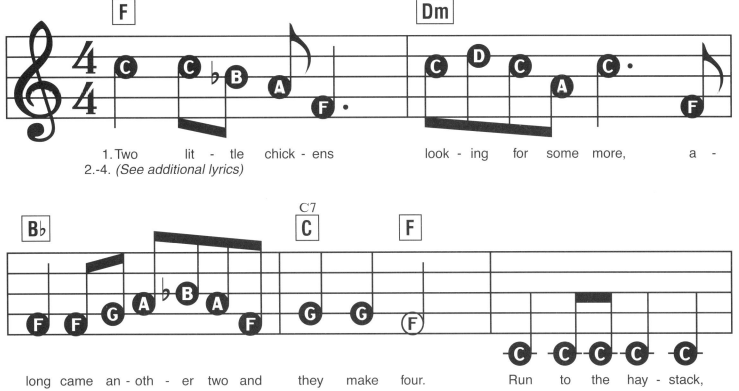

1. Two lit - tle chick - ens look - ing for some more, a -
2.-4. *(See additional lyrics)*

long came an - oth - er two and they make four. Run to the hay - stack,

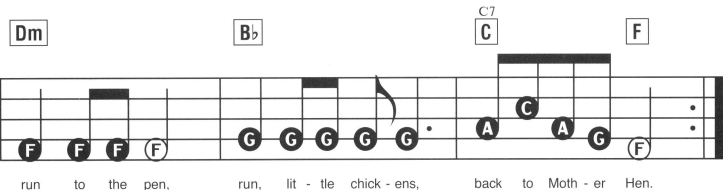

run to the pen, run, lit - tle chick - ens, back to Moth - er Hen.

Additional Lyrics

2. Four little chickens getting in a fix,
   Along came another two and they make six.
   Run to the haystack, run to the pen,
   Run, little chickens, back to Mother Hen.

3. Six little chickens perching on a gate,
   Along came another two and they make eight.
   Run to the haystack, run to the pen,
   Run, little chickens, back to Mother Hen.

4. Eight little chickens run to Mother Hen,
   Along came another two and they make ten.
   Run to the haystack, run to the pen,
   Run, little chickens, back to Mother Hen.

Two Little Dickie Birds

Registration 8
Rhythm: 6/8 March

Traditional

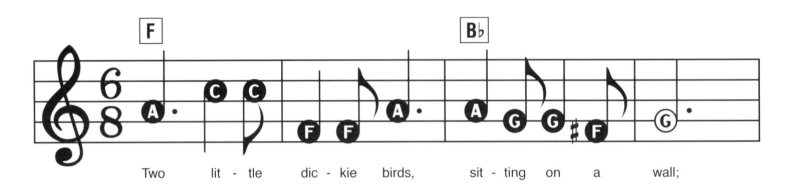

Two lit - tle dic - kie birds, sit - ting on a wall;

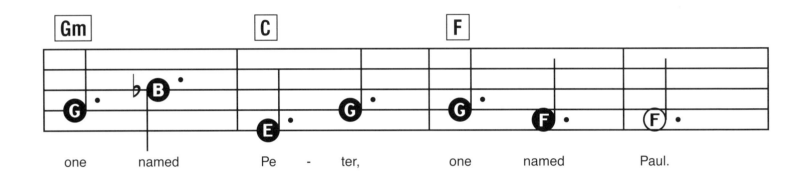

one named Pe - ter, one named Paul.

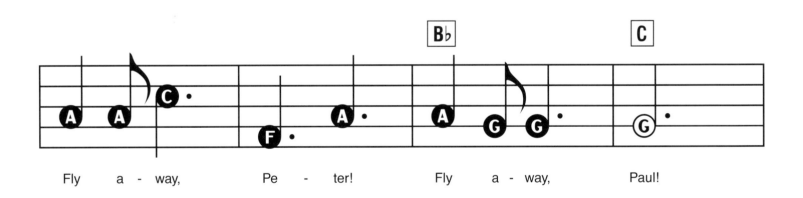

Fly a - way, Pe - ter! Fly a - way, Paul!

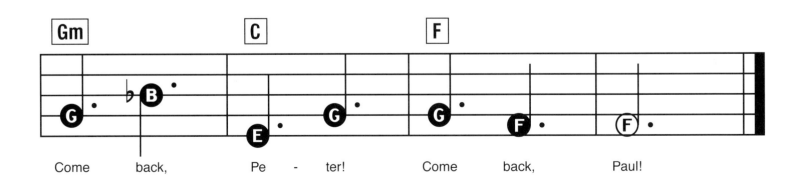

Come back, Pe - ter! Come back, Paul!

Underneath the Spreading Chestnut Tree

Registration 4
Rhythm: March

Traditional

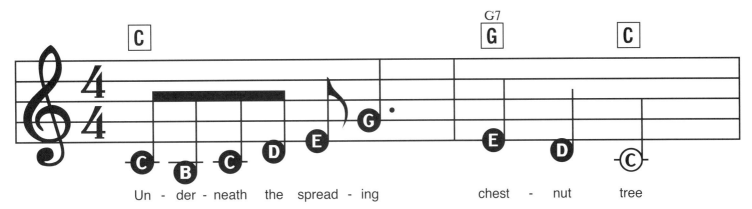

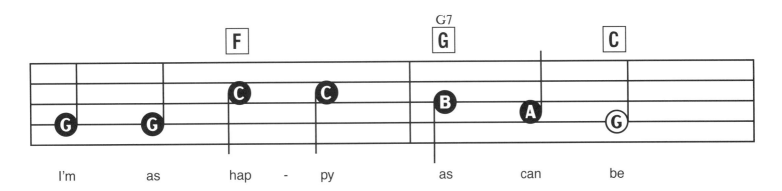

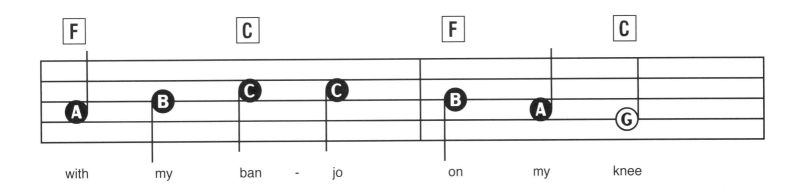

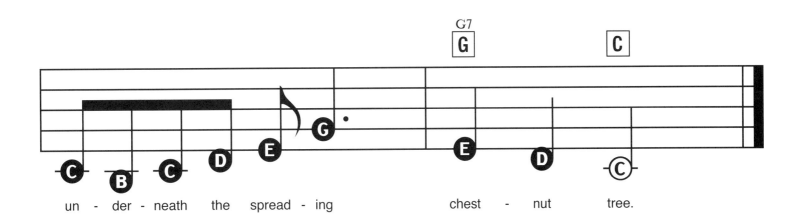

Wee Willie Winkie

Registration 10
Rhythm: Fox Trot

Traditional

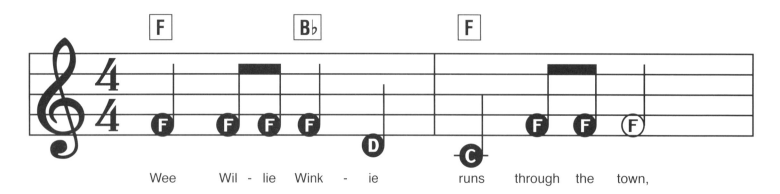

Wee   Wil - lie   Wink - ie   runs   through   the   town,

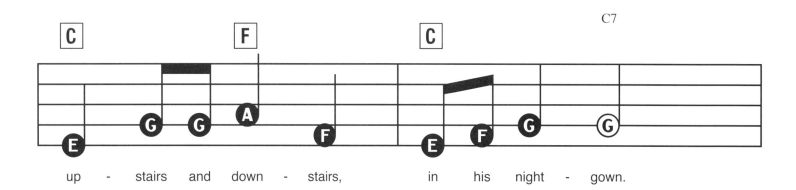

up - stairs   and   down - stairs,   in   his   night - gown.

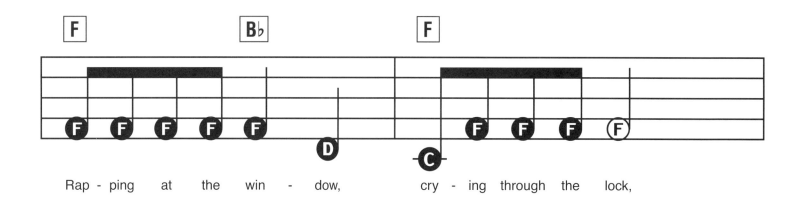

Rap - ping   at   the   win - dow,   cry - ing   through   the   lock,

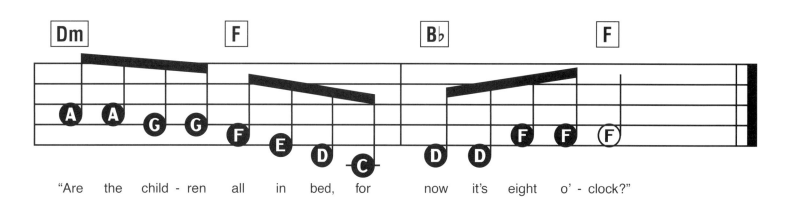

"Are   the   child - ren   all   in   bed,   for   now   it's   eight   o' - clock?"

What Are Little Boys Made Of?

Registration 4
Rhythm: 6/8 March

Traditional

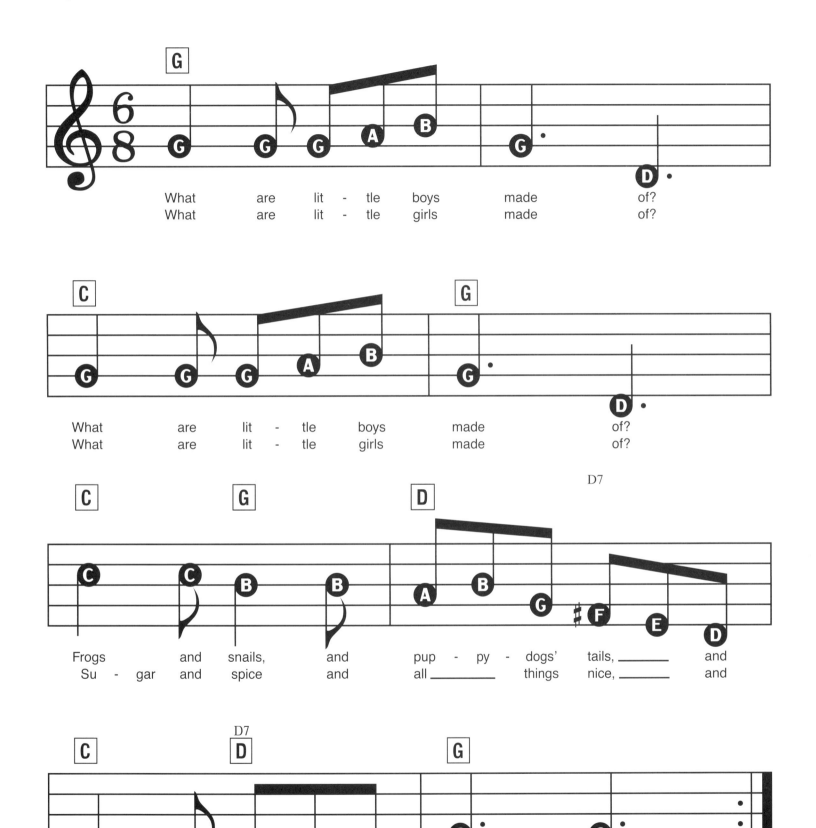

The Wheels on the Bus

Registration 9
Rhythm: Fox Trot or Swing

Traditional

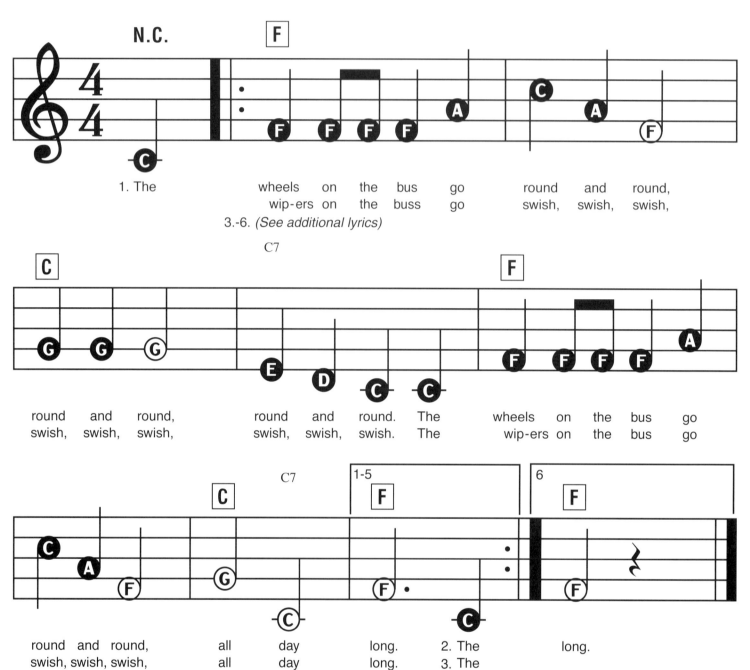

Additional Lyrics

3. The horn on the bus goes beep, beep, beep,
   Beep, beep, beep, *etc.*

4. The children on the bus goes chatter, chatter, chatter,
   Chatter, chatter, chatter, *etc.*

5. The people on the bus bounce up and down, *etc.*
   Up and down, up and down, *etc.*

6. The babies on the bus fall fast asleep,
   Fast asleep, fast asleep, *etc.*

Where Are You Going To, My Pretty Maid?

Registration 3
Rhythm: Waltz

Traditional

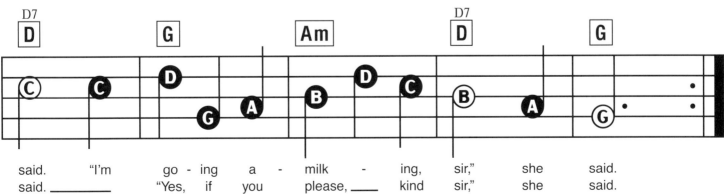

When Johnny Comes Marching Home

Registration 2
Rhythm: 6/8 March

Words and Music by
Patrick Sarsfield Gilmore

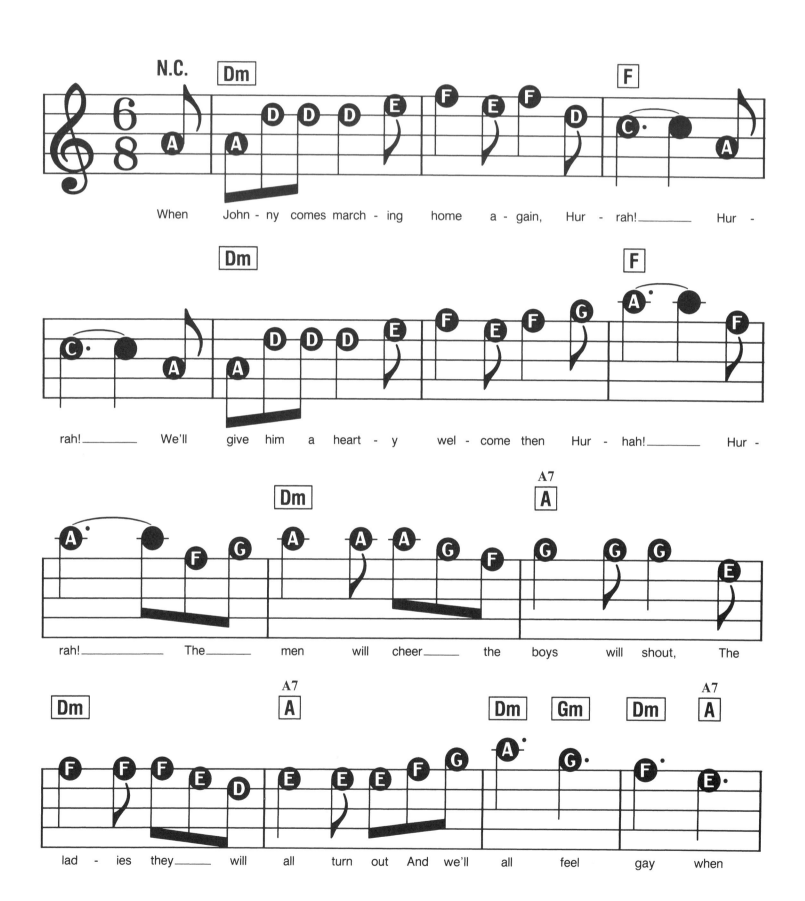

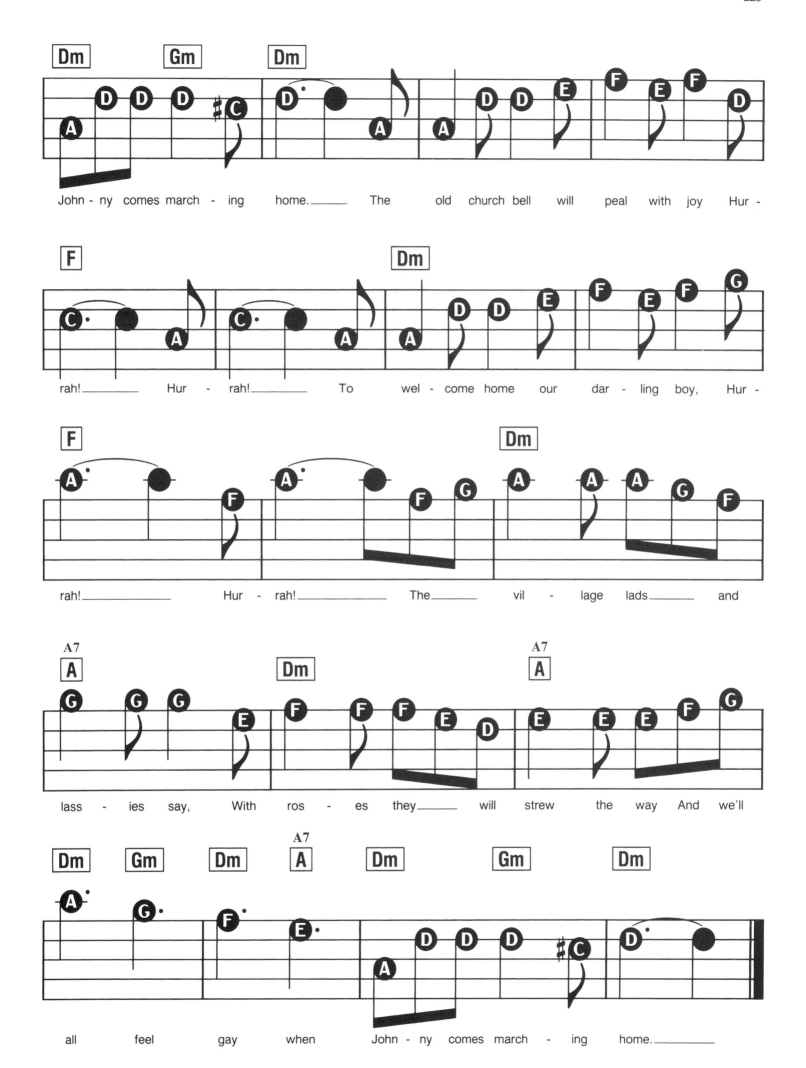

Where Is Thumbkin?

Registration 7
Rhythm: March or Fox Trot

Traditional

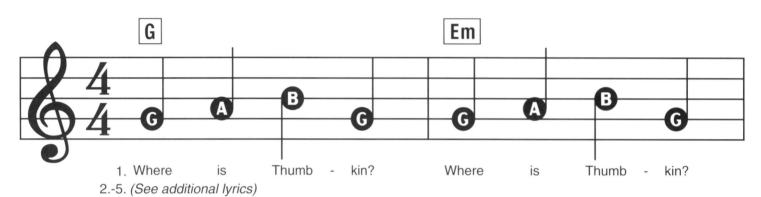

1. Where is Thumb - kin? Where is Thumb - kin?
2.-5. *(See additional lyrics)*

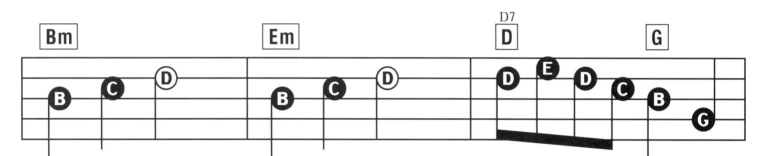

Here I am, here I am. How are you to - day, sir?

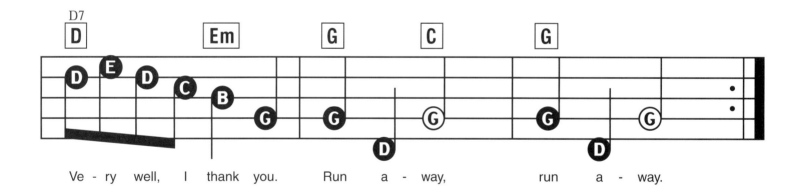

Ve - ry well, I thank you. Run a - way, run a - way.

Additional Lyrics

2. Where is Pointer? *etc.*

3. Where is Middle-man? *etc.*

4. Where is Ring-man? *etc.*

5. Where is Little-man? *etc.*

You'll Never Get to Heaven

Registration 7
Rhythm: Swing

Traditional

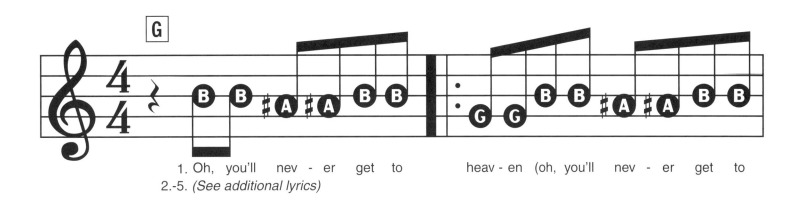

1. Oh, you'll nev - er get to heav - en (oh, you'll nev - er get to
2.-5. *(See additional lyrics)*

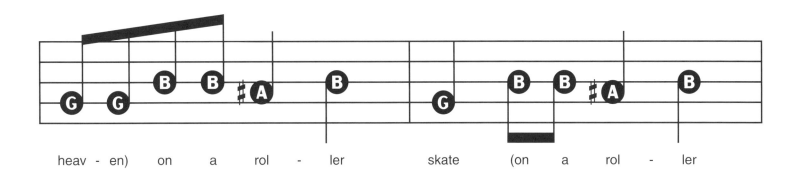

heav - en) on a rol - ler skate (on a rol - ler

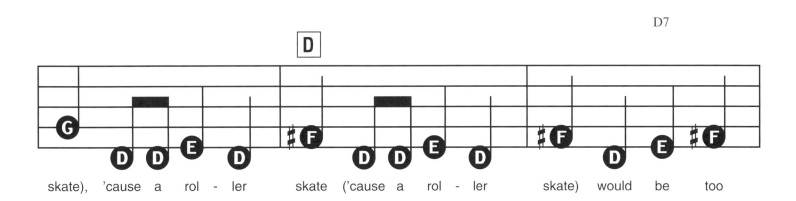

skate), 'cause a rol - ler skate ('cause a rol - ler skate) would be too

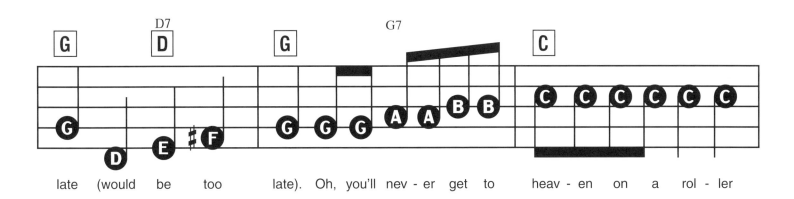

late (would be too late). Oh, you'll nev - er get to heav - en on a rol - ler

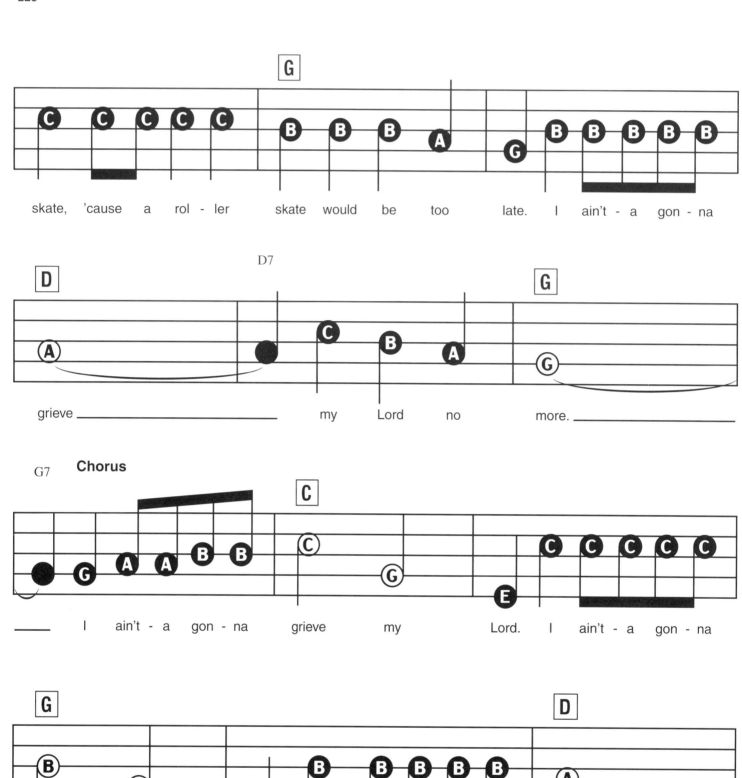

skate, 'cause a rol - ler   skate would   be   too   late. I   ain't - a gon - na

grieve _____   my   Lord   no   more. _____

Chorus

_____   I ain't - a gon - na   grieve   my   Lord. I   ain't - a gon - na

grieve   my   Lord.   I   ain't - a gon - na   grieve _____

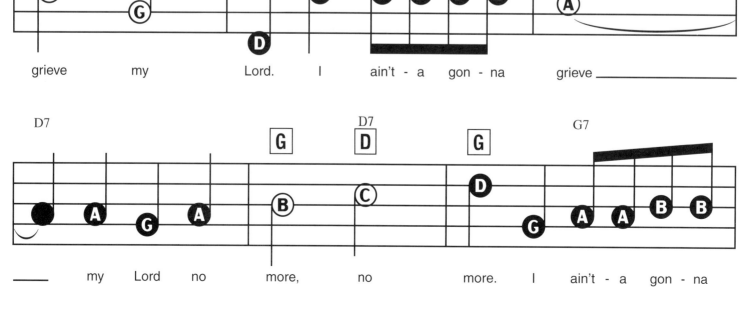

_____   my   Lord no   more,   no   more.   I   ain't - a gon - na

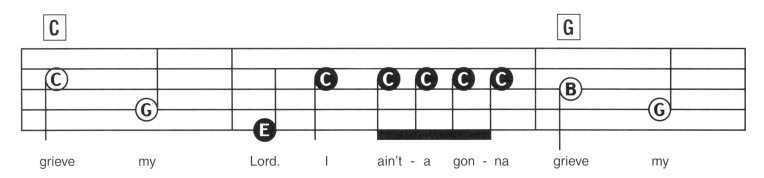

grieve   my   Lord.   I   ain't - a   gon - na   grieve   my

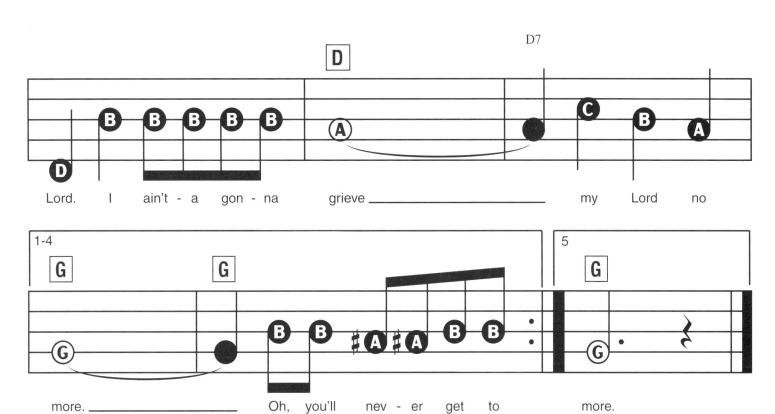

Lord.   I   ain't - a   gon - na   grieve _____   my   Lord   no

more. _____   Oh,   you'll   nev - er   get   to   more.

Additional Lyrics

2. Oh, you'll never get to heaven
   (oh, you'll never get to heaven)
   In a rocket ship (in a rocket ship)
   'Cause a rocket ship ('cause a rocket ship)
   Won't make the trip (won't make the trip).
   Oh, you'll never get to heaven in a rocket ship
   'Cause a rocket ship won't make the trip.
   I ain't-a gonna grieve my Lord no more.
   Chorus

3. Oh, you'll never get to heaven
   (Oh, you'll never get to heaven)
   On an old tram car (on an old tram car)
   'Cause an old tram car ('cause an old tram car)
   Won't get that far (won't get that far).
   Oh, you'll never get to heaven on an old tram car
   'Cause an old tram car won't get that far.
   I ain't-a gonna grieve my Lord no more.
   Chorus

4. Oh, you'll never get to heaven
   (oh, you'll never get to heaven)
   With Superman (with Superman)
   'Cause the Lord He is ('cause the Lord He is)
   A Batman fan (a Batman fan).
   Oh, you'll never get to heaven with Superman
   'Cause the Lord He is a Batman fan.
   I ain't-a gonna grieve my Lord no more.
   Chorus

5. Oh, you'll never get to heaven
   (Oh, you'll never get to heaven)
   In a limousine (in a limousine)
   'Cause the Lord don't sell ('cause the Lord don't sell)
   No gasoline (no gasoline).
   Oh, you'll never get to heaven in a limousine
   'Cause, the Lord don't sell no gasoline.
   I ain't-a gonna grieve my Lord no more.
   Chorus

Who Killed Cock Robin?

Registration 1
Rhythm: Ballad

Traditional

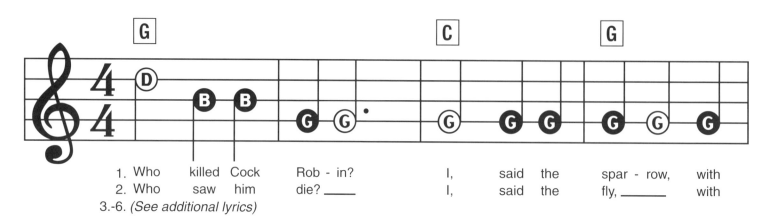

1. Who killed Cock Rob - in? I, said the spar - row, with
2. Who saw him die? _____ I, said the fly, _____ with
3.-6. *(See additional lyrics)*

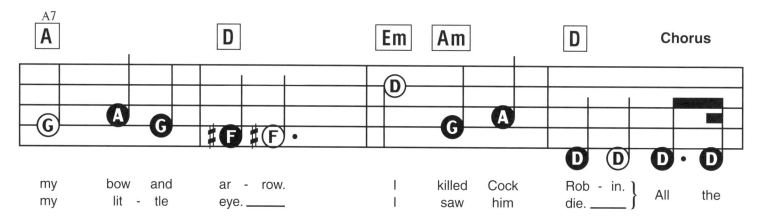

my bow and ar - row. I killed Cock Rob - in.} All the
my lit - tle eye. _____ I saw him die. _____} All the

Chorus

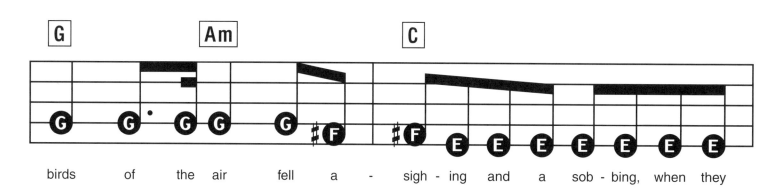

birds of the air fell a - sigh - ing and a sob - bing, when they

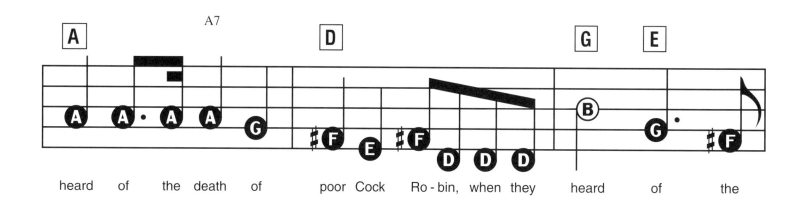

heard of the death of poor Cock Ro - bin, when they heard of the

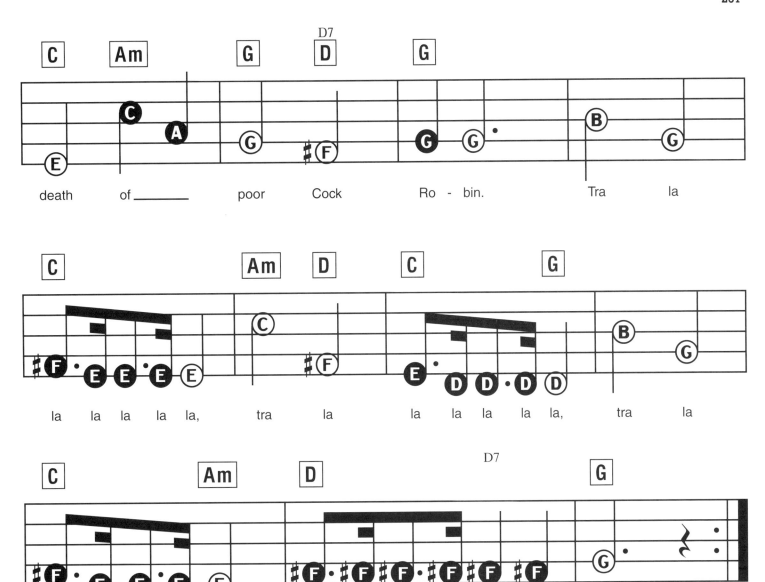

Additional Lyrics

3. Who'll toll the bell?
   I, said the bull.
   Because I can pull,
   I'll toll the bell.
   Chorus

4. Who'll dig his grave?
   I, said the owl.
   With my little trowel,
   I'll dig his grave.
   Chorus

5. Who'll be the parson?
   I, said the rook.
   With my bell and book,
   I'll be the parson.
   Chorus

6. Who'll be chief mourner?
   I, said the dove.
   I'll mourn for my love,
   I'll be chief mourner.
   Chorus

Yankee Doodle

Registration 9
Rhythm: March

Traditional

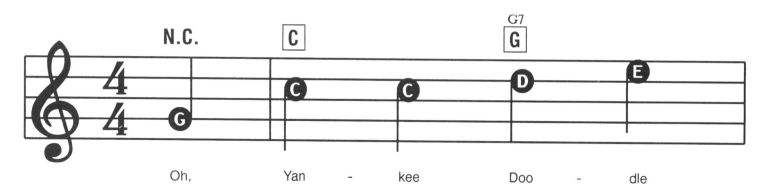

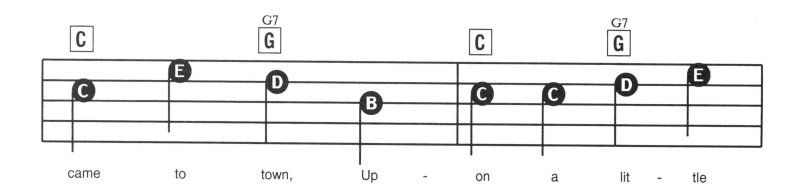

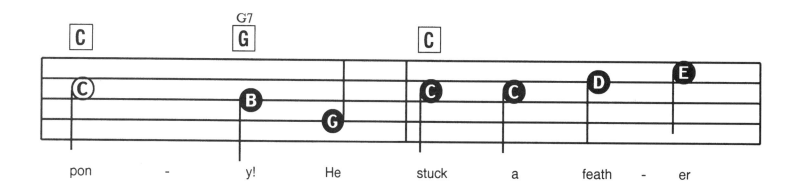

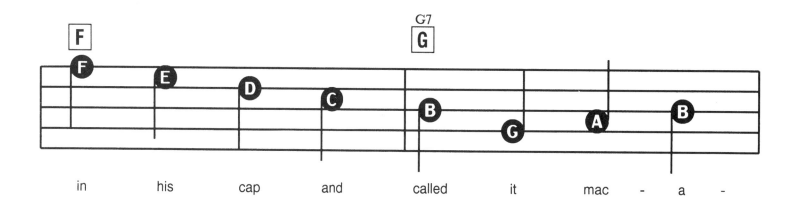

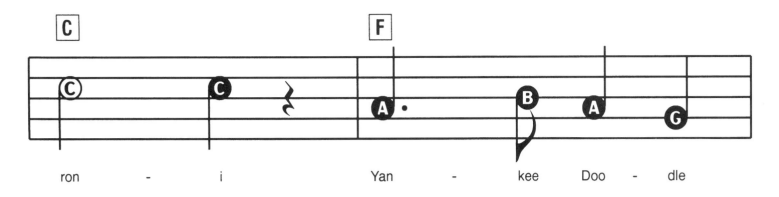

ron - i   Yan - kee Doo - dle

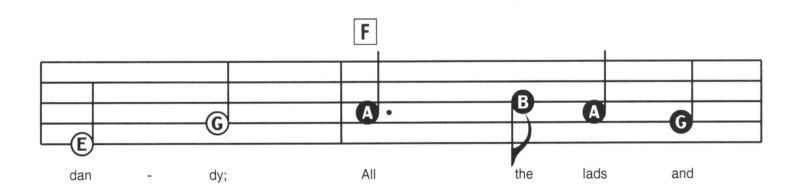

doo - dle do,   Yan - kee Doo - dle

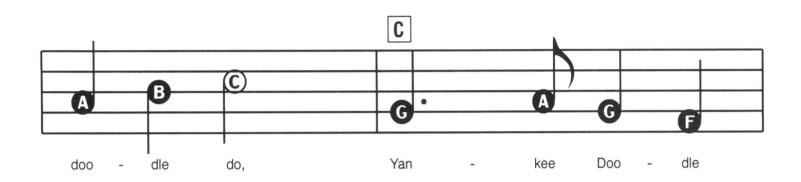

dan - dy;   All   the   lads   and

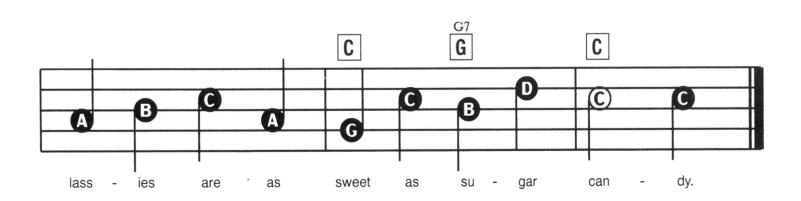

lass - ies   are   as   sweet   as   su - gar   can - dy.

Registration Guide

- Match the Registration number on the song to the corresponding numbered category below. Select and activate an instrumental sound available on your instrument.

- Choose an automatic rhythm appropriate to the mood and style of the song. (Consult your Owner's Guide for proper operation of automatic rhythm features.)

- Adjust the tempo and volume controls to comfortable settings.

Registration

1	Mellow	Flutes, Clarinet, Oboe, Flugel Horn, Trombone, French Horn, Organ Flutes
2	Ensemble	Brass Section, Sax Section, Wind Ensemble, Full Organ, Theater Organ
3	Strings	Violin, Viola, Cello, Fiddle, String Ensemble, Pizzicato, Organ Strings
4	Guitars	Acoustic/Electric Guitars, Banjo, Mandolin, Dulcimer, Ukulele, Hawaiian Guitar
5	Mallets	Vibraphone, Marimba, Xylophone, Steel Drums, Bells, Celesta, Chimes
6	Liturgical	Pipe Organ, Hand Bells, Vocal Ensemble, Choir, Organ Flutes
7	Bright	Saxophones, Trumpet, Mute Trumpet, Synth Leads, Jazz/Gospel Organs
8	Piano	Piano, Electric Piano, Honky Tonk Piano, Harpsichord, Clavi
9	Novelty	Melodic Percussion, Wah Trumpet, Synth, Whistle, Kazoo, Perc. Organ
10	Bellows	Accordion, French Accordion, Mussette, Harmonica, Pump Organ, Bagpipes

FOR ORGANS, PIANOS & ELECTRONIC KEYBOARDS

E-Z PLAY® TODAY PUBLICATIONS

The E-Z Play® Today songbook series is the shortest distance between beginning music and playing fun! Check out this list of highlights and visit www.halleonard.com for a complete listing of all volumes and songlists.

HAL•LEONARD® CORPORATION

7777 W. BLUEMOUND RD. P.O. BOX 13819 MILWAUKEE, WI 53213

Prices, contents, and availability subject to change without notice.

0312

CD PLAY-ALONG SERIES

Each book in this exciting new series comes with a CD of complete professional performances, and includes matching custom arrangements in our famous E-Z Play® Today format. With these books you can:

• Listen to complete professional performances of each of the songs

• Play the arrangements along with the recorded performances

• Sing along with the full performances; and/or play the arrangements as solos, without the disk.

SONG FAVORITES WITH 3 CHORDS • VOLUME 1
15 songs, including: Can Can Polka • For He's a Jolly Good Fellow • Kum Ba Yah • Oh! Susanna • On Top of Old Smoky • Ta-Ra-Ra-Boom-De-Ay • When the Saints Go Marching In • Yankee Doodle • and more. 00100180

CHILDREN'S SONGS • VOLUME 2
16 songs, including: Alphabet Song • Chopsticks • Frere Jacques (Are You Sleeping?) • I've Been Working on the Railroad • Jack and Jill • Looby Loo • Mary Had a Little Lamb • The Mulberry Bush • This Old Man • Three Blind Mice • and more. 00100181

HYMN FAVORITES • VOLUME 3
15 songs, including: Abide with Me • Blessed Assurance • The Church's One Foundation • Faith of Our Fathers • The Old Rugged Cross • Onward, Christian Soldiers • Rock of Ages • Sweet By and By • Were You There? • and more. 00100182

COUNTRY • VOLUME 4
14 songs, including: Crazy • Gentle on My Mind • Green Green Grass of Home • I Walk the Line • Jambalaya (On the Bayou) • King of the Road • Make the World Go Away • Son-Of-A-Preacher Man • Your Cheatin' Heart • and more. 00100183

LENNON & McCARTNEY • VOLUME 7
10 songs, including: Eleanor Rigby • Hey Jude • In My Life • The Long and Winding Road • Love Me Do • Nowhere Man • Please Please Me • Sgt. Pepper's Lonely Hearts Club Band • Strawberry Fields Forever • Yesterday. 00100240

THE SOUND OF MUSIC • VOLUME 8
10 songs, including: Climb Ev'ry Mountain • Do-Re-Mi • Edelweiss • The Lonely Goatherd • Maria • My Favorite Things • Sixteen Going on Seventeen • So Long, Farewell • Something Good • The Sound of Music. 00100241

WICKED • VOLUME 9
10 songs, including: As Long as You're Mine • Dancing Through Life • Defying Gravity • For Good • I'm Not That Girl • No One Mourns the Wicked • Popular • What Is This Feeling? • The Wizard and I • Wonderful. 00100242

LES MISÉRABLES • VOLUME 10
10 songs, including: Bring Him Home • Castle on a Cloud • Do You Hear the People Sing? • Drink with Me (To Days Gone By) • Empty Chairs at Empty Tables • A Heart Full of Love • I Dreamed a Dream • On My Own • Stars • Who Am I?. 00100243

HAL•LEONARD® CORPORATION

7777 W. BLUEMOUND RD. P.O. BOX 13819 MILWAUKEE, WI 53213

Visit Hal Leonard Online at **www.halleonard.com**

Prices, contents and availability subject to change without notice.

BOOK/CD PACKAGES ONLY $12.95 EACH!

HAL•LEONARD®

0312